KINGDOM FUNDAMENTALS

What the Kingdom of God Means
and
What it Means for You

SEBASTIEN RICHARD

Kingdom Fundamentals: What the Kingdom of God Means and What it Means for You

THRIVING PURPOSE

On the Web at: thrivingonpurpose.com

ISBN: 978-1-7777784-0-8

First Edition: July 2021

10 9 8 7 6 5 4 3 2 1

I DEDICATE THIS LITERARY OFFERING TO

THE LORD JESUS CHRIST,

MY ONE AND MY ALL,

MY SAVIOR AND MY LORD.

HE IS THE KING OF GLORY

WHO GAVE US THE KEYS TO THE KINGDOM.

HE IS FOREVER WORTHY OF

OUR PRAISE, WORSHIP, AND HONOR!

TO HIM BE ALL THE GLORY FOREVER AND EVER.

AMEN

TABLE OF CONTENTS

ACKNOWLEDGEMENTS

PREFACE

INTRODUCTION 1

PART ONE

CHAPTER 1: THE GLORIOUS GOVERNMENT OF GOD 31

CHAPTER 2: MAN'S DOMINION MANDATE 69

CHAPTER 3: THE KING TO THE RESCUE! 83

CHAPTER 4: THE MISUNDERSTOOD GOSPEL
OF JESUS CHRIST 111

CHAPTER 5: GOD IS GOOD... ALL THE TIME! 137

CHAPTER 6: GOD'S RULES OF ENGAGEMENT. 161

PART TWO

CHAPTER 7: FAITH—THE KINGDOM'S CURRENCY 189

CHAPTER 8: YOUR BESTOWED KINGDOM
AUTHORITY 213

CHAPTER 9: WHAT YOU SAY IS WHAT YOU GET 237

CHAPTER 10: TRUSTING IN KINGDOM WEALTH
AND PROVISION 263

CHAPTER 11: EMBRACING YOUR KINGDOM
IDENTITY 285

CONCLUSION 315

ACKNOWLEDGEMENTS

A work the likes of *Kingdom Fundamentals* is impossible without the help of Almighty God. I have relied on Him and His Word throughout the writing of this book for insight, inspiration, and direction. On many occasions, His Holy Spirit has given me powerful *downloads* that only made me look up and gratefully say, *"Thank You!"*

Furthermore, I could never have done it without those who, prior to myself, were dedicated to studying and spreading the message of the Kingdom. Just like Isaac Newton, I too can say:

> *"If I have seen further, it is by standing on the shoulders of Giants."*

In my research and study, I discovered that *the Gospel of the Kingdom* had fascinated many people throughout history. I found it interesting that aside from being tackled by men and women of God, the subject has also ignited interest among thinkers, philosophers, and even scientists across history and from all backgrounds. I even came across powerful thoughts on the Kingdom from supposed enemies of Christianity, such as Friedrich Nietzsche. The German philosopher, known to believers as the man who said *"God is dead,"* surprised me and showed tremendous insight when he said:

> *"The 'kingdom of God' is not something one waits for; it has no yesterday or tomorrow, it does not come 'in a thousand years'—it is an experience within a heart; it is everywhere, it is nowhere."*

However, there have been a handful of men and women which God has used to reel me in to the truth and transformative power of this message, but two people stand out in particular: the late Dr. Myles

Munroe, and Gary Keesee—pastor and author at Faith-Life church in New Albany, Ohio.

It was primarily through the tireless work of these two men that I learned the fundamentals (and the not-so-fundamentals) of the Kingdom of God and how it operates in the earth realm.

Myles Munroe had made it his life mission to teach the concepts and principles of the Kingdom of God to as many people as possible. Unfortunately, he died tragically back in 2014 and went to be with the Lord. But, thanks to technology, I found his popular teachings on YouTube and also purchased many of his books. These were life-changing materials for me. I literally devoured their content.

As for pastor Gary Keesee, I found him during a Kingdom Quest of my own. Ignited by Dr. Munroe's teachings, I became curious to see if I could find more Bible teachers who taught Kingdom, and while I was disappointed to see how few teachers out there taught about the Kingdom, I did find pastor Gary. What I loved about his teachings was how relatable and applicable he made them to real-life situations. He basically made the more complex theological teachings of Dr. Munroe come alive through a somewhat simpler theology and application. He offered a unique and relatable lens through which all could see the Kingdom better. I was so blessed by his teaching videos that I enrolled in his Provision Institute to learn even more about *"how the Kingdom operates."*

And then, of course, there is Elisabeth, my beloved wife and partner. Our mutual passion for the Kingdom of God message ignited the project of putting the fundamentals in book form. She is the one who came up with the title for this book. She really desired a compilation that would teach believers all over the world the fundamentals, or basics, of what the Kingdom is all about. Her constant encouragement and zeal for the Kingdom made her push me for the completion of this work. Furthermore, our continuous exchanges of ideas, which we call *masterminds*, bore much fruit that found its way within these pages.

PREFACE

The reason I wrote *Kingdom Fundamentals* is quite simple. As a believer, when I was taught about the *Kingdom of God* and how it operates in the earth realm, it literally changed my life. This knowledge ignited my walk with God and my faith to such a degree that I knew the message of the Kingdom was not only needed for the Church at this time but *absolutely crucial.*

Someone once said that Religion is like a playpen: it is made to keep us safe until we can climb over the bars and explore God's truth on our own.

The message of the Kingdom does this. It enables believers to climb over the bars of religion and experience the full power and glory of God's Kingdom truth here and now.

> Religion is like a playpen: it is made to keep us safe until we can climb over the bars and explore God's truth on our own.

We are living in unprecedented times. We may very possibly be the final generation before the return of The Lord Jesus Christ in glory! And which is more, Jesus told us that in the final days of mankind:

> *"... this gospel of the kingdom shall be preached in all the world for a witness unto all nations; and then shall the end come"* ~ Matthew 24:14 (NKJV).

He also said,

> *"... when the Son of Man comes, will He really find faith on the earth?"* ~ Luke 18:8 (NKJV).

In Greek, this passage contains an article before the word 'faith,' so it should read, *"will He really find THE faith on the earth?"* So, what is implied here is that Jesus was asking, *"will I find the right kind of faith?"* or *"will I find the right kind of believer?"*

Dear friend, I believe that His long-awaited return has been postponed... by us, *His Church!*

By the time the New Testament Church was in its infancy, after the death of the apostles, the early Christians had undergone so much trouble and persecution with the Kingdom of God message that they slowly began abandoning the use of the term itself. Indeed, after the destruction of Jerusalem by the Roman armies in 70 A.D., the preaching of the Kingdom started to change and morph into the more widely accepted message of salvation and making heaven that has now permeated our theology and religion.

I believe that for centuries, we (the Church) have dropped the ball and have not preached the FULL Gospel of the Kingdom, which was Jesus' intention from the get-go. If we had, we might have sped up His return and avoided much of the struggles experienced throughout human history. But this is merely a conjecture.

Better Late than Never

My first brush with his Kingdom teachings came from a teaching series he called: *Rediscovering the Kingdom*. It spanned over 40 sermons—all about the Kingdom, how it operates, and our place in it. When I listened to this series, I had been a 'Christian' for over 30 years, and yet, it changed my life. It shifted my identity from Christian to Kingdom citizen and son of the King. The message of the Kingdom, when properly taught and understood, can do that— no matter how long you've been a believer. In fact, I tend not to call myself a Christian anymore. I now consider myself a Kingdom citizen and child of the Most High.

The true gospel of the Kingdom helps us to clarify and redefine our identity as believers. It blesses us and corrects many misconceptions we may have about God, the Scriptures, the gospel, our world, and ourselves. It shifts our thinking back into alignment through proper thinking, perspective, and understanding. In short, no matter how long you've been a believer, it will change your life if you've never heard it before.

The message of the Kingdom is a transformative one.

Since the passing of Dr. Myles Munroe in 2014, the message of the Kingdom has been steadily spreading. More and more, this *'Gospel of the Kingdom'* is being preached throughout the world, on many different platforms, through many different people. It is becoming known and experienced by a growing number of believers. As a result, we are gradually witnessing a worldwide revival, and another 'great awakening' is definitely brewing. I believe this will be the final great awakening. Indeed, I believe this is the Holy Spirit's greatest move yet on our behalf and that the message will reach the confines of the earth (finally), and then the end will come.

Defining *'Fundamentals'*

Like me, my wife, Elisabeth, greatly benefited from the Kingdom message. So, it was no surprise when, as we discussed the writing of this book and what we should call it, she said: *"Since you're teaching the basics about the Kingdom in the book, why don't you call it Kingdom Fundamentals?"* And just like that, a book concept was born.

But what exactly is a fundamental?

The Merriam-Webster dictionary defines fundamentals as follows: *General or basic truths on which other truths or theories can be based.*

It also gives us the following synonyms: "ABC(s), alphabet, basics, elements, essentials, grammar, principles, rudiments."

The word, *fundamentals*, also comes from the French root word: *fondation*, which means, you guessed it, *foundation*.

So, a fundamental is something upon which we can build up—a foundation.

Therefore, *Kingdom Fundamentals* are foundational truths upon which you can build your faith and understanding of God's Kingdom. Those fundamentals are the ABCs or the building blocks of the Good News of the Kingdom. Actually, there is so much information provided here that you'll get more than just the ABCs. You'll get the DEFs, and maybe even the GHIs as well.

In writing this book, my goal was simple: *Equip believers with the necessary knowledge of the Kingdom of God to correct their thinking, beliefs and improve their lives.* In turn, this will equip them better to preach the gospel of the Kingdom and spread its message all over the earth, and hopefully hasten His return in the process.

The subtitle of this book says it all; *Kingdom Fundamentals* is about *What the Kingdom of God Means and What it Means for You.* Or, as a clever friend of mine wrote on social media once, referring to the New Jerusalem:

Step 1: Know that there is a literal 1500 miles squared Kingdom above your head.

Step 2: Find out how that relates to you.

I sincerely hope *Kingdom Fundamentals* fulfills its mission statement. I hope it blesses and transforms you like it has me. I hope it enhances your life and that it makes you bold in proclaiming the FULL gospel that Jesus Christ came to bring–*The Gospel of the Kingdom.*

If this book is successful in fulfilling its mission, more than ever, we will be shouting in unison, "*Maranatha, come, Lord Jesus!*" (Revelation 22:20).

 # INTRODUCTION

The Kingdom of God: A Primer

"The Kingdom of God is not a matter of getting individuals to heaven, but of transforming the life on earth into the harmony of heaven." ~ Walter Rauschenbusch

Introducing people, even seasoned believers, to the Kingdom of God, is no small task. The Kingdom is many things to many people. It is so vast, so simple, and yet so complex that I need to do so in a way it will really set the tone for the rest of this book.

The simplicity of the Kingdom requires us to be like a small child—trusting, believing, and open-minded. And yet, the complexity of the message of the Kingdom requires us to re-learn much of what we have learned as adults. It requires fresh revelation and understanding.

The introduction to *Kingdom Fundamentals* is perhaps a bit longer read than you would expect from a typical book intro. Keep this in mind as you read this lengthy but important introduction into this equally complex and wonderful subject.

My First Steps Into the Kingdom

"All of those who would be forgiven of their sins, it's possible. Don't delay! Receive Jesus Christ today!"

With those urgency-flavoured words, the pastor of our church launched an irresistible invitation that would forever change my life. It was 1983, and I was just nine years old.

He then added:

1

"If you want God to forgive you of your sins, and if you believe in your heart that Jesus sacrificed Himself for you and then rose from the dead three days later, I invite you to come forward. Come and join me, and we'll pray for you."

As a shy nine-year-old, walking to the front of a filled church was not on my agenda that Sunday. But God was calling me—lovingly, powerfully, and irresistibly. Although just a youth, my life hadn't been easy, and He was calling me to Himself, *to so much more!*

You should know that I came from a poor and broken household. I had experienced multiple moves, and I had lived my young life at times raised by my parents (who divorced twice) and grandparents.

So, this invitation to have a relationship with a loving God was irresistible for a kid like me. He was an anchor, and I needed stability. So, regardless of my shyness, I walked all the way to the front, without my parents. My dad later confided that it happened so fast he hardly had time to notice me getting out of my seat.

And then, the pastor, seeing my young age, probed by asking a very simple question. He asked,

"Do you really understand what I said today and what you are doing right now?"

I said, *"Yes."* I was sincere.

Well, in hindsight, I realize I didn't fully understand (no one really does). I didn't really understand much of it at all. Like all of those who come to Christ, we have only an inkling of understanding about God's greatness and His unfathomable wisdom, power, and love.

The truth is, I'm still learning about what happened that day. In truth, we cannot ever reach the end of knowing God and His Word—30 lifetimes wouldn't suffice. He is unfathomable, and so is His Word.

Nevertheless, we can know more of Him every day if we are intentional about it.

This book, dear friend, is about what I didn't understand back then and for the following 30 years of my walk with Christ. It is also about what we all desperately need to understand: *The Kingdom of God.*

This book is about *His Kingdom,* its reality, and what it means to be a citizen in it.

More than just Salvation

I was saved on that wonderful day. But truth be told, I was pretty clueless as to what I had just stepped *into.* Indeed, I had just stepped into the palace of the King of kings, the Kingdom of God! Nevertheless, for years, I remained *stuck in the lobby* because I misunderstood *the Gospel of the Kingdom.*

I couldn't, as a nine-year-old boy, from a broken household, fathom what my newness of life as a Kingdom citizen fully meant. And I know I'm not alone.

Many believers have been walking with Christ for 5, 10, or 30+ years and still don't understand the fullness of *God's Kingdom purpose for man.* Many even pastor megachurches!

In fact, most don't even understand that *they are operating in the Kingdom right now.*

For most Christians, it is all about being saved and going to heaven someday. It is all about the cross and the salvation attached to it. And it is about going to heaven when you die, right? And let's be frank… it is also about avoiding hell when we die too.

So, growing up in the Church, I was taught that after you're saved, it's all about letting others know about Jesus, the cross, and the message of salvation. We want to get them into the Kingdom through the door (Jesus is the door; John 10:7-9). We want to make sure they get to heaven, someday when they die, just as we will.

Sadly, for many, that's it.

We teach about Jesus, His sacrifice, His shed blood, and the precious redemption attached to it. We teach about *the Gospel of salvation*. For many churches, ministries, and denominations, that's what it's all about: salvation, and then heaven... someday. It's about getting through that door and then helping others find the same door.

But there's only one problem with this gospel. It's not the Gospel (or Good News) that Jesus taught.

A careful reading of the synoptic Gospels shows us that for Jesus, it was all about the *Gospel of the Kingdom*; to be understood as *the Good News of the Kingdom*.

So, what ended up happening is that we created many evangelism tools, courses, and programs that teach people about the gospel of salvation but *neglect the Gospel of the Kingdom that Jesus was so on fire about.*

Unfortunately, for centuries, we failed to teach the FULL Gospel.

As a result, we teach people how to get into the Kingdom, but for most of them, they have no clue what to do once they're inside. Basically, they get saved by entering 'through the door,' but then, like me, they get stuck in the lobby thinking this is the Christian life because they were taught very little about the Kingdom.

> We teach people how to get into the Kingdom, but for most of them, they have no clue what to do once they're inside.

And then, since we are told to 'make disciples,' we set out to teach them the same things: *How to get people through the door.* The problem is that you cannot teach effectively what you do not know and understand.

4

I'm pretty sure that when Jesus told us to make disciples of all nations (Matthew 28:19-20), what He had in mind was more akin to getting *the Gospel of the Kingdom* preached and taught all over the world (Matthew 24:14), of which the gospel of salvation is only a fraction.

What the Kingdom of God is *NOT*

"When man fell from grace, he lost a kingdom, not a religion. He lost dominion over the earth; He did not lose Heaven. Therefore, mankind's search is not for a religion or for Heaven but for his Kingdom." ~ Myles Munroe

Much of my effort in writing this book was aimed at providing the best possible explanation of what the Kingdom of God is and how it operates. As I do this, you will notice throughout the book that I also cover, while not as extensively, what the Kingdom of God is NOT. This is important because many believers have become ensnared, as I had, into misconceptions about the Kingdom of God. So, while not giving exhaustive explanations for each point, here is what the Kingdom of God is NOT:

- ♛ ***The Kingdom of God is NOT heaven.*** *Heaven is a place.* The Kingdom of God is the government of that place extending its influence in the earth realm and within the heart of man. This is expressed whenever and wherever the King's will and authority are revered.

- ♛ ***The Kingdom of God is NOT church.*** Those who believe this are confusing religion with the Kingdom. While there is Kingdom influence wherever believers assemble, your local church is not to be mistaken for the Kingdom of God.

- ♛ ***The Kingdom of God is NOT only spiritual.*** While it is accessed in the spirit and its manifestation begins in the Spirit, it doesn't necessarily stay there. The Kingdom's influence can greatly transform the physical world as well. Its power can heal the sick, grow crops, raise the dead, stop the rain, etc. Its influx and power can even fix cars (I have witnessed such stories). To quote Mark Shaw: "To insist that the kingdom of God is only spiritual is to promote the status quo."

> "To insist that the kingdom of God is only spiritual is to promote the status quo." ~ Mark Shaw

- ♛ ***The Kingdom of God is NOT words only.*** That is what I used to believe. I used to believe that if I memorized Scripture (words), evangelized a lot (words), and talked to others about Jesus (more words), I was living out the Kingdom. While I was doing valuable *Kingdom work*, I wasn't seeking the Kingdom first, nor was I necessarily experiencing the Kingdom's power in my life. Rightly did Jesus rebuke the Pharisees when He told them:

"You search the Scriptures because you think they give you eternal life. But the Scriptures point to me!" ~ John 5:39 (NLT)

So, what is the Kingdom of God then? What should we be seeking first? Or doing? Paul gave us a clue in 1 Corinthians 4:20 (NLT) when he wrote:

"The Kingdom of God is not just a lot of talk; it is living by God's power."

The great reformer, Martin Luther, said it this way:

"The Kingdom of God does not consist in talk, but in power, that is, in works and practice. God loves the 'doers of the word' in faith and love, and not the 'mere hearers,' who, like parrots, have learned to utter certain expressions with readiness."

And 17th-century preacher and writer, John Bunyan, said:

> *"Beware of resting in the word of the kingdom, without the spirit and power of the kingdom of that gospel, for the gospel coming in word only saves nobody, for the kingdom of God or the gospel, where it comes to salvation, is not in word but in power."*

I also like what A.W. Tozer said:

> *"The kingdom of God is not in words. Words are only incidental and can never be fundamental. When evangelicalism ceased to emphasize fundamental meanings and began emphasizing fundamental words, and shifted from meaning to words and from power to words, they began to go down hill."*

These Signs Shall Follow Those Who Believe...

In the beginning of Jesus' ministry, John (the Baptist) had been imprisoned, and he began having doubts concerning Jesus. He wasn't entirely sure Jesus was the Messiah anymore.

The account is told in Matthew 11:2-6 (NIV):

> *"When John, who was in prison, heard about the deeds of the Messiah, he sent his disciples to ask him, 'Are you the one who is to come, or should we expect someone else?'*
>
> *Jesus replied, 'Go back and report to John what you hear and see: The blind receive sight, the lame walk, those who have leprosy are cleansed, the deaf hear, the dead are raised, and the good news is proclaimed to the poor. Blessed is anyone who does not stumble on account of me.'"*

Jesus was basically saying, *"Here is the proof that the Kingdom has come through me: everywhere I go, miracles happen, and the power of the Kingdom is made manifest."*

And so, with great noise, signs, wonders, and excitement, Jesus was confirming that the Kingdom of God had come. When Jesus came preaching the Gospel of the Kingdom, it was made manifest with *power!*

Likewise, the disciples brought the visible manifestation of the power of the Kingdom of God after Pentecost and throughout the Book of Acts. They replicated the same miracles that Jesus did.

So, what about today? Some say that these things are now passed. They say that these signs were only to authenticate the Church's Kingdom call in its beginning. And yet, all over the world, faith-filled believers are still healing, casting out demons, and even raising the dead!

That's the power of the Kingdom of God! And it's no surprise since Jesus Himself told us in Mark 16:17-18 (NKJV):

> *"And these signs will follow those who believe: In My name they will cast out demons; they will speak with new tongues; they will take up serpents; and if they drink anything deadly, it will by no means hurt them; they will lay hands on the sick, and they will recover."*

And

> *"Most assuredly, I say to you, he who believes in Me, the works that I do he will do also; and greater works than these he will do, because I go to My Father." ~ John 14:12 (NKJV)*

So, if the Kingdom is still manifesting and expanding, and if its power is still available to believers, how come so many believers are not manifesting the signs and power of the Kingdom?

It's because they simply do not believe nor understand the Gospel of the Kingdom and how the Kingdom of God operates. While they are citizens of the Kingdom, they have no clue about the rights, privileges, and laws that apply to their heavenly citizenship and its inherent authority and power.

They are comparable to people who booked a stay at a five-star hotel and who are…

Stuck in the Lobby

Dr. Myles Munroe once compared the Kingdom of God to a Grand Hotel. He also deplored the fact that most believers have entered the Hotel upon salvation, but through ignorance of what the Hotel has to offer, remain in the lobby for the length of their stay. Likewise, most Christians have come through the door of the Kingdom (Jesus Christ), but once in the Kingdom, they have very little knowledge of how to operate in it and of everything made available to them.

Think about it; if you were to go to a grand hotel and remain in the lobby for the length of your stay, what would you be missing out on? When a believer gets 'stuck in the lobby' of The Grand Kingdom Hotel, he misses out on a lot. If you were stuck in the lobby, you'd be missing out on…

- A comfy king-sized bed
- Room service
- Fancy restaurants on site
- A private bathroom
- A giant-screen TV in your room
- The pool, sauna, gym, etc.

As a believer stuck in the lobby, here is what I thought I was on earth for:

- I thought that once saved, my purpose was just to evangelize.

- ⚜ I thought my only hope was pretty much limited to going to heaven someday.

- ⚜ I thought the Glory of God could only be witnessed once in heaven.

- ⚜ As a Christian, I thought that the only things (aside from salvation) differentiating me from others were supposed to be my joy and my peace, which I often lacked.

So, the question I always had at the back of my mind was: *Is this it?* Is this all there is to my life as a believer? This faith? Reading this book daily? My walk with God? The drudgery of my day-to-day? Is this the abundant life Jesus promised? Somehow, I knew I came up short. I had the nagging feeling I was missing out on something. Something *BIG*. That was the Holy Spirit, stirring me out of my religious slumber. He was wooing me towards more—*towards the abundant life Jesus promised.*

For the Christian, being stuck in the lobby of the Kingdom doesn't mean he's not enjoying a big screen TV or the pool. No. It means he's missing out on:

- ⚜ God's miraculous Kingdom provision.

- ⚜ Seeing the Kingdom of God influence the earth here and now.

- ⚜ A stronger and more defined sense of purpose.

- ⚜ Witnessing the supernatural so often that it becomes natural.

- ⚜ Being used mightily by the King.

- ⚜ Hearing from God regularly through many different channels, not just Scripture.

- ⚜ Seeing the joy of others when they witness the Kingdom's glory.

- ⚜ Exercising tremendous God-given authority, and so much more!

This book is a call to believers everywhere to get out of the lobby and into the marvellous Kingdom "prepared for them since the foundation of the world."

This Kingdom is accessible *here and now* in all its glory through the Holy Spirit-led manifestation of the sons of God. Yes, this means you! The Kingdom is within you and beckons to burst forth! You only need

This book is a call to believers everywhere to get out of the lobby and into the marvellous Kingdom "prepared for them since the foundation of the world."

to gain understanding, believe, and step outside the lobby of dead religion and live out your faith through His Spirit.

Ushering in the Kingdom

When John the Baptist came in the desert, preaching and teaching men to repent, his message was a simple one. Day in and day out he shouted:

> "Repent, for the kingdom of heaven is at hand!"
> ~ Matthew 3:2 (NKJV)

The Kingdom of God is at hand (Or the kingdom of heaven has come near)? Really?

This was a *new* message. It was unlike anything the Israelites had ever heard. It was so new, in fact, that the religious leaders of the time thought John might be the long-awaited Messiah. They sent a delegation to question him concerning his identity, message, and mission.

He then confirmed he was not the Messiah and that the one coming after him (Jesus Christ) would baptize people with fire and the Holy Spirit. Shortly after this, Jesus began His ministry.

The ministry of Jesus began while His cousin, John, was put in prison. In Mark 1:14-15 (NIV), we read these words:

After John was put in prison, Jesus went into Galilee, proclaiming the good news of God. "The time has come," he said. "The kingdom of God has come near. Repent and believe the good news!"

So, Jesus kicked off His ministry exactly where John had left off his: *by proclaiming the Kingdom of God and urging people to repent.* The Bible says:

"From that time on (when John was put in prison) Jesus began to preach, 'Repent, for the kingdom of heaven has come near.'" ~ Matthew 4:17 (NIV)

But what John couldn't do, Jesus came to fulfill. He brought the Kingdom with Him. And so it was that with great noise, signs, miracles, wonders, and excitement, Jesus was confirming that *The Kingdom of God* had come. He brought it with Him. It has been with us ever since; near, accessible, powerful… *and within!*

If You Fail to Go Within…

"The kingdom is where the King reigns. If He is reigning in my heart, then the Kingdom of Heaven has come to me." ~ Eric Liddell, athlete and missionary

"The kingdom is where the King reigns. If He is reigning in my heart, then the Kingdom of Heaven has come to me." ~ Eric Liddell, athlete and missionary

In the Gospel of Luke, Jesus says something about the Kingdom of God that is unique, shocking, and quite misunderstood.

In Luke 17:21 (NKJV), He says:

*"Now when He was asked by the Pharisees when the kingdom of God would come, He answered them and said, 'The kingdom of God does not come with observation; nor will they say, 'See here!' or 'See there!' For indeed, **the kingdom of God is within you.'"***

The Kingdom of God is within you? Um, *say what?!*

Many commentators have been somewhat stumped by this verse in Luke. As a result, you will likely find a different interpretation and explanation of its meaning for every commentator you read. Furthermore, many hyper-spiritualizers and New Agers have taken the verse to validate their belief in their own inner godhood or personal divinity. So, this verse has become quite the popular quote in the esoteric/New Age/New Thought community.

Whether you believe the Greek was mistranslated, or whether you have taken the verse and made it into an esoteric gobbledegook, the fact remains that this verse is in our Bibles, and in red letters, no less. These are the very Words of Jesus.

I believe the verse should be taken at face value: *The Kingdom of God is within you.*

It has been said by many wise men: "*If you fail to go within, you will go without.*" This definitely is in line with Jesus' statement about the Kingdom.

First, it is true that for the believer who has the Holy Spirit residing within, this makes all the sense in the world. The plenitude of the whole Kingdom of God accompanies the indwelling of the Holy Ghost. And if the fulness of the Kingdom accompanies the Spirit of God, what can be said of Him residing in the hearts of men? Simply this: Through the presence of the Holy Spirit, the Kingdom of God is within you indeed!

Furthermore, Jesus did tell us that He came to accomplish the law and the prophets, did He not? Well, that being the case, it was prophesied by Jeremiah what the Kingdom of God would be like in the New Covenant:

> "*Behold, the days are coming, says the Lord, when I will make a new covenant with the house of Israel and with the house of Judah—not according to the covenant that I made*

> *with their fathers in the day that I took them by the hand to lead them out of the land of Egypt, My covenant which they broke, though I was a husband to them, says the Lord. But this is the covenant that I will make with the house of Israel after those days, says the Lord: I will put My law in their minds, and write it on their hearts; and I will be their God, and they shall be My people. No more shall every man teach his neighbor, and every man his brother, saying, 'Know the Lord,' for they all shall know Me, from the least of them to the greatest of them, says the Lord. For I will forgive their iniquity, and their sin I will remember no more."*
> *~ Jeremiah 31:31-34 (NKJV)*

With the New Covenant, God wanted to bring His Kingdom and government into the hearts of men. This is what is so amazing about the Kingdom of God: It emanates from Him, flows into His children, and back out into the earth realm through their influence and God-given authority.

Wherever God is honored as King, there is the Kingdom of God made manifest.

The famous missionary doctor, Albert Schweitzer, said: *"There can be no Kingdom of God in the world without the Kingdom of God in our hearts."*

> **Wherever God is honored as King, there is the Kingdom of God made manifest.**

The Kingdom: The Long-Awaited Unseen Realm

The Bible tells us that the Kingdom of God is something that not only was expected but long-awaited.

Joseph of Arimathea is described in the Bible as a man who *was also waiting for the kingdom of God* (Mark 15:43; Luke 23:51).

He wasn't alone. Judea back then had been under Roman

occupation since 63 B.C. by the time John (the Baptist) came on the scene in A.D. 29, preaching about the Kingdom. That's close to a century! Furthermore, the Hebrew people had suffered all throughout their history of slavery, exile, oppression, and now Roman occupation.

So, those who, like Joseph, held on to the hope of God's Kingdom being made manifest, eagerly anticipated the day when God would finally bring freedom from the evil powers of the world. They desired to see His righteous Kingdom established on the earth NOW—with power and glory.

However, when the Kingdom of God came near, they failed to recognize it for the most part. They expected it to come through politics and power. They expected a Messiah who would break the chains of physical oppression. And, in some weird way, even after 2000 years, we still fail to recognize it today! This explains why Christianity is plagued (yes, *plagued*) with over 250 denominations worldwide, and growing.

Jesus told the Pharisees in Luke 17:21 (NKJV): *the Kingdom of God is within you.* Obviously, most of the Pharisees of the day didn't know what to make of this. They were befuddled. Likewise, in the non-canonical Gospel of Thomas, we read these interesting lines attributed to Jesus when He was questioned about the Kingdom by His disciples. These words align with what Christ said in Luke 17:21:

> *"His disciples said to him, 'When will the kingdom come?' 'It will not come by watching for it. It will not be said, 'Look, here!' or 'Look, there!' Rather, the Father's kingdom is spread out upon the earth, and people don't see it.'"*
> *~ Gospel of Thomas 113*

The Kingdom Always Leaves a Trail

Although the Kingdom is not visible to the naked eye, it always leaves a trail.

During the time of Jesus' budding ministry, John the Baptist, from the confines of his jail cell, began having some doubts concerning his beloved cousin. He wondered if Jesus was truly the Messiah. It says in Matthew 11:1-3 (NIV):

> "After Jesus had finished instructing his twelve disciples, he went on from there to teach and preach in the towns of Galilee. When John, who was in prison, heard about the deeds of the Messiah, he sent his disciples to ask him, 'Are you the one who is to come, or should we expect someone else?'"

In this passage, we see that John, although hailed by Jesus to be the greatest man ever born of women (Matthew 11:11), was fallible and yes, human. He had his doubts. But Jesus didn't hold it against him. Instead, He reassured Him through these words of Kingdom confirmation in the following verses (v. 4-6; NIV):

> Jesus replied, "Go back and report to John what you hear and see: The blind receive sight, the lame walk, those who have leprosy are cleansed, the deaf hear, the dead are raised, and the good news is proclaimed to the poor. Blessed is anyone who does not stumble on account of me."

In other words, Jesus was telling John that there was great confirmation of who He was and what He was bringing. He was bringing the manifestation of the Kingdom. In essence, Jesus was saying that the Kingdom of God, although invisible, always leaves a visible trail.

And, in turn, He charged His disciples to be trailblazers. Wherever they would set foot, they too would leave a trail:

"And these signs will follow those who believe: In My name they will cast out demons; they will speak with new tongues; they will take up serpents; and if they drink anything deadly, it will by no means hurt them; they will lay hands on the sick, and they will recover."
~ *Mark 16:17-18 (NKJV)*

These are the signs that follow the preaching of the Kingdom of God on earth. The Gospel of the Kingdom is what has been referred to in certain circles as *The Full Gospel*. It is complete. It lacks nothing. It shows up with power, authentication, and confirmation—through signs, wonders, and miracles. And it leaves no doubt for those who witness it.

Glory to God! This is still true today—*for you and me!*

Seek First the Kingdom

When Jesus instructed His disciples to *seek first the Kingdom* (Matthew 6:33), He was saying that the Kingdom is not overtly obvious for all to find or to know.

Remember what Solomon said in Proverbs 25:2 (NIV):

"It is the glory of God to conceal a matter; to search out a matter is the glory of kings."

And we are assured by our Lord that:

"Ask, and it will be given to you; seek, and you will find; knock, and it will be opened to you. For everyone who asks receives, and he who seeks finds, and to him who knocks it will be opened." ~ *Matthew 7:7-8 (NKJV)*

Within the context of this passage, there is a strong indication of *persistence* here. We are to persistently seek, ask, and knock, in order to find or receive what we seek. We are to persistently seek the Kingdom of God.

Back when I completed my John Maxwell Team leadership training years ago, Paul Martinelli, who was president of the organization at the time, told us:

> *"Understand that the content and teachings you are given access to here are gold. They are so life-changing that many of you will want everybody to get these teachings. Since everybody needs personal growth and leadership, your enthusiasm will make you want to go out and give this to everybody— sometimes even for free. But, here is my advice to you in order to avoid disappointment: Don't give it to the people who need it (everybody needs it), give it to those who want it."*

This one piece of advice changed my approach regarding so many things when it comes to people—whether they are believers or not. It is a failsafe against giving your pearls to swine.

This principle also makes me think of the Kingdom of God.

Strangely, the dichotomy of the Kingdom is that while God wants to get everyone into the Kingdom, He made the Kingdom hard to find. It's like He hid it only for those who really want it. Only those who diligently seek it will find it. It is found only through the narrow way.

Here is what Jesus said of *the hidden Kingdom* in Matthew chapter 13 (NKJV):

> *"The kingdom of heaven is like leaven, which a woman took and <u>hid</u> in three measures of meal till it was all leavened."* *(v. 33)*

> *"Again, the kingdom of heaven is like treasure <u>hidden</u> in a field, which a man found and <u>hid</u>; and for joy over it he goes and sells all that he has and buys that field."* *(v. 44)*

> *"Again, the kingdom of heaven is like a merchant <u>seeking</u> beautiful pearls, who, <u>when he had found</u> one pearl of great price, went and sold all that he had and bought it."* *(v. 45-46)*

The leaven is *hidden* in the dough. The treasure was *hidden* in the field. The pearl of great price was sought out and hard to find.

Also, in Matthew 13:11-13 (NLT), Jesus told His disciples the following after they asked Him why He spoke in parables:

> *"You are permitted to understand the secrets of the Kingdom of Heaven, but others are not. To those who listen to my teaching, more understanding will be given, and they will have an abundance of knowledge. But for those who are not listening, even what little understanding they have will be taken away from them. That is why I use these parables."*

Indeed, *the secrets of the Kingdom* are given to the disciples who are willing to ardently seek out these matters. The mere fact that you are now reading this book is proof-positive that you want *'the glory of kings'* by seeking out matters.

We mustn't be afraid to get our hands dirty, so to speak, when it comes to finding out more about the Kingdom of God.

For lack of a better comparison, we must become like *Indiana Jones*. How would Indie seek the Kingdom? How did he seek the artifacts in the Indiana Jones movies? For example, picture yourself as Indiana Jones featured in a movie called: *Indiana Jones and the Hidden Kingdom*. As the main character, what would you be doing in such a movie? You'd be researching, reading, planning, asking, seeking, knocking; right? That's how intentional you have to become when seeking any hidden Kingdom.

When Jesus told us to seek first the Kingdom, it was an invitation into obsession.

Do you remember the scene of 'The breath of God' at the end of *Indiana Jones and the Last Crusade*? In the movie, there were three final

> **When Jesus told us to seek first the Kingdom, it was an invitation into obsession.**

19

riddles/tests that needed to be overcome by any who sought the Holy Grail. Men were sent by the bad guys in order to get through. They all failed. Each one of them was decapitated by an unseen and mysterious booby trap. The single clue Indie had to go with to get through were these cryptic words: *Only the penitent will pass.*

As he was advancing nervously, at the very last second, he understood what the clue meant, and to avoid certain death by decapitation, Indiana Jones fell to his knees (penitent, praying), avoided the booby trap, and passed the test. Phew!

Well, in a similar fashion, to find the hidden Kingdom, we have a clue. Our clue is: *only the diligent and humble will find it.* Diligence is careful and persistent work. That's our clue to Kingdom discovery and advancement. That's how we seek it, find it, and operate in it— in diligence and humility. That's how we find hidden treasures. All believers are called to seek the Kingdom this way.

Canadian social worker, Catherine Doherty, said:

> *"To pass through the door that leads to God's kingdom, we must go down on our knees."*

And Jonathan Edwards said:

> *"The seeking of the kingdom of God is the chief business of the Christian life."*

Hidden, and What Else?

> *"Jesus made clear that the Kingdom of God is organic and not organizational. It grows like a seed and it works like leaven: secretly, invisibly, surprisingly, and irresistibly."*
> ~ Os Guinness

So, the Kingdom of God is hidden, but what else characterizes the Kingdom? Well, Jesus gave numerous comparisons when He spoke of the Kingdom of God. It is...

👑 **Not of this world:** When answering Pilate's questions, Jesus said:

> *"My kingdom is not of this world. If it were, my servants would fight to prevent my arrest by the Jewish leaders. But now my kingdom is from another place." ~ John 18:36 (NIV)*

In Philippians 3:20 (ESV), we are told:

> *"Our citizenship is in heaven, and from it we await a Savior, the Lord Jesus Christ."*

And Jesus also said:

> *"They are not of the world, just as I am not of the world. Sanctify them in the truth; your word is truth." ~ John 17:16-17 (ESV)*

👑 **Invisible:** When He was asked by the Pharisees when the kingdom of God would come, He answered them and said, *"The kingdom of God does not come with observation; nor will they say, 'See here!' or 'See there!' For indeed, the kingdom of God is within you." ~* Luke 17:20-21 (NKJV)

Also, during His famous nightly chat with Nicodemus, He told him:

> *"The wind blows where it wishes, and you hear the sound of it, but cannot tell where it comes from and where it goes. So is everyone who is born of the Spirit." ~ John 3:8 (NKJV)*

In other words, people become citizens of the Kingdom *invisibly*. Kingdom citizenship is acquired from above, yes. But it also happens within—invisibly, spiritually.

👑 **Expansive:** Expansiveness (i.e., the tendency to expand) is an inherent property of the Kingdom. The Kingdom of God is always growth-oriented. It never regresses and always progresses. It follows a simple law of the God of the living, summed up by John Henry Newman when he said, *"Growth is the only evidence of life."* In Matthew 13:31-33, Jesus compared the Kingdom to a *mustard* *seed* and to *leaven* to explain how the Kingdom grows and expands from within a man to many outward manifestations and fruit.

👑 **Far-Reaching:** The Kingdom of God has an extended reach. Like any great Kingdom, it always conquers new territory farther and farther. In Matthew 13:47-50 (NIV), Jesus spoke of the Kingdom thus:

> *"Once again, the kingdom of heaven is like a net that was let down into the lake and caught all kinds of fish. When it was full, the fishermen pulled it up on the shore. Then they sat down and collected the good fish in baskets, but threw the bad away. This is how it will be at the end of the age. The angels will come and separate the wicked from the righteous and throw them into the blazing furnace, where there will be weeping and gnashing of teeth."*

And when he called Simon (Peter) and Andrew, Jesus implied this comparison by saying:

> *"Follow me, and I will make you fishers of men."*
> *~ Matthew 4:19 (ESV)*

Even later, when He issued His Great Commission, He said,

> *"Go into all the world and preach the gospel to every creature." ~ Mark 16:15 (NKJV)*

And...

> *"... Make disciples of all nations..." ~ Matthew 28:19 (ESV)*

So, with characteristics such as the aforementioned, the Kingdom of God, while making itself desirable, is proving quite elusive, nonetheless.

The Kingdom of God is vast as an ocean and tiny as a droplet. It is both universal and exclusive at the same time. This is how it weeds out the lukewarm and unintentional seekers. It is, indeed, found only through the narrow way (Matthew 7:13-14).

> The Kingdom of God is vast as an ocean and tiny as a droplet. It is both universal and exclusive at the same time.

Furthermore, this keeps in line with the ways of the Kingdom, where everything seems to be operating paradoxically to the natural world we are used to:

- The last shall be first

- The servant shall lead

- The humble shall be elevated

- The poor shall be rich, etc.

Your Kingdom Quest

Today, right now, in reading these lines, you are undertaking an important journey—your very own quest for Kingdom knowledge, revelation, and understanding. As it did for me, this quest will make you grow in faith and knowledge and will lead you to a more intimate revelation of the King within you through God's Spirit. I believe the fruit of this quest will:

- Open your mind

- Open your eyes

- Strengthen your faith

- Boost your confidence

- Sharpen your mindset

- Bring blessings and favor into your life

- Enable you to let go of false religious thinking

- Give you understanding

- Bring you to expect miracles in your life...daily

Fifteen years ago, when my wife Elisabeth and I began our own journey into *deeper biblical understanding*; our own Kingdom Quest, it changed our lives. It did for us all of the above, and still does.

I believe it will change your life as well.

There is a prayer frame set on my wall that I have read many times in my own life. It has been in my office for over ten years. I have prayed this prayer many times in the course of my walk with Christ. It reads as follows:

"My journey out of deception began with a prayer,
an innocuous prayer that hardly seemed life-changing in its scope.
In fact, at the time, it hardly seemed much of anything at all.

"Dear Lord," I prayed, "If I am believing any lies in my life,
or am deceived in any areas of my Christian life and what I believe,
can You show me? I want Your truth at all costs,
even if knowing it destroys my entire worldview.
Oh, and I mean it Lord, even if part of me doesn't and is scared."

That was the prayer; the prayer that changed my world
and set me free.
In retrospect, it was a silly child-like prayer, but God honored it."

The (unknown) author who wrote this says it changed his life. Well, I can say it changed my life too. It takes guts to sincerely utter such a prayer. I believe, however, that it is a necessary one for believers today. Many of us have been ensnared by religious teachings and bound by dogma. And these beliefs and 'traditions of men' are keeping us not only in the dark but have enslaved us and brought fruitless results.

It's nothing new. Remember what Jesus told the Pharisees in Mark 7:6-9 (ESV):

> *"Well did Isaiah prophesy of you hypocrites, as it is written, 'This people honors me with their lips, but their heart is far from me; in vain do they worship me, teaching as doctrines the commandments of men.' You leave the commandment of God and hold to the tradition of men." And he said to them, 'You have a fine way of rejecting the commandment of God in order to establish your tradition!'"*

The Bible also says in Hosea 4:6 (ESV): "

> *My people are destroyed for lack of knowledge; because you have rejected knowledge, I reject you from being a priest to me. And since you have forgotten the law of your God, I also will forget your children."*

God doesn't want any of us to be in ignorance. Just like Paul told the Athenians in Acts 17:30 (ESV):

> *"The times of ignorance God overlooked, but now he commands all people everywhere to repent."*

Much of believers' plight today comes from misunderstanding His Word and how His Kingdom operates, including who they are in it and how they should live.

This misunderstanding of God's truth, plan, and how they fit in it has led many into bondage:

- 👑 **Emotional bondage**
- 👑 **Doctrinal or dogmatic bondage**
- 👑 **Falsehood bondage**
- 👑 **Religious bondage**
- 👑 **Financial bondage**

Yahushua Ha'Mashiach, Jesus the Messiah, came to set the captives free. And the truth, *His truth*, will set you free.

The main message He came to teach was about a gospel, which means 'Good News'. But not just any good news or gospel...*the Good News of the Kingdom of God!*

The word *'Kingdom,'* or term *'Kingdom of God'* or *'Kingdom of Heaven'* is mentioned well over 100 times in the New Testament—especially in the synoptic Gospels of Matthew, Mark, and Luke.

Go re-read the gospels, and you will realize that the 'Kingdom of God' was the central message of Jesus during His ministry and even after His Resurrection. You could even say it was what He was most passionate about.

Dr. Myles Munroe put it this way:

> *"The mission of Jesus was to establish God's Kingdom on earth in the hearts of men."*

"The mission of Jesus was to establish God's Kingdom on earth in the hearts of men." ~ Myles Munroe

In Luke 4:43 (ESV), Jesus said to His disciples:

> *"I must preach the good news of the kingdom of God to the other towns as well; for I was sent for this purpose."*

And after His resurrection, He appeared for forty days to the disciples, and the Bible says in Acts 1:3 (NIV):

> *"After his suffering, he presented himself to them and gave many convincing proofs that he was alive. He appeared to them over a period of forty days <u>and spoke about the kingdom of God</u>."*

Since it was evidently so important to Jesus to teach about the Kingdom, one question remains...

Why are we so seldom taught about the Kingdom of God in Church?

Since the Kingdom of God was Jesus' central teaching, shouldn't it be ours as well? This is a rhetorical question, of course.

We cannot undermine the importance of teaching and learning the Kingdom of God and everything pertaining to it.

It is vital to every believer to understand these matters.

Just to be clear, although I am happy to share what I do know, I am still learning much and will learn till the day I die. Therefore, I urge you to verify and test everything you will read in these pages. Don't just gobble it up or reject it, but seek it out for yourself. Get confirmation from God on all matters.

Just as Paul says,

> *"Test everything that is said. Hold on to what is good." ~ 1 Thessalonians 5:21 (NLT)*

Come Up Hither

I love how in Revelation 4:1 (NIV), the apostle John hears a voice (most probably the Lord), which tells him:

> *"Come up here, and I will show you what must take place after this."*

In our walk with God, we are constantly beckoned by God to *come up higher*. God wants to reveal new things to us regularly.

When Jesus came to earth, He came for the purpose of *revealing the Kingdom of God to men* (Luke 4:43). This was a call for believers to come up higher.

This book's purpose is to accompany you and help you to go higher in your understanding of God, His government, and your role in it here and now.

I believe the information and wisdom shared herein will enable you to go higher in your walk with the Lord.

In all honesty, I am humbled and honored to have written this book. I feel it is making me take an active part in sharing the Gospel of the Kingdom before the End comes. And to me, the fact that you're reading it right now is no small thing.

From the time Jesus began proclaiming the Kingdom of God, believers have been called to come up higher. That is just the way of the Kingdom.

From the time Jesus began proclaiming the Kingdom of God, believers have been called to come up higher. That is just the way of the Kingdom.

You, dear friend, are no exception. It's time to come up higher, and it all begins with your understanding of the Kingdom, its King, its citizens, and its laws.

So, by all means, continue reading and *"come up higher."*

PART 1
THE KINGDOM:

ITS ATTRIBUTES,
ITS MAJESTY,
AND ITS KING

THE GLORIOUS GOVERNMENT OF GOD

Exploring the Constituents of God's Kingdom

"It is impossible to rightly govern a nation without God and the Bible." ~ George Washington

There is this story told about Moses leading the Israelites out of Egypt:

When he came to the Red Sea, he asked God for help. God told him that there was good news and there was bad news:

"The good news," said the voice from on high, "is that I will part the sea so you and your people can escape."

"And the bad news?" asked Moses.

"You will have to file an environmental impact statement."
~ *Ozzie St. George*

Like many people, perhaps even like you, I have never been a big fan of government.

I used to believe (and to a large extent still do) that government and politics were strictly man's inventions stemming from a selfish desire for control and power.

I would jokingly say: The word *'politics,'* is composed of two Latin words, *poly*, meaning *many*, and *ticks*, which are blood-sucking parasites.

I also thought that God had little to do with man's politics, government, and laws. These, in my understanding, were man-made means of mass control and deceit. I held, and still do, a conspiratorial view of governments.

Notwithstanding, I believe I misunderstood in part where government really comes from—its origins, if you will.

Man's penchant to establish laws, rules, and governments is not because he is inherently wicked or seeking power. It is not a haphazard quirk in his personality either. No. Rather, it is an expression of the God in whose image we were made. God is a lover of just laws and just government. These ideals stem from Him. In fact, the Kingdom of God is established on just laws, and yes, also just government. It is now my understanding that man's governments are in many ways imperfect reflections of the government of the Kingdom of Heaven. The concepts and principles of Heaven's government have found their way into man's psyche, and ultimately, into our reality.

While man's government is obviously flawed, it does in many ways parallel the realities of God's system of governance.

Now, are there some bad people in the government who entered politics with twisted and selfish motives? Of course, there are! But the desire to implement governments in cities, states, and countries is not in itself wicked. It is an expression of the divine order and God's ways and will through man.

The Bible reminds us of these facts not only in Romans chapter 13:1-7, but also in 1 Peter 2:13-14, 17b (NKJV):

> *"Therefore submit yourselves to every ordinance of man for the Lord's sake, whether to the king as supreme, or to governors, as to those who are sent by him for the punishment of evildoers and for the praise of those who do good. [...] Fear God. Honor the king."*

And yes, obedience to authorities, for the believer, should be done provided it doesn't interfere with our duties and allegiance to God our King, and the Kingdom of Heaven.

Although the Bible does tell us that the wicked governments of the earth will be judged and ultimately destroyed, the Scriptures, surprisingly, are far from being anti-

> Obedience to authorities, for the believer, should be done provided it doesn't interfere with our duties and allegiance to God our King, and the Kingdom of Heaven.

government per se. That is because there is such a thing as good government. And for this reason, we should familiarize ourselves with it more. When we understand what good government is, we can better identify and point out bad government and avoid deception.

Kingdoms and Monarchy: Forgotten Concepts

For those of us who live in western civilization, the concept of a Kingdom has become hazy at best. Instead, we have become familiar with governments, presidents, prime ministers, et al.

You talk to a westerner about Monarchy, and he will look at you as if you were talking about fairy tales in a faraway land from times past. We just have a tough time wrapping our minds around it. This is no fault of our own since most of us didn't grow up under a distinct monarchy. Or, if we have, it is like that of the British Commonwealth, where, while it is still in effect, its legislation has given way to a more modern administration in the guise of modern government.

All this to say that clearing up the fog about Kingdom concepts is necessary for believers to better understand the rule of the Kingdom of God.

The Kingdom of God is a *theocracy*. The definition of a theocracy, according to Britannica, is:

"A government by divine guidance or by officials who are regarded as divinely guided. In many theocracies, government leaders are members of the clergy, and the state's legal system is based on religious law."

God's theocracy, His Kingdom, is the only form of government that can redeem and save mankind. For this reason alone, I feel it is necessary that every person should be instructed as to its nature and general characteristics.

And so, it is with this first chapter that I decided to elucidate the Kingdom of God's nature and describe some of its general characteristics, concepts, and elements. This will set the stage, so to speak, and serve as a solid foundation for the rest of the book's contents.

Kingdom knowledge and awareness are something I have found severely lacking in our churches' teachings in general and individual believers' lives.

To know how to operate in the Kingdom of God, you need to know how the Kingdom of God operates.

Those who seek to understand and know more about the Kingdom of God will reap tremendous rewards for their lives.

> To know how to operate in the Kingdom of God, you need to know how the Kingdom of God operates.

Jesus said:

"Therefore every scribe instructed concerning the kingdom of heaven is like a householder who brings out of his treasure things new and old." ~ Matthew 13:52 (NKJV)

I believe Jesus was saying here that everyone (especially teachers and scholars) who get instructed in the things of the Kingdom will grow in their understanding of both the Old and New Covenants. Kingdom instructions bring more clarity into the ways of God and into His will for man.

God is indeed involved in government—His government for His Kingdom.

Kingdom = Government

In the Book of Isaiah, we are given an amazing prophecy regarding Jesus and His role as the ultimate ruler:

> *"For unto us a Child is born, unto us a Son is given; And the government will be upon His shoulder. And His name will be called Wonderful, Counselor, Mighty God, Everlasting Father, Prince of Peace. Of the increase of His government and peace There will be no end, Upon the throne of David and over His kingdom, to order it and establish it with judgment and justice from that time forward, even forever. The zeal of the Lord of hosts will perform this." ~ Isaiah 9:6-7 (NKJV)*

The prophecy above concerning Jesus Christ as the coming Messiah portrays Him as *a bringer of Government* and as a ruler… as a *Prince*, no less! It speaks of the coming Kingdom of God as a *governing authority through its Messiah.*

We are all quite familiar with the words of The Lord's prayer: *"Thy Kingdom Come."* But it was Shakespeare who said, *"Familiarity breeds contempt."* We have become so familiar with the words of the Lord's prayer that we seem to take them for granted, or worse, we ignore their meaning.

I like the words of N.T. Wright when he says:

> *"The phrase 'kingdom of heaven,' which we find frequently in Matthew's Gospel where the others have 'kingdom of God,' does not refer to a place, called 'heaven,' where God's*

people will go after death. It refers to the rule of heaven, that is, of God, being brought to bear in the present world. Thy kingdom come, said Jesus, thy will be done, on earth as in heaven. Jesus' contemporaries knew that the creator God intended to bring justice and peace to his world here and now. The question was, how, when and through whom?"

When Jesus came to earth, He brought the Kingdom with Him, but He hadn't died, gone to heaven, and sent the Holy Spirit *yet*. The Kingdom was '*at hand*', but it still needed ushering in. This explains, at least partly, why He taught the disciples to pray, *"Thy Kingdom come."* That's because, at the time, more of it needed to be made manifest. And although much of it has been made manifest since Pentecost, more needs to come still. In other words, the Lord's prayer is definitely still needed and hasn't been done away with.

Furthermore, the passage in Isaiah 9:6-7 tells us that Jesus Christ would have the government on His shoulders and that there would be no end to the increase and peace of His government.

Encyclopedia Britannica had this to say about the Kingdom of God:

"Behind the Greek word for kingdom (basileia) lies the Aramaic term malkut, which Jesus may have used. Malkut refers primarily not to a geographical area or realm nor to the people inhabiting the realm but, rather, to the activity of the king himself, his exercise of sovereign power. The idea might better be conveyed in English by an expression such as kingship, rule, or sovereignty."

So, according to the (arguably) most prestigious body of secular knowledge, *Encyclopedia Britannica*, the Kingdom of God refers to the activity of the King Himself and His exercise of sovereign power. That's a powerful statement! In fact, the very term *'Kingdom of God'* is interchangeable with *'the Government of God.'*

I have found this idea to be helpful for myself as a Westerner to better grasp the concept of a Kingdom. I have also found that most other people understand it better this way as well. I suppose this has to do with our familiarity with the concept of government.

> The very term 'Kingdom of God' is interchangeable with 'the Government of God.'

Most people grew up within a system of government instead of within a monarchy.

Colonizing a New Realm

Many believers fail to understand why God created the earth and man. And no, it wasn't because God was bored. Most of us are like David, who penned the following words:

> *"When I consider Your heavens, the work of Your fingers, the moon and the stars, which You have ordained, what is man that You are mindful of him, and the son of man that You visit him? For You have made him a little lower than the angels, and You have crowned him with glory and honor. You have made him to have dominion over the works of Your hands; You have put all things under his feet, all sheep and oxen—even the beasts of the field, the birds of the air, and the fish of the sea that pass through the paths of the seas." ~ Psalm 8:3-8 (NKJV)*

In all honesty, I also have had similar thoughts from time to time as to our relevancy in His grand cosmic plan of the ages.

But we must keep in mind that the modus operandi of any Kingdom in order to prosper is *expansion*. I don't know of any successful kingdom in earth's history that wished to remain static. The essence of life is growth. The God of life always seeks to expand

His Kingdom, its glory, and its influence. Like it says in Isaiah: *Of the increase of His government and peace there will be no end.*

This concept of expansion began way before the coming of Christ. It is simply one of the characteristics of God to expand His influence and that of His Kingdom. In fact, we also observe the same bent in man. Man, who was made in the image of God, has done the same thing here on the earth—he has sought to expand his influence all over the earth. It is in man's nature to do so because it is part of his prerogative.

When God created the earth, He wanted to create a realm that would be completely different from heaven although an expansion of heaven. *He wanted to create a new thing.* He wanted to create a *physical* realm. He wanted to create a colony from heaven that would be physical in nature. He desired to populate this new realm with a new spirit-creature that would inhabit a physical body and extend His rule over this realm. So, in His delight and sovereignty, He chose to create *man.*

> 'Then God said, 'Let Us make man in Our image, according to Our likeness; let them have dominion over the fish of the sea, over the birds of the air, and over the cattle, over all the earth and over every creeping thing that creeps on the earth.' So God created man in His own image; in the image of God He created him; male and female He created them. Then God blessed them, and God said to them, 'Be fruitful and multiply; fill the earth and subdue it; have dominion over the fish of the sea, over the birds of the air, and over every living thing that moves on the earth.'" ~ Genesis 1:26-28 (NKJV)*

Heaven's Influence

So, this is how the earth became a colony of the Kingdom of Heaven. The intent of God was to make earth an extension of His kingdom in a physical realm. God is the ultimate innovator!

Merriam-Webster describes a colony as *a body of people living in a new territory but retaining ties with the parent state.*

I live in Canada. Canada is a colony of the British Empire, of Great Britain. Although much of our ties with Great Britain have waned throughout the centuries, we have retained much of the influence of our parent state. We have a common crown; a parliamentary system of government; the same language (with the addition of French), and a similar set of habits, ideals, philosophies, and values.

The same could be said of the earth after God formed Adam and put him there. Adam, along with Eve, was to colonize the realm by being fruitful and multiplying. They were to rule over the realm and colonize it with Heaven's influence. Influence means '*to flow into*'. Man is meant to *flow* Heaven's influence *into* the Earth Realm the same way God breathed life (flowed) into him.

> Influence means 'to flow into'. Man is meant to flow Heaven's influence into the Earth Realm the same way God breathed life (flowed) into him.

While we know they (Adam and Eve) made a mess of things, it is important to understand God's original intent when He made the earth and man. He didn't make heaven for man; He made the earth for man. He doesn't want man to populate heaven; He wants him to populate the earth.

Too many believers live with their sight set almost exclusively on heaven.

- ♛ **They long for heaven**
- ♛ **They think of heaven**
- ♛ **They sing of heaven**
- ♛ **They cry for heaven**
- ♛ **They dream of heaven**
- ♛ **They wish to go 'home' to be with the Lord**

I call these rocket-ship Christians: *They're so set on heaven that they're of little earthly use.* Or, to use the words of Oliver Wendell Holmes: *"Some people are so heavenly minded that they are no earthly good."*

That's unfortunate and yet undeniable. We've all met such Christians. Even I have been guilty of this mindset and conduct for a few seasons. Such unbridled desires for *Heaven* (or what heaven is perceived as) are due to a lack of biblical understanding about the purpose of man and what it means to be here.

Here is an unpopular truth: God made man to dominate and populate the earth... not heaven.

In Genesis 2:15 (ESV), we read: *"The Lord God took the man and put him in the garden of Eden to work it and keep it."*

So, contrary to popular belief, you and I were not expatriated here; *we were put here* for a powerful and distinct purpose. And this overarching purpose was to bring the influence of the Kingdom (government) of God and spread it to every nook and cranny of this realm by being fruitful and multiplying—both physically and spiritually (as stated in Genesis 1:26-28).

I love this quote by J.A. Hardgrave:

> *"What if the goal of Jesus was not just to get us from earth to heaven after we die, but to empower us to bring heaven to earth before we die?"*

> "What if the goal of Jesus was not just to get us from earth to heaven after we die, but to empower us to bring heaven to earth before we die?" ~ J.A. Hardgrave

Make no mistake. This book is meant to make you understand the Kingdom of God. Understanding the Kingdom of God will shift your outlook, shake your beliefs, and influence your actions—as well it should. This is what Kingdom knowledge does to a person. It is what it did for me.

Central Elements of Every Kingdom

Every kingdom in all of history, in order to be qualified as such, was composed of *four main elements*. The Kingdom of God is no exception. These four elements that are found in every Kingdom on earth and throughout history are *a king, a territory, laws, and subjects*.

A King: The King of the Kingdom of God is, of course, God Himself. There are plenty of instances in the Scripture where God is clearly identified as the undisputed monarch of earth and heaven. Here are just a few:

> *"Sing praises to God, sing praises! Sing praises to our King, sing praises! For God is the King of all the earth; sing praises with a psalm!"* ~ Psalm 47:6-7 (ESV)

> *"Your throne, O God, is forever and ever. The scepter of your kingdom is a scepter of uprightness."* ~ Psalm 45:6 (ESV)

> *"The Lord sits enthroned over the flood; the Lord sits enthroned as king forever."* ~ Psalm 29:10 (ESV)

> *"On his robe and on his thigh he has a name written, King of kings and Lord of lords."* ~ Revelation 19:16 (ESV)

The Kingship of God over all that exists is indisputable, and that, no matter where you stand theologically.

A Territory: Every kingdom has a territory. It is the piece of land owned by the king, over which he extends his rule. Even the word *kingdom* itself defines what a kingdom is. It is composed of two words: king-dom, a shortened version of *king-domain*, i.e., the *king's domain*. A domain is defined as the *territory over which dominion is exerted*.

Some kingdom territories are huge, such as the kingdom of the

British Empire, also known as the United Kingdom. During the 19th century, the United Kingdom ruled from London, England, and stretched over five continents!

Other kingdoms can be quite small. Take the kingdom of Brunei, for example; it is smaller than the state of Delaware, and yet, it still qualifies as a kingdom because it is spread over a delimited territory and is under the rule of a king.

As for the Kingdom of God, since its King is God Himself, there are not limits to the extent of its territory. Since He is the Creator and inceptor, God's ownership and rule extends all over heaven, earth, and beyond! Or, as Toy Story's Buzz Lightyear would say: *"To infinity, and beyond!"*

However, it was God's initial desire to appoint man as the dominating presence and as ruler of the earth realm. We'll dive into this truth even more in the next chapter.

Laws: God, our King, is a lawmaker. This is no surprise since every Kingdom has laws. And as the King, He makes and decrees those laws. His Kingdom is governed by His laws, which are expressed when He speaks, and thus by His Word.

There are three categories of laws that God gave in order to enable man to operate at full capacity and understanding in the earth realm: physical (natural law), moral (commandments and ethics), and spiritual (supernatural/Kingdom-related laws).

In the Bible, we read of God's *laws, commandments, decrees, statutes, testimonies, and ordinances.* These all have legal ramifications and point to a Holy Creator—God, who delights Himself in law and order.

The first five books of the Bible attributed to Moses, also known as the Pentateuch, are called the *Torah* in Hebrew. Torah has a range of meanings but is narrowed down to "Instruction," "Teaching," or "Law."

Although there are three categories of laws, there are two distinct categories that are earth-bound and familiar to us all: the physical laws (natural) and moral laws (commandments). The third category of laws (spiritual), which comes from the Kingdom of heaven, is not earth-bound. These heavenly laws are made manifest when we pray, when miracles are performed or witnessed, or when spiritual laws are accessed.

I made a good case study of spiritual laws in my book, *The Law of Attraction: Is It for Christians?* As I pointed out then, God is no respecter of persons when it comes to His established spiritual laws. Those who know how they work can make them work on their behalf—*whether they are Christians or not.* These spiritual laws and their working are not necessarily attached to one's salvation. Although I know this statement is controversial for some, I will not expand on it here.

And now, let's talk about God's natural laws.

In an article titled *God and Natural Law* (https://answersingenesis. org/is-god-real/god-natural-law/), Dr. Jason Lisle wrote the following concerning God's physical-natural laws:

> *Everything in the universe, every plant and animal, every rock, every particle of matter or light wave, is bound by laws which it has no choice but to obey. The Bible tells us that there are laws of nature—"ordinances of heaven and earth" (Jeremiah 33:25). These laws describe the way God normally accomplishes His will in the universe.*
>
> *God's logic is built into the universe, and so the universe is not haphazard or arbitrary. It obeys laws of chemistry that are logically derived from the laws of physics, many of which can be logically derived from other laws of physics and laws of mathematics. The most fundamental laws of nature exist only because God wills them to; they are the logical, orderly way that the Lord upholds and sustains the universe He has created.*

These "laws of nature" are embedded within creation itself and attract inherent consequences when broken. For example, we know that you cannot break the law of gravity. Well, you can try, but it will bring you a world of hurt if you do so.

Human sexuality is also part of God's natural order and has inherent natural laws attached to it. When speaking of sexual sin, Paul wrote of the inherent consequences of going against the natural order. Of homosexuality, he said that those who committed such acts *"received in themselves the due penalty for their error"* Romans 1:27 (NIV). And of the sin of fornication, in 1 Corinthians 6:18 (NIV), he said:

> *"Flee from sexual immorality. Every other sin a person commits is outside the body, but the sexually immoral person sins against his own body."*

In other words, sexual sins are not just the breaking of God's moral law but also the breaking of His natural law.

Only recently has science confirmed just how true these passages are. A little over a decade ago, scientists found out about a scientific phenomenon called *male microchimerism.*

"What is male microchimerism," you ask?

Well, it is the phenomena by which some women may retain the DNA of every man they have ever slept with within their own bodies. *Yikes!*

Of course, the ramifications of this phenomenon are far-reaching and honestly quite scary. But suffice it to say that this gives even more meaning and credence to the Bible when it says that *"the two shall become one flesh."*

Furthermore, many deliverance ministers have confirmed that demons can be transferred through illicit sexual union. This is yet another thing they don't teach us in Sunday school.

As for the moral laws of God, His commandments and precepts, we know they were given to man for just conduct, peace, and as an expression of God's holiness reflected through His people as they obey Him. Furthermore, it is interesting to note that the Bible's definition of sin *is the transgression of the law* or the breaking of His law (1 John 3:4; KJV).

As citizens of the Kingdom, in order to benefit fully of our rights and privileges, we must, just like King David, delight ourselves in the laws of God—which are found in His Word. They are also to be found throughout His Creation, for those willing to look around and learn. This subjection and delight in His ways are what bring blessings to our lives. This is what gives us the favor of the King.

David said it this way:

> *"The law of the Lord is perfect, converting the soul; the testimony of the Lord is sure, making wise the simple; the statutes of the Lord are right, rejoicing the heart; the commandment of the Lord is pure, enlightening the eyes; the fear of the Lord is clean, enduring forever; the judgments of the Lord are true and righteous altogether. More to be desired are they than gold, yea, than much fine gold; sweeter also than honey and the honeycomb. Moreover by them Your servant is warned, and in keeping them there is great reward." ~ Psalm 19:7-11 (NKJV)*

Subjects (citizens): Every kingdom has subjects. A king's rule is not just over a given territory but also extends to the people living within that territory—to its citizens. It is also interesting to note that, in a kingdom, the citizens are called subjects. The word is from the Latin *subjectus,* which means 'brought under.' This indicates that they are *subjected* to the King's decisions, laws, and decrees. They are *brought under* his rule—for better or worse.

But this definition may sound pejorative to some. So, keep in mind that conversely, subjects are also brought under the king's favor, benevolence, magnanimity, and blessings. And this is even truer when your king is the King of kings, such as is the case for Kingdom citizens.

Furthermore, people become citizens of any given kingdom by birth. I am a citizen of Canada because I was born here. Therefore, I am subject to its laws, constitution, but I also have rights and privileges. Similarly, you and I must be born into the Kingdom of God by being born again or born 'from above.' I cover this in detail in chapter 4.

Every citizen in every kingdom has rights and privileges, but also duties and responsibilities.

As a citizen, I am required to uphold and obey my country's laws (provided they agree with God's laws). I am required to pay taxes. I am required to be a productive citizen and to contribute, etc.

> Every citizen in every kingdom has rights and privileges, but also duties and responsibilities.

The same can be said of the Kingdom of God. We have rights, privileges, duties, and responsibilities. We were granted the highest blessings available and given all things that pertain to life and godliness (Ephesians 1; 2 Peter 1:3). However, we are mandated to bear fruit and charged as ambassadors to fulfill a Great Commission (John 15; Matthew 28:19-20).

The Bible says that we were given the *power* to become not just mere subjects but actual children of the King (John 1:12). And such power cannot be taken lightly.

More Kingdom Concepts

Aside from the four main kingdom elements described previously, there are even more concepts to be found in the Bible that confirm just how real and tangible God's Kingdom is. In fact, after I understood the fundamentals of the Kingdom for myself, I was amazed at how much the Bible reads like a constitution for believers. I was also amazed at how many kingdom parallels can be woven between the Kingdom of God and earthly kingdoms and governments.

So, there is that: *every Kingdom has a constitution.*

A Constitution is defined as *the basic principles and laws of a nation, state, or social group that determine the powers and duties of the government and guarantee certain rights to the people in it.*

Every country has a written constitution, and if you're like me, you've...um, well, probably never read it. Yes, I can be neglectful in some matters. But I do know I should read it, though. I never read it because I am more enthralled with my Kingdom citizenship than with my earthly citizenship. I prefer reading my Kingdom constitution because it bears a greater impact on my life than the earthly one I am under. The Kingdom of God overarches any earthly kingdom. Its constitution supersedes anything else you may be under in the earthly realm. You will understand this more fully by the end of this book.

By now, you've probably made the connection that *the Bible is the constitution of the Kingdom of God and for its citizens.* But unlike any other constitution, you don't want to let this one gather dust. Read it, meditate on it, study it, and decree it over your life every day!

> The Bible is the constitution of the Kingdom of God and for its citizens.

Rights: In any given country, citizens have rights. According to Wikipedia, rights are *legal, social, or ethical principles of freedom or entitlement; that is, rights are the fundamental normative rules about what is allowed of people or owed to people according to some legal system.*

The Kingdom of God is a kingdom that operates by law. When a citizen's rights are infringed upon, it is his privilege to claim those rights in the courts. We will examine this further in the chapters on authority and faith. But suffice it to say that as citizens of the Kingdom of God, we were given by law tremendous privileges and rights that we can boldly claim before the King through declaration, intercession, and prayers. Just as there is a due process in any government to claim your rights, so it is with the Kingdom of God.

Interestingly, the apostle Paul appealed to his rights as a Roman citizen twice in the Book of Acts (Acts 16:37-38; Acts 22:25-28). In the latter passage, Paul states that he was born a Roman citizen. His citizenship status by birth is why he can successfully appeal to the emperor (Acts 25). We can surmise that if he understood his earthly rights, he most certainly understood his Kingdom rights as well.

Ministries: The word *ministry* is a familiar one for most believers today. In fact, it is very familiar in the Kingdom of God vernacular. In our churches, we have different ministries: youth ministries, worship ministries, singles' ministries, hospitality ministries, food pantry ministries, etc. Our pastors and paid leaders are following their call to *minister* or into the *ministry*. We often see ministries bearing the names of their founders in North America; ex: so-and-so ministries. My own ministry is called *Thriving on Purpose Ministries*.

Likewise, Kingdoms (governments) have different ministries.

The word *ministry* simply means, in the middle English *ministerie*, *minstri*, which is to say: *personal service*. Also, it is from the middle French *ministère*, which means *service* and *duty*. Going back to Old French, it is borrowed from the Latin *ministerium*, meaning: activity of a servant, duty, task, support.

In Canada, as in most governed territories, kingdoms, and countries, we have different *ministries*, or services, for the citizens:

- ♛ **Ministry of Health**
- ♛ **Ministry of Education**
- ♛ **Ministry of Defense**
- ♛ **Ministry of Environment**
- ♛ **Ministry of Employment, etc.**

It is useful, in order to understand these terms better, to replace them with the word 'service.' The service of education or the service of environment, etc.

Good governments are always put in place to serve the people. Their ministries (services) are put in place to help the citizens.

The Kingdom of God also has different branches in its government or ministries, if you will. These are established governmental services that are made readily available to all Kingdom citizens.

Consider how these differing services bless us regularly...

Ministry of Justice: The Kingdom of God has a judicial system—a ministry of justice. There are, indeed, *courts in heaven.* Surprised? You shouldn't be. God is called a Judge in many places throughout Scripture. And, as a judge, He does preside over a court. The Bible says, in Psalm 82:1-2 (NKJV):

"God stands in the congregation of the mighty; He judges among the gods. How long will you judge unjustly and show partiality to the wicked?"

And the New Living Translation (NLT) renders it this way:

"God presides over heaven's court; He pronounces judgment on the heavenly beings: 'How long will you hand down unjust decisions by favoring the wicked?'"

Furthermore, the Bible also tells us that Jesus is our advocate (our lawyer) before the Father in court (1 John 2:1). He defends us against the accuser of the brethren, Satan, who accuses believers day and night before the Father (Revelation 12:10).

In Daniel and Revelation, we are told that there are judicial proceedings involving open books (plural) in the heavenly courts.

Daniel's vision in chapter 7 of the book bearing his name is that of a courtroom—the courts of heaven!

> *"I watched till thrones were put in place, and the Ancient of Days was seated; His garment was white as snow, and the hair of His head was like pure wool. His throne was a fiery flame, its wheels a burning fire; a fiery stream issued and came forth from before Him. A thousand thousands ministered to Him; ten thousand times ten thousand stood before Him. The court was seated, and the books were opened." ~ Daniel 7:9-10 (NKJV)*

And in Revelation 20:11-15 (NKJV), we get a clear picture of the Final Judgement:

> *"Then I saw a great white throne and Him who sat on it, from whose face the earth and the heaven fled away. And there was found no place for them. And I saw the dead, small and great, standing before God, and books were opened. And another book was opened, which is the Book of Life. And the dead were judged according to their works, by the things which were written in the books. The sea gave up the dead who were in it, and Death and Hades delivered up the dead who were in them. And they were judged, each one according to his works. Then Death and Hades were cast into the lake of fire. This is the second death. And anyone not found written in the Book of Life was cast into the lake of fire."*

There is so much to learn about God's laws, His administration, and the courts of heaven! Too much to write about here. However, Christian teacher and author, Robert Henderson, has written a whole series of books to help believers better understand how the courts of heaven operate and how believers can access this particular heavenly realm through prayer and intercession to plead cases and receive justice from the King.

Here is what Robert Henderson said about the power and impact of these heavenly proceedings:

> *"Once the court is in session and the books are open, cases can be presented, legal precedents set and the dominion rights of principalities removed from nations."*

Ministry of Defense: Every kingdom, or nation, has an army. The purpose of the ministry of defense is to protect the country and its citizens from all threats and enemies, "foreign and domestic." The Kingdom of God has an immensely powerful army serving the King.

Honestly, I used to believe I was part of God's army. As a man seeking a testosterone rush, a clearer identity, and validation, this gave me a great sense of worth. I told myself I was *'a warrior in the army of the Lord'!* And while I do wage warfare against the Enemy on occasion, the Bible doesn't support this notion very much— especially under the New Covenant.

As New Covenant believers, we are not usually referred to as an army. Rather, we are said to be His bride (the Church). We are also compared in many instances to… sheep. So yes, in this war, we are more akin to civilians than soldiers. I know… bummer, right?

So, although we were given tremendous authority and power as citizens, *we are not His army per se.*

Nonetheless, you can be sure it doesn't mean that we shouldn't learn spiritual warfare. There are aspects of Kingdom warfare that beckon civilians to bravely take up arms. While the Kingdom's war is fought on a cosmic scale, we are nevertheless involved in a very civil war here in the earth realm. And I know many civilians who can kick some serious spiritual butt! So, every believer should learn spiritual self-defense and *put on the whole armor of God* (Eph. 6:11). In fact, I strongly advise my listeners and readers to learn spiritual warfare, spiritual self-defense and offense, and learn how to counter Enemy tactics.

Nevertheless, and as disappointing as this can be to some of you (as it was for me), *we are not the main army in God's Kingdom.* We are more like a militia.

As a testimony to His Kingdom, Jesus told Pilate:

> *"My kingdom is not of this world. If my kingdom were of this world, my servants would have been fighting, that I might not be delivered over to the Jews. But my kingdom is not from the world." ~ John 18:36, (ESV)*

Now, obviously, we see from this passage that Jesus' fighting servants were *not His disciples.* He was referring to *other servants.* In Matthew, we are told who these are. After the disciples put up a fight, sword in hand, to prevent Jesus from being captured, He said:

> *"Put your sword in its place, for all who take the sword will perish by the sword. Or do you think that I cannot now pray to My Father, and He will provide Me with more than twelve legions of angels?" ~ Matthew 26:52-53 (NKJV)*

Here, Jesus was saying to Peter, *"Civilian, this is not your job!"*

Yes, by now, you've surely guessed that the angels act as the main military force in God's Kingdom. In fact, *they are the military, the secret service, and the royal guard!*

Angels, whom we will cover more fully in chapter 6, come in various shapes, sizes, ranks, and fulfill many roles for the King. Although they are all servants, some are messengers, some are warriors, some are guardians, and some are secret service and intelligence (spies).

Angels possess many enviable "superpowers" such as superstrength, near invulnerability, superspeed, superintelligence, and shape-shifting abilities, among other things. They use these in the service of the King and on behalf of you and me on a daily basis.

Sometimes, I like to reflect on how many times angels have come to help or rescue me without being aware. I know of a few that I am certain of and remember fondly. However, I also know without a doubt that many times, I got rescued or helped while I was unaware of an angelic presence.

And the good news is that there are at least twice as many good angels as fallen ones (Revelation 12:4, 7-9)! We are therefore, as Hebrews 12:22 says, blessed with *"an innumerable company of angels."*

> Angels possess many enviable "superpowers" such as superstrength, near invulnerability, superspeed, superintelligence, and shape-shifting abilities, among other things.

So, as citizens, we are never outnumbered or outgunned. Our King has blessed us with the most powerful military ever with beings of tremendous power. Most of the time, they act on our behalf, unseen or unrecognized, to protect us from evil and harm. The Bible says that the King Himself:

> *"Shall give His angels charge over you, to keep you in all your ways. In their hands they shall bear you up, lest you dash your foot against a stone." ~ Psalm 91:11-12 (NKJV)*

Ministry of Education: The apostle Paul tells us about the ministry of education and how it relates to the citizens of the Kingdom.

> *"He Himself gave some to be apostles, some prophets, some evangelists, and some pastors and teachers, for the equipping of the saints for the work of ministry, for the edifying of the body of Christ, till we all come to the unity of the faith and of the knowledge of the Son of God, to a perfect man, to the measure of the stature of the fullness of Christ; that we should no longer be children, tossed to and fro and carried about with every wind of doctrine, by the trickery of men,*

in the cunning craftiness of deceitful plotting, but, speaking the truth in love, may grow up in all things into Him who is the head—Christ—from whom the whole body, joined and knit together by what every joint supplies, according to the effective working by which every part does its share, causes growth of the body for the edifying of itself in love." ~ Ephesians 4:11-16 (NKJV)

This aptly called fivefold ministry (apostles, prophets, evangelists, pastors, teachers) is meant to be our *Kingdom Ministry of Education*.

But what's more, is that we were all given the Ultimate Teacher residing within, who teaches us all things (John 14:26; 1 John 2:27). The Holy Spirit is meant to guide us into ALL truth (John 16:13).

More Kingdom Elements

As you get to know your constitution better (The Bible), you will get to know more about all the Kingdom is and has to offer you as a citizen. I remember how exciting it was for me when I began to understand Kingdom elements, principles, and concepts. It made the Scriptures pulsate with new life and revelation for me.

The Kingdom of God also has:

- **A Currency:** The Kingdom's currency is not the dollar, the yen, or the euro. No. The currency used by Kingdom citizens is their *faith*. We will dive deeper in this truth in latter chapters.

- **Ambassadors:** As citizens of the Kingdom living in a foreign land (earth), we act as ambassadors for the King of Glory. As such, we represent the King's will, His rule, and His authority wherever we go.

- **An Economy:** The wealth of the King is limitless. He owns it all. There are over 2000 passages that relate to money, wealth, or possessions in our constitution—the Bible. And, as any good King would, *God delights in the prosperity of His servants* (Psalm 35:27).

♛ **A Secret Service:** Some of God's angels act as the military, others as guards, others as messengers, others are part of the secret service. They go undercover on secret missions to inform, warn, help, assist, or rescue God's children daily.

Clash of Kingdoms

Another element that most worthwhile Kingdoms have is: an adversary.

Kingdom Fundamentals was meant to dig deeper in the understanding of the Kingdom—Our Kingdom. Therefore, it was on purpose that I tried to avoid, as much as possible, giving too much attention to *the kingdom of darkness*. Nevertheless, since as believers we find ourselves at the crossroads of two kingdoms clashing, it is necessary to address it.

All great kingdoms in history were at war at one time or another. The Kingdom of God is no exception. Although spiritual in nature, the Kingdom is and has been at war for millennia. This war does contain some similarities with earthly kingdoms clashing, but it also has major differences. Earthly wars are fought over wealth or territory, and while these elements are part of the biblical conflict, the major difference is found in this: *this is a war over men's souls.*

Make no mistake about it, Satan does indeed have a kingdom of his own. Consider these Scriptures:

> *"The devil took him up and showed him all the kingdoms of the world in a moment of time, and said to him, 'To you I will give all this authority and their glory, for it has been delivered to me, and I give it to whom I will. If you, then, will worship me, it will all be yours.'"* ~ Luke 4:5-7 (ESV)

> *"Every kingdom divided against itself is laid waste, and no city or house divided against itself will stand. And if Satan casts out Satan, he is divided against himself. How then will his kingdom stand?"* ~ *Matthew 12:26-26 (ESV)*

> *"For he (God) has rescued us from the kingdom of darkness and transferred us into the Kingdom of his dear Son."* ~ *Colossians 1:13 (NLT)*

Furthermore, the devil, as the general of the enemy army, has acquired quite a following over the centuries and since his original rebellion. He is not leading a haphazard group of disorganized factions. No. He leads a highly organized, hierarchical, and efficient force that is hell-bent (pun intended) on dethroning the King. Keep in mind that Satan used to be a general in the hierarchy of heaven. That is where he learned the rank and file of an efficient fighting force. In other words... he learned how a kingdom operates while in heaven; therefore he learned from the best.

The apostle Paul clearly warned us and reminded us of this fact in His epistle to the Ephesians:

> *"Our struggle is not against flesh and blood, but against the rulers, against the authorities, against the powers of this dark world and against the spiritual forces of evil in the heavenly realms. Therefore put on the full armor of God, so that when the day of evil comes, you may be able to stand your ground, and after you have done everything, to stand."* ~ *Ephesians 6:12-13 (NIV)*

Paul talks here of *rulers, authorities, powers,* and *spiritual forces of evil.* In other words, we struggle against fallen angels, Satan's angelic generals assigned over territories (towns, cities, states, and countries), demonic entities of all kinds who influence, indoctrinate, tempt, and torment believers and unbelievers alike.

Also, while Satan has a spiritual army, he has a very human

one as well: the tares among the wheat. Just as God has servants and children upon the earth, so does the devil have distinct human agents doing his will on the earth to counter the Kingdom of God at every turn.

Jesus spoke of *the wheat and the tares, the sheep and the goats, the brood of vipers*, and *the wolves in sheep's clothing*.

Concerning the parable of the wheat and the tares, Jesus explained it to His disciples and said:

> *"His disciples came to Him, saying, 'Explain to us the parable of the tares of the field.'*
>
> *He answered and said to them: 'He who sows the good seed is the Son of Man. The field is the world, the good seeds are the sons of the kingdom, <u>but the tares are the sons of the wicked one. The enemy who sowed them is the devil</u>, the harvest is the end of the age, and the reapers are the angels. Therefore as the tares are gathered and burned in the fire, so it will be at the end of this age. The Son of Man will send out His angels, and they will gather out of His kingdom all things that offend, and those who practice lawlessness, and will cast them into the furnace of fire. There will be wailing and gnashing of teeth. Then the righteous will shine forth as the sun in the kingdom of their Father. He who has ears to hear, let him hear!'" ~ Matthew 13:36-43 (NKJV)*

Indeed, if we are willing to have eyes to see and ears to hear, we will recognize that there are tares on the earth. There are those who are not of God but are of the devil. They serve him and him alone. They infiltrate, subdue, divide, and conquer for their master–Satan. They look just like wheat, but are not. Jesus said:

> *"You will know them by their fruits." ~ Matthew 7:16 (NKJV)*

It shocks most Christians when I tell them that these people known as *"tares"* cannot be redeemed. And yet, this is strongly indicated in Scripture.

Respected theologian, J.I. Packer, said:

> *"The idea that all are children of God is not found in the Bible anywhere."*

So, as you engage further in serving God's Kingdom, always keep these things in mind, as you will surely encounter many tares who will oppose you forcefully.

God is King, Period.

Let's now get back to the King of the Kingdom.

The Bible makes it clear that *God is in charge*. He is the King. The opening verse of this chapter, taken from Isaiah 9:6-7, is just one of the many which testify to God's rulership as King and Lord over all.

Another verse says it this way:

> *"The Lord has established his throne in the heaven, and his kingdom rules over all." ~ Psalm 103:19 (NKJV)*

Every kingdom has a king. The word '*King*-dom' itself indicates the presence of a king. For many believers though, the concept of God as King over a determined Kingdom suffers somewhat of a lack of understanding.

Most of us have no problem seeing God as creator, as redeemer, or even as Father, but for some reason, our imagination suffers when it comes to having a clear understanding of God as King.

As I mentioned before, most of us in the West live in a democracy where the people elect a president or prime minister. We have, for the most part, parted ways with the notion of a *monarchy*. We have become (or always were) unfamiliar with it. Oh, sure, there is still a queen in England, and we are familiar with the royal family because of the tabloids and the news media. But our understanding of royalty is skewed and now limited to a glamorous and entertaining one—not an experiential, and dare I say, *real* one.

A pastor friend of mine once said: *"The people who hate monarchy better get over it quick. God is all about monarchy, and Christ is the King. And when He comes back to set up His permanent rule, there will be no question about that."*

Indeed, when the Lord returns, there will be no question that He's the King—the *King of kings and the Lord of lords.* Jesus hinted quite a few times during His ministry on earth that He was indeed a King.

The prophet Daniel saw it in a vision too:

> *"I was watching in the night visions, and behold, one like the Son of Man, coming with the clouds of heaven! He came to the Ancient of Days, and they brought Him near before Him. Then to Him was given dominion and glory and a kingdom, that all peoples, nations, and languages should serve Him. His dominion is an everlasting dominion, which shall not pass away, and His kingdom the one which shall not be destroyed." ~ Daniel 7:13-14 (NKJV)*

And Jesus, when brought before Pilate, confirmed His Kingship when pressed by the Roman governor:

> *'Jesus answered, "My Kingdom is not of this world. If My Kingdom were of this world, My servants would fight, so that I should not be delivered to the Jews; but now My Kingdom is not from here."*

> *Pilate therefore said to Him, "Are You a king then?"*

> *Jesus answered, "You say rightly that I am a king. For this cause I was born, and for this cause I have come into the world, that I should bear witness to the truth. Everyone who is of the truth hears My voice."' ~ John 18:36-37 (NKJV)*

Throughout this book, I speak of many things. I bring to light many Kingdom principles. These will serve you well if you understand and apply them. Nevertheless, never forget throughout that if you pursue Kingdom principles above His presence, you are looking for the Kingdom without its King. May it never be!

> **Anyone who seeks first the Kingdom must seek it through its King.**

Anyone who seeks first the Kingdom must seek it through its King.

The Culture of the Kingdom

Every Kingdom has a culture. Here in Canada, we are often identified as *"Unarmed Americans with free healthcare… who are nice."*

While humorous, this description does indeed aptly define Canadians, in general anyway. We are known as people who say "sorry" all the time. It sometimes behooves me just how nice (naively so) we can be. Our southern American neighbours love to jest with us concerning this fact. I think they see us as pushovers. Nevertheless, while generalized, it paints an accurate picture of our culture.

We could define other cultures similarly, even using just one word. For example, perhaps you are familiar with the following stereotypes (and I am not trying to offend anyone here): American grandiloquence, French snobbism, Japanese ingenuity, Indian tech-savviness, German efficiency, Danish gloom, etc. These cultures can pretty much all be defined using just one word.

Well, just like earthly kingdoms, the Kingdom of God also has its distinct culture. In fact, its culture is extraordinarily strong, defined, and recognizable. But before I define the culture of the Kingdom, allow me to answer the question: What exactly is *culture*?

The best definition I have ever heard of culture is: *This is how we do things here.*

Indeed, culture is the answer to the question: *How are things done here?* How are things done in your house, in your organization, in your company, in your country?

The culture of the Kingdom of God has many defining characteristics that would take me a long time to expound. In fact, the subject would make for a great book on its own. I can only give you the crux of it here.

When you think about it, culture is prevalent everywhere we go. In other words, there is a way we conduct ourselves, or how things are done, everywhere we go. Every country has a culture. Every company and organization has a culture. Every household has its own definite culture. Your family and mine have our own way of doing things. In fact, even elevators have a culture, and I can prove it.

> Culture is the answer to the question: *How are things done here?* How are things done in your house, in your organization, in your company, in your country?

If you enter an elevator, would you get in and face all the people while standing with your back to the door? No? Why not? Because that's not how we usually behave in an elevator, is it? Usually, in an elevator, we get in, turn around, and face the door. We also tend to avoid eye contact with others, right? So, simply put, this is part of the culture of an elevator. This is *how we do things* in an elevator.

So, what defines the culture of the Kingdom of God? What is *the way we do things* as citizens of the Kingdom? That's a good question.

To know the culture of a kingdom, you look at what its citizens embrace and practice.

When you tell people you are a born-again Christian, what image do you think comes to their mind? Well, right away, their concept of who you are becomes clearer, right? For example, they know that you probably:

- ♛ **Are good-natured**
- ♛ **Attend a church**
- ♛ **Read the Bible**
- ♛ **Believe in God and Jesus**
- ♛ **Pray regularly**

Additionally, knowing you are a believer makes them expect certain things from you. How many of those you work with, knowing you're a Christ-follower, would be shocked if you cussed? Probably all of them. Why? Because cussing isn't part of the culture of the Kingdom or its citizens.

How many would be shocked or confused if you told dirty jokes all the time? Probably all of them. They would probably even call you on it.

That's the culture of the Kingdom of God. Citizens of the Kingdom of God are expected to have certain beliefs and behaviours congruent with the Kingdom's culture. They are held to a higher standard. The culture of the Kingdom is one of godly fruit. The culture of the Kingdom represents the King Himself.

Citizens of the Kingdom are to bear the fruit of the culture which are the fruit of the Spirit of its King, stated in Galatians 5:22-23:

> *Joy, peace, forbearance, kindness, goodness, faithfulness, gentleness, and self-control.*

While this help to identify the culture of the Kingdom of God, I believe Jesus gave us the best answer to this question when He said to His disciples:

"A new commandment I give to you, that you love one another; as I have loved you, that you also love one another. By this all will know that you are My disciples, if you have love for one another." ~ John 13:34-35 (NKJV)

By commanding a level of love that goes above and beyond normality, Jesus established the cultural benchmark of the Kingdom. It is by this that others are to be stirred and enticed to become citizens themselves. In other words, they will know you by your fruit and desire to know how you got it.

Australian missiologist, Michael Frost, said:

"If your neighbors did an analysis of your life, what would they learn about the kingdom?"

Love is the overarching cultural characteristic of the Kingdom of God. By it, people feel the King's presence, acknowledge His servants, and desire to become citizens themselves.

We are to live as committed Kingdom citizens so that it provokes questions for which the Gospel of Christ is the answer.

Myles Munroe said:

"The Kingdom is the love of God prevailing in politics, in business, in government, in media. It is all the impact of the laws of God creating a social environment where the strong help the weak, where those who have give to those who don't. It's a society where relationships are built on love."

Love is the overarching cultural characteristic of the Kingdom of God. By it, people feel the King's presence, acknowledge His servants, and desire to become citizens themselves.

The apostle Paul, in 1 Corinthians 13:1-13, also gave us a good reminder of how central love is to the Kingdom of God's campaign. In his epic description of the

63

importance of *agape* (transcendent, from God) love, he makes it quite clear that *if we have not love, we are nothing* (v.2). In other words, as Kingdom citizens, if we do not have love, we are not bringing the culture of the Kingdom with us.

Now, it has been said that *"Love conquers all."* If so, how does this translate for us as Kingdom citizens?

Many Mountains Left to Conquer

There are many characters I love in the Bible—warts and all. One such character is Caleb, in the Old Testament.

I've always pictured him as a flinty old warrior, what we would call a *badass* today. And that he was!

Of the twelve spies who returned from Canaan, he was the only one, along with Joshua, who believed they could take the land—even though it was populated with… *giants!* He told Moses, *"Let us go up at once and occupy it, for we are well able to overcome it."* ~ Numbers 13:30 (ESV)

The least we can say is that the man was not easily intimidated.

Even in his old age, after he had fought and won many hard battles for Israel, he still had much fight in him. He remained undeterred in his faith and capabilities.

In the Book of Joshua, chapter 14:6-15 (NLT), he says the following to his leader (Joshua):

> *"Remember what the Lord said to Moses, the man of God, about you and me when we were at Kadesh-barnea. I was forty years old when Moses, the servant of the Lord, sent me from Kadesh-barnea to explore the land of Canaan. I returned and gave an honest report, but my brothers who went with me frightened the people from entering the Promised Land. For my part, I wholeheartedly followed the Lord my God. So that day Moses solemnly promised me, 'The land of Canaan on which you were just walking will*

be your grant of land and that of your descendants forever, because you wholeheartedly followed the Lord my God.'

"Now, as you can see, the Lord has kept me alive and well as he promised for all these forty-five years since Moses made this promise—even while Israel wandered in the wilderness. Today I am eighty-five years old. I am as strong now as I was when Moses sent me on that journey, and I can still travel and fight as well as I could then. So give me the hill country that the Lord promised me. You will remember that as scouts we found the descendants of Anak living there in great, walled towns. But if the Lord is with me, I will drive them out of the land, just as the Lord said."

So Joshua blessed Caleb son of Jephunneh and gave Hebron to him as his portion of land. Hebron still belongs to the descendants of Caleb son of Jephunneh the Kenizzite because he wholeheartedly followed the Lord, the God of Israel. (Previously Hebron had been called Kiriath-arba. It had been named after Arba, a great hero of the descendants of Anak.)

And the land had rest from war."

Kingdom expanders are like Caleb. They want to conquer for the Lord and His Kingdom—and they do not care who or what stands in their way. They have faith; they are brave, and they are bold.

Likewise today, there are mountains left to conquer. And in the sight of many believers, these seem hard to take. We see these mountains as belonging to giants. And in many ways, they do. Nevertheless, we need to choose this day if we will be like Caleb and Joshua, or like the other ten spies, who were fearful and afraid to engage the enemy.

I very much like the scene in the movie *Troy*, where a young boy exchanges a few words with the Greek champion, Achilles (played by Brad Pitt), right before an important duel.

In the movie, Achilles is summoned by his king to go toe to toe with the greatest and most accomplished warrior of the rival army of Thessaly: Boagrius. Boagrius is a muscle-bound mountain of a man, not unlike what we would have imagined Goliath to look like. The winner of the duel will spare his own army further harm.

As Achilles is mounting his horse and getting ready to head into battle, the young boy says to him:

"The Thessalonian you're fighting... he's the biggest man I've ever seen. I wouldn't want to fight him."

To which Achilles gives the epic reply: *"That's why no one will remember your name."*

Now, let me ask you a question…

Do you remember the names of all twelve spies who were sent out to spy on the land in Numbers chapter 13, or just the names of Joshua and Caleb?

Like me, you probably only remember Joshua and Caleb. And yet, the names of all twelve spies are listed in the chapter. But no one remembers their name.

So, if we desire to leave a godly legacy of Kingdom influence, we too, like Caleb, have mountains to conquer.

The mountains that are before us have been listed in certain circles as *"The Seven Mountains of Influence"* or *"The Seven Mountains of Culture."* This concept was revealed to men of God back in the 1970s. Yes, despite it being deemed controversial, I believe the concept is God-given and part of His last-days plan for His Church.

Here are the seven mountains, according to the seven-mountain mandate:

- Education
- Religion
- Family
- Business
- Government/Military
- Arts & Entertainment
- Media

In order to take on the task of *"taking the land"* or taking the mountain or killing the giant, we first need to see it. And secondly, we need to want it. And when I say *want it*, I mean *really want it!*

This, then, begs the question…

Are You All In?

The disciples, and especially the apostles, were willing to *'leave it all behind for the sake of the Kingdom'*.

The same couldn't be said of the rich young ruler, though. His story is told in Matthew 19:16-22; Mark 10:17-27; and Luke 18:18-23. After Jesus had tested him, the rich young ruler proved incapable of entering the Kingdom of God because he was overly attached to his wealth and unwilling to part with it.

Back then (and today still), wealth was seen as evidence of God's favor. So, when Jesus, referring to the young man, said that it was *"harder for a rich man to enter the Kingdom of God than for a camel to go through the eye of a needle,"* it made the disciples worried about their own salvation. *"Who then can be saved?"* they asked.

One of my favourite passages of scriptures is the ensuing conversation between a worried Peter and Jesus:

> *"Peter said, 'See, we have left all and followed You.' So He said to them, 'Assuredly, I say to you, there is no one who has left house or parents or brothers or wife or children, for the sake of the kingdom of God, who shall not receive many times more in this present time, and in the age to come eternal life.'" ~ Luke 18:29 (NKJV)*

In effect, Peter was asking: *"Look Jesus, we're all 100% in. We left it all behind as proof. So, if you don't mind my asking; what's in it for us?"*

A few years back, I thought I was, just like the disciples in Jesus' day, all in for the Kingdom's sake. On top of my full-time job with

Canada Post, I had my podcast going. I used most of my free time to create content for *Thriving on Purpose* and write more books. I really thought I was an active and engaged Kingdom citizen…until one night when the Lord gave me a dream…

In the dream, I was walking in a field going up a hill. Suddenly, coming up from the ground was an immense and beautiful treasure chest. As I beheld it, it opened up to reveal a blinding light emanating from it. Then, behind me, I heard a voice, which I knew was the Lord's. He asked: *"Are you all in?"* And then I woke up.

It was then that I understood that my version of being all in for the kingdom and Jesus' version were two vastly different things. Ever since then, I have been striving to seek the Kingdom first, even more, to be 'all in' and find this hidden treasure in the field.

Whether we like to admit it or not, many of us are like the rich young ruler. He served as a cautionary tale. Many of us want to keep something back from God—our time, money, and effort. And yet, the price for entry into the Kingdom and access to its glory is *everything*.

> 'He said to them, *"Whoever desires to come after Me, let him deny himself, and take up his cross, and follow Me. For whoever desires to save his life will lose it, but whoever loses his life for My sake and the gospel's will save it."'* ~ Mark 8:34-35 (NKJV)

It's a hefty price tag for sure, but the rewards are, well… *Out of this world!*

MAN'S DOMINION MANDATE

Understanding Man's Place in Creation

*"And God blessed them, and God said unto them, Be
fruitful, and multiply, and replenish the earth, and subdue
it: and have dominion over the fish of the sea, and over the
fowl of the air, and over every living thing that moveth upon
the earth." ~ Genesis 1:28 (KJV)*

T
o understand God's Kingdom Purpose for Man, we must go
back to the beginning of our story… in Genesis.

In the Bible, God says:

*"Remember the former things of old, for I am God, and there
is no other; I am God, and there is none like Me, declaring
the end from the beginning, and from ancient times things
that are not yet done, saying, 'My counsel shall stand, and I
will do all My pleasure." ~ Isaiah 46:9-10 (NKJV)*

I know many of my readers do not like to read extra-biblical
accounts of Jesus. They perceive them as untrue, potentially
dangerous, and choose to steer clear. Nevertheless, if we choose
to remain open-minded, we can find some real gems in some of
those texts–whether or not they are (or are considered) canon. For
example, in the extra-biblical *Gospel of Thomas*, the following is
written in part 18:

*"The disciples said to Jesus, "Tell us how our end will be."
Jesus said, "Have you discovered, then, the beginning, that*

you look for the end? For where the beginning is, there will the end be." ~ Gospel of Thomas, part 18

"The disciples said to Jesus, "Tell us how our end will be." Jesus said, "Have you discovered, then, the beginning, that you look for the end? For where the beginning is, there will the end be."
~ Gospel of Thomas

This saying, attributed to Jesus, is reminiscent of what He said in Matthew 24:37-39, where He compared the days of the end with the days of Noah.

Many modern evangelicals give too much importance to the Book of Revelation—*to the end*. And yet, our understanding of the beginning is so flawed, so incomplete. The first few chapters of Genesis, in modern Evangelical circles, are often neglected; and that, to our own demise.

Truthfully, as believers, we cannot possibly grasp the end unless we acquire a solid understanding of the beginning.

Back when I was 28 years old, I had become arrogant and complacent in my walk with God. I was in my spiritual adolescence, and I had been blessed with a little bit of knowledge.

Unfortunately, though, I didn't know it was just that: *a little knowledge.* I believed I knew my Bible very well–even better than most pastors, I thought. I was becoming very prideful. As a result, I was also becoming unteachable. But the Lord showed me the folly of my ways. He brought me back to reason by using just one verse in just one book. He brought me to the book of Beginnings, the book of our genes… a.k.a. *Gene*-sis.

He showed me a verse in there that completely baffled me, and then He spoke to my spirit, saying: *"You see, you don't even understand the first book—the beginning. So, how can you pretend to understand the rest of the story?"*

One word from the Lord is all it took for me to humbly seek forgiveness and repent.

As you know, the Word of God tells us that the Lord corrects and reproves us for our own good and because He loves us (Psalm 119:67, 71; Hebrews 12:6-11).

From that moment on, I was humbled, and I became a committed lifelong student of the Bible, a lifelong learner. Ironically, I became especially fond of Genesis in the process.

In the Beginning

When God created the earth realm and man, He had a unique mandate for him.

The earth realm was a distinct realm in God's creation. It was to be a realm of carbon-based beings with bodies differing from those found in the heavens.

This earth realm was made for a specific type of creation and beings. It was to be physical in nature, and as such, quite unique.

It was the realm of organic bodies. Notice how the plants, the trees, the birds, the fish, all the animal, and man… all have organic bodies.

The earth realm is specifically designed to harbour and benefit beings who are alive and organic. This was a first in God's creation. And this is notable. We will see why later.

Now, man was appointed a special status in this new realm called the earth realm.

In Genesis 1:26-28 (ESV), we read the following:

> *"Then God said, 'Let us make man in our image, after our likeness. And let them have dominion over the fish of the sea and over the birds of the heavens and over the livestock and over all the earth and over every creeping thing that creeps on the earth.' So God created man in his own image, in the image*

of God he created him; male and female he created them. And God blessed them. And God said to them, 'Be fruitful and multiply and fill the earth and subdue it, and have dominion over the fish of the sea and over the birds of the heavens and over every living thing that moves on the earth.'

In this whole passage, the two most important words are found when God blesses mankind, in the person of Adam and Eve, and says to them, *"Have Dominion."*

Yes, *Have Dominion!*

Now, to understand what this means precisely, we need a definition of the word 'Dominion.'

The dictionary tells us that dominion means: Sovereignty or control.

Synonyms for dominion include *supremacy, ascendency, superiority, pre-eminence, primacy, authority, mastery, control, command, direction, power, rule, government, jurisdiction, lordship.*

So, when God gave man dominion, He made mankind to be *rulers* over this earth realm, this 'domain', which is where we get the word *dominion* from.

> When God gave man dominion, He made mankind to be rulers over this earth realm, this 'domain', which is where we get the word dominion from.

Notice also, whether it is used as a prefix or suffix, the word *'dom'* means *'to rule.'*

This gives us a better understanding of words like:

- ♛ **king-dom (the domain of the king; where a king rules)**
- ♛ **free-dom (the domain of the free; where the free rule)**
- ♛ **dom-estic (the domain of the house; under house rules)**

So, God assigned man with the rulership of this place called earth. He also gave man rulership over all the beings He created. Man was to rule it all!

The birds, the fish, the plants, the trees; all the animals and the territory itself were put under man's dominion. In Genesis 2:19-20 (NIV), we read the following:

> *"Now the Lord God had formed out of the ground all the wild animals and all the birds in the sky. He brought them to the man to see what he would name them; and whatever the man called each living creature, that was its name. So the man gave names to all the livestock, the birds in the sky and all the wild animals."*

There is a fascinating principle at work in this passage. It is a dominion principle. It is the Kingdom dominion principle of naming. By naming it, we become *authors* over it. Whatever we name, we have authority over.

- ♛ We name our *children*
- ♛ We name our *businesses*
- ♛ We name our *books*
- ♛ We name our *towns, rivers, cities, lakes, territories*

We are told here that Adam exercised his dominion by naming the animals. It is also interesting to note that Eve herself was named by Adam. God could have named Eve, but He let Adam do it (Genesis 3:20). This further explains why man was given the headship of the household in marriage (Ephesians 5:22-24; 1 Timothy 2:12-13).

So, the earth and everything in it were given over to man for him to exercise his authority.

The Bible says in psalm 115:16 (NIV):

> *"The highest heavens belong to the Lord, but the earth he has given to mankind."*

The Message translates it this way:

> *"The heaven of heavens is for God, but he put us in charge of the earth."*

Furthermore, just a quick parenthesis here…

I find it interesting to note that God, appointing man a dominion mandate, makes us understand God's second commandment even better. In Exodus 20, in the Ten Commandments, we read this:

> *"You shall not make for yourself a carved image, or any likeness of anything that is in heaven above, or that is in the earth beneath, or that is in the water under the earth. You shall not bow down to them or serve them, for I the Lord your God am a jealous God, visiting the iniquity of the fathers on the children to the third and the fourth generation of those who hate me, but showing steadfast love to thousands of those who love me and keep my commandments." ~ Exodus 20:4-6 (ESV)*

Isn't it interesting that God not only wants us to worship Him only but doesn't want us to demean ourselves by worshipping images of creatures we were given dominion over?

When we make for ourselves graven images, we elevate what we should dominate. It severely demeans our status as rulers.

The Sovereignty of God

At this point, I feel it is necessary to address the subject of *The Sovereignty of God*.

If you have been a believer for long enough, as I have, no doubt that you have heard how God rules over everything, right? He is sovereign. This is an undeniable truth and a cornerstone of the Christian faith.

Another main attribute of God is His omnipotence. Omnipotence means that *God can do all things*. He is all-powerful. So, let's be clear: God is sovereign and all-powerful.

No one can dispute the sovereignty of God. He is the Creator of all. He also has indisputable sovereignty in heaven and on earth. So, how can we reconcile man's rulership of the earth realm with the sovereignty of God Almighty?

That is a fantastic question!

Well, the first thing we can say on the matter is that *sovereignty always trumps dominion.*

God, in His sovereignty, has given man dominion. And the giver is always greater than the receiver. Sovereignty means *"supreme power or authority."* It is unlimited in scope, especially when relating to God. Dominion, however, has limits. It is always over a determined domain, beings, or things but has limits delineated by size, influence, or numbers.

But let's take it further.

Have you ever been asked the childish question: *If God is all-powerful, can He create a rock that even He wouldn't be able to move?*

Believe it or not, I actually have the answer to that cryptic question of the ages. The answer is *YES, He can.* In fact, He already *has* created a rock that He cannot move.

The rock that God cannot move is (drumroll)... *His own WORD!*

The only One who can dispute the sovereignty of God... is God Himself.

The Bible says this concerning God's authoritative Word:

> *"Forever, O Lord, your word is firmly fixed in the heavens."*
> ~ *Psalm 119:89 (ESV)*

And in Numbers 23:19-20 (ESV), we read these words from Balaam, the non-Israelite prophet:

> *"God is not man, that he should lie, or a son of man, that he should change his mind. Has he said, and will he not do it? Or has he spoken, and will he not fulfill it? Behold, I received a command to bless: he has blessed, and I cannot revoke it."*

Balaam here says, *"He has blessed and I cannot revoke it."*

God's word is irrevocable. His blessing seals the deal.

In Matthew chapter 5:17-19, we read:

> *"Do not think that I have come to abolish the Law or the Prophets; I have not come to abolish them but to fulfill them. For truly I tell you, until heaven and earth disappear, not the smallest letter, not the least stroke of a pen, will by any means disappear from the Law until everything is accomplished. Therefore anyone who sets aside one of the least of these commands and teaches others accordingly will be called least in the kingdom of heaven, but whoever practices and teaches these commands will be called great in the kingdom of heaven.*

Now, do you remember back in Genesis 1:28? It said:

"He blessed them, <u>and said… let them have dominion</u>."

So, here is a vital thing you need to understand about God's sovereignty:

God is as sovereign as His Word.

Let me repeat that:

God is as sovereign as His Word.

What does this mean?

Simply this: God is bound by His own Word because He is perfect. God is so good, so just, so Holy, and so perfect that *He cannot break His Word.*

> God is as sovereign as His Word.

You've probably heard sayings such as: *"My word is my bond."* Or *"A man is only as good as his word."*

Well, these apply even more so to God! His word and His blessing are unbreakable. When He gave man dominion on the earth realm, it was irrevocable.

Respected faith teacher, Charles Capps, in *God's Image of You*, puts it this way:

> *"It's illegal for God to come to earth and destroy the work of the devil with His divine Godhead powers. He delivered the authority of this earth to man and has never taken it back. It's still in the hands of man. Adam turned it over to Satan, but Jesus took it from the devil and gave it back to the believer before He ascended to heaven. He said, all power is given unto me in heaven and in earth. Go ye therefore ... (Matt. 28:18, 19). He delivered that authority back to man."*

I am convinced that your understanding of how God gave man dominion is the main key to your understanding of how God's Kingdom operates. If you fail to understand this Kingdom cornerstone set in Genesis, you will fail to grasp the rest of the story. You will have major holes in your understanding of the whole Bible. The dominion concept has blessed and empowered my walk with God in ways that would have been impossible without its understanding. I sincerely hope it will do the same for you.

> Your understanding of how God gave man dominion is the main key to your understanding of how God's Kingdom operates.

Unbreakable

Do you remember back in the story of how Jacob stole Esau's blessing from Isaac?

It's in Genesis 27:30-37.

When Esau found out, he went and pleaded with Isaac, his father:

> *"Now it happened, as soon as Isaac had finished blessing Jacob, and Jacob had scarcely gone out from the presence of Isaac his father, that Esau his brother came in from his hunting. He also had made savory food, and brought it to*

*his father, and said to his father, "Let my father arise and eat
of his son's game, that your soul may bless me."*

And his father Isaac said to him, "Who are you?" So he said, "I
am your son, your firstborn, Esau." Then Isaac trembled exceedingly,
and said, "Who? Where is the one who hunted game and brought it
to me? I ate all of it before you came, and I have blessed him—and
indeed he shall be blessed." When Esau heard the words of his father,
he cried with an exceedingly great and bitter cry, and said to his father,
"Bless me—me also, O my father!" But he said, "Your brother came
with deceit and has taken away your blessing."

> And Esau said, "Is he not rightly named Jacob? For he has
> supplanted me these two times. He took away my birthright,
> and now look, he has taken away my blessing!" And he
> said, "Have you not reserved a blessing for me?" Then Isaac
> answered and said to Esau, "Indeed I have made him your
> master, and all his brethren I have given to him as servants;
> with grain and wine I have sustained him. What shall I do
> now for you, my son?" ~ Genesis 27:30-37 (NKJV)

Isaac, after he had blessed Jacob instead of Esau, could not break
his own word. It had been decreed. Now, if the words and blessings
of Isaac were unbreakable, how much more the Words and Blessings
of God!?

In chapter 9, we will look further into the taming of the tongue
and the power of our words.

The Ecclesia: Called to Rule and Conquer

Now that I have made clear our individual dominion calling,
what about our collective one? What about the calling of the Church?

In the New Testament, the Greek word *Ekklesia* (which, in my
opinion, was poorly translated as *Church*) appears 114 times.

Here is how Encyclopedia Britannica has defined the Greek root word, *Ecclesia*:

> *"Ecclesia, Greek Ekklēsia, ("gathering of those summoned"), in ancient Greece, assembly of citizens in a city-state. Its roots lay in the Homeric agora, the meeting of the people. The Athenian Ecclesia, for which exists the most detailed record, was already functioning in Draco's day (c. 621 BC). In the course of Solon's codification of the law (c. 594 BC), the Ecclesia became coterminous with the body of male citizens 18 years of age or over and had final control over policy, including the right to hear appeals in the hēliaia (public court), take part in the election of archons (chief magistrates), and confer special privileges on individuals." ~ Encyclopedia Britannica*

I like this particular definition (Encyclopedia Britannica) because it conveys so much more than the regular ones we've heard about the church being a mere *"assembly"* or being composed of *"the called-out ones."*

It is interesting to note that in the days of early America, in the 13 colonies, racial and gender prejudices aside, only men who exemplified these traits of the *Ecclesia* were given the right to vote: they were required to be Christian and own property in order to have the power to influence the republic. In other words, they needed to have faith in God and "skin in the game" in order to have a voice. I believe this kept political leaders much more accountable to both God and the people.

I believe the *'ecclesia'* is much more than just the assembly of those who believe or called out of the world. Jesus meant for the Church to be much more than that when He said:

> *"But who do you say that I am?"*

> *Simon Peter answered and said, "You are the Christ, the Son of the living God."*

Jesus answered and said to him, "Blessed are you, Simon Bar-Jonah, for flesh and blood has not revealed this to you, but My Father who is in heaven. And I also say to you that you are Peter, and on this rock [this declaration] <u>I will build My church, and the gates of Hades shall not prevail against it.</u> And I will give you the keys of the kingdom of heaven, <u>and whatever you bind on earth will be bound in heaven, and whatever you loose on earth will be loosed in heaven."</u> ~ Matthew 16:15-19 (NKJV)

This remarkable statement Jesus made about His Church indicates much more than an *assembly* of like-minded people, as it is often defined. It underlies much power, authority, and influence. In other words, I believe Jesus meant for the Church to exert much more Kingdom influence and dominion than we do in reality.

In my book, titled *5 Reasons God Wants You to Prosper*, I give the following analogy about the Church:

"In most religious circles, they understand this passage as Jesus saying that His Church will resist the attacks of the enemy—that it will stand strong. And yet, it means quite the opposite.

When He says: The gates of Hell shall not prevail against it, He means that the strongholds of hell shall not resist the power of the advancing Church—of the expanding Kingdom of our God. It means the Church is the aggressor!

Have you ever seen medieval movies where soldiers are trying to take a fort or castle? In such instances, a battering ram was commonly used to break down the door of the tightly guarded fortress. This was a huge log-like contraption that was held by several men and used to repeatedly smash the door until it broke open under the assault.

This is the Church that Jesus came to establish. It is bold, strong, and contrary to what most believe… it is intended for assault!

The Church is not intended to sit idly under the attacks of the enemy. Rather, it is meant to smash the gates of hell and takes back territory for the King and His Kingdom. The Kingdom of God is meant to be proactive and not reactive."

Now, what I wrote about the Church back then definitely conveys more accurately the definition of *Ecclesia* given to us by Britannica, which mentions:

> "Having control over policy, including the right to hear appeals in the hēliaia (public court), take part in the election of archons (chief magistrates), and confer special privileges on individuals."

As a body of believers and the body of Christ on the earth, the Church has a lot more power, authority, and influence than we have dared to operate in. Furthermore, we know that when He comes back, *Jesus is coming as judge and conqueror*:

> The Church has a lot more power, authority, and influence than we have dared to operate in.

> "Then I saw heaven opened, and behold, a white horse! The one sitting on it is called Faithful and True, and in righteousness he judges and makes war." ~ Revelation 19:11 (ESV)

Again, this indicates an establishing of undeniable dominion (dominance).

But, as we will see in the next chapter before the Church became empowered to take back what the Enemy had stolen, God Himself initiated a lengthy re-entry and re-conquest processes when He established multiple covenants (partnerships) with man. This was to serve as His way of *legally, righteously,* and *fully* re-entering the arena.

3

THE KING TO THE RESCUE!

The History of God's Salvation

"And I will establish my covenant between me and you and your offspring after you throughout their generations for an everlasting covenant, to be God to you and to your offspring after you." ~ Genesis 17:7

So far, I have made it clear that the whole message of the Bible is not about a religion. It is about a Kingdom.

The whole Bible is an epic story about a Kingdom and its King (God), the citizens of the Kingdom (mankind), the loss of the earth realm to an enemy (Satan), the subsequent enslavement of the citizens under an accursed system, and finally, the ultimate re-conquering of the kingdom of the world by the King Himself (in the person of Jesus Christ) to redeem His citizens, free them, and ultimately make them co-heirs of the Kingdom of God.

And now, dear reader, we continue with this chapter, which is the most theologically inclined in this book, and in all honesty, probably the driest. Nevertheless, these first two chapters are of the utmost importance since they serve to establish a firm understanding of the intents and purposes of God in creating and establishing mankind. We will also cover why His redemptive plan took place the way it did. Keep this in mind as we lay the groundwork of this understanding.

Also, in the previous chapter, we explored how God put man in charge of the earth realm and gave him dominion. This begs the question…

With man officially in charge in the earth realm, what did this imply when man fell?

We will now dig deeper into this and more.

Necessary Theology

I am not, nor ever claimed to be, a seminary trained or certified theologian. However, to set the groundwork for Kingdom understanding, we need to get into some *theological stuff*. Therefore, this chapter will explore a broad scope overview of how Adam lost the Kingdom and why God adopted a gradual process to restore it unto mankind.

Most of us know this basic scriptural concept, and yet, we do not fully understand the intricacies of God's lengthy redemptive process throughout history. For example, some of you might have wondered...

- ♛ Why didn't God intervene in Eden to prevent the fall?

- ♛ Why couldn't God just kick Satan out of the earth realm?

- ♛ Why did it take so long for God to send Christ?

- ♛ What was the whole purpose of God's covenants with Noah, Abraham, Moses, and David?

Let us now examine the different covenants of God with man. While it is mostly an overview and far from theologically exhaustive, it is nonetheless necessary. This might make this chapter appear a bit dryer or unexciting. But no matter how you receive it, I urge you to stick with it. This understanding is needed to see the whole tapestry that God was weaving in bringing about the Kingdom in partnership with man.

The Bible: An Epic Story

When they undertake to teach the Bible as a whole, most Bible teachers teach it as an epic story. However, it is interesting to note that the theology behind their teaching depends largely on how God is portrayed in the epic story.

We learn in the Bible that God wears many different hats. He is a Creator, a Judge, a Father, and a Redeemer. But for us to understand the Kingdom of God and how it unfolds in the Bible, we need to perceive God as a *King*.

As I stated earlier, this is not always easy for people in most western countries. There is even, dare I say it, a certain contempt for monarchy held by many people. This is mostly due to some historical records of abuse by worldly kings and queens. Some of them were ruthless and didn't treat the people fairly. Nevertheless, make no mistake about it: God is King! He sits on the throne and rules over all. Or, as David puts it in 1 Chronicles 29:11-12 (ESV):

> *"Yours, O Lord, is the greatness and the power and the glory and the victory and the majesty, for all that is in the heavens and in the earth is yours. Yours is the kingdom, O Lord, and you are exalted as head above all. Both riches and honor come from you, and you rule over all. In your hand are power and might, and in your hand it is to make great and to give strength to all."*

Therefore, in order to grasp what the Kingdom of God is and our place in it, we need to perceive God as a Monarch. He is the King of kings and Lord of lords over all. He is, in fact, an Emperor.

Emperors are generally recognized to be of the highest monarchic honor and rank, surpassing even kings. So, in the technical sense and because of the vastness of His rule, God is indeed an emperor, although not referred to as such.

So, we need to examine the epic story of the Bible through the lens of the story of a King (God), His Kingdom (His government), and His subjects (angels, men). We also need to consider it from the perspective of a King who willed His Kingdom to be expanded from heaven into a newly created physical realm (the earth). He thus created a race of physical beings to have dominion in this new realm to colonize it. But this new realm, and these new creatures, had an Enemy lurking in the shadows—the Fallen One, Lucifer, Satan, also known as the Devil.

The Devil's plan was to usurp this new realm by tricking man into disobeying and rebelling against the King. By bringing man to disobey the King's orders (to sin and fall), the Devil stole dominion from man and became the Prince of this world (John 14:30). He has since been the prince of the power of the air (Ephesians 2:2).

Right away, the King put in motion his contingency plan (which was pre-existing) to bring this world back into alignment with His Heavenly Kingdom. He needed to bring man back on top, back in the dominion of the earth realm, to re-establish His Kingdom's rule on the earth. But, with man in rebellion against God through sin, how would that be achieved?

This is the crux of the Bible story. It is about a mighty King, His Kingdom, His not-so-faithful subjects, a powerful and wicked enemy, and the King's ultimate sacrifice and restoration of His subjects.

This is what this chapter will examine.

Where Did Man Fall From?

First, let's talk about the fall.

We've all been taught that the fall is when sin or disobedience entered the world, and with it, separation from God ensued, and ultimately… death. That is true, but the fall encompasses even more than that.

Here is a question for you… *What did man fall from?* Or perhaps, *Where did man fall from?*

Some would say that man fell from grace. Some would say that man fell out of favor with God. Others would argue that man fell from perfection into sinfulness. Those observations are all correct. But while these do apply to the whole event of the fall, they fail to capture the extent of the fall of man.

The ultimate fall of man was a fall from *dominion*—physical, yes, but even more so spiritual.

Man fell from dominion, and everything else fell with him as a result.

> The ultimate fall of man was a fall from dominion—physical, yes, but even more so spiritual.

When Eve decided to obey the serpent's voice (The 'Nachash' in Hebrew), and Adam listened to her, *they fell from dominion.* And with that fall came a nasty transfer of authority in the earth realm.

To gain legality in this realm, Satan needed to *usurp* it from man and through man. Because man was granted dominion of the earth realm, everything that is to be done in the earth realm needs man's co-operation—conscious or unconscious, voluntary or not, willing or unwilling. According to Wikipedia: "

> *A usurper is an illegitimate or controversial claimant to power, often but not always in a monarchy. In other words, a person who takes the power of a country, city, or established region for themselves, without any formal or legal right to claim it as their own."*

The Serpent, the devil, took over the earth realm through deception, cunning, and by making man doubt *the Word of God.* He still uses the same tactic to this day. To render us ineffective, all he has to do is make us doubt the Word of God.

And here is something else you need to understand:

God, having given man dominion, could not intervene directly while Eve and Adam were being tempted. If He had, He would have broken His Word. And His Word stated and established that Man was put in charge here. Did God have the power to do it? To intervene? Of course, He did. But He didn't have the *legal right*... being restrained by His own Word.

So, here is what I could compare this to...

At the time of penning these words, I've been married to my wife Elisabeth for 18 years. When her father gave her away to me on our wedding day, he promised her to me. He did so willingly and accepting that the headship of Elisabeth was now my responsibility as a Christian husband.

So, this meant that technically, he decided to stay out of our affairs. He transferred his authority onto me. Therefore, as a good father-in-law, he respects our life decisions. Whether it's about where we live, the house we live in, how we spend our money, or where our kids go to school—and *whether or not he approves of our decisions.* If he budded in all the time, he would be breaking his own word. He would be acting as if he had not given her away. He would be breaking his promise—his word.

Notwithstanding all this, if we consult him on these matters, he will gladly help us, advise us, or give us his two cents.

It was the same thing with God when the serpent came to tempt Eve. By giving man dominion, God had what we could call a *'Non-intervention without invitation clause'* in His contract with man.

He was bound by His Word.

He could have easily stopped Eve from being deceived. After all, He's God. However, if he had intervened and stopped Eve from taking the fruit, He would have broken His own Word, and then Satan would have had a field day, legally speaking, in the courts of heaven.

In fact, the whole plan of God's redemption of man would have been made impossible if He had broken His own Word. The consequences would have been disastrous, to say the least.

Another example I could give you is this:

Imagine if you were renting a house from a landlord. This is where you live with your loved ones and all your goods. Even if the landlord owns the house and the land it is on, he cannot just come into your house uninvited whenever he wishes. Every renting agreement comes with a special clause stating that the landlord cannot come into your house whenever he wants. You have to invite him in, even if he owns it. You have legal rights in this house, even if the house doesn't really belong to you. He can only come in when you give him permission. I will discuss this example further in the chapter titled *God's rules of engagement*.

So, what you need to understand is that *the Kingdom of God is ruled by law*. And the law in the Kingdom, in any kingdom, is whatever the King says. God is King, and His Word is the law. So, when He gave dominion to man—this became law.

We will see more about the laws of the Kingdom as we advance in this book.

For now, here are the main things we need to know that happened at the fall:

1. Man lost his dominion. This is the main thing. In doing so, man transferred official rulership of the realm over to Satan who became, according to Jesus in John 14:30, *'the prince of this world,'* and also *'the god of this world'* (2 Corinthians 4:4), and *'the prince of the power of the air'* (Ephesians 2:2).

By the way, this implies indirectly that man, before his fall, was all these things. Prince, ruler, and even, dare I say it… little gods (small 'g'), according to Psalm 82, and restated by Jesus in John 10:34-35 (ESV):

Jesus answered them, "Is it not written in your Law, 'I said, you are gods'? If he called them gods to whom the word of God came—and Scripture cannot be broken — do you say of him whom the Father consecrated and sent into the world, 'You are blaspheming,' because I said, 'I am the Son of God?'

Now, to be clear, the *'You are gods'* statement above shouldn't be misunderstood. Many New Agers and New Thought adepts believe they are gods, in a literal sense and with an inflated self-image, because they misunderstand the more profound implications of this verse. This is, of course, a fallacy. What I am saying, however, is that when we fell from *dominion*, we fell from a very elevated position and estate.

2. Man inherited a sinful state. From the point of the fall to today, man is born in sin. This means that man is born with an unregenerate spirit—sinful and guilty before God. As a result, man needs faith, repentance, and God's grace to be put back in a right relational status with Him. Our spirits need to be re-born for us to be called born-again. This is our redemption. Christ came to earth, died, and rose again to give man this opportunity. This is the message of salvation that has enabled so many of us to be redeemed and walk as Kingdom citizens.

Faith in the sacrifice of Christ and His subsequent resurrection is the only door, the only way...

- To inherit the Kingdom of God
- To become a Kingdom citizen with rights and privileges here and now on earth
- To have the Kingdom of God made alive within you by the indwelling of the Holy Spirit (remember that Jesus said the Kingdom is within you), and
- To live in the Kingdom of Heaven in the presence of God once you die.

3. Sin, death, suffering, and sickness came into the world. We are told in Genesis chapter 3 that the consequences for mankind were dire.

First, we became mortal, physically limited, and vulnerable to illnesses.

Second, we became sinners from birth and by nature. We became genetically flawed, soulishly deviant, and spiritually dead, i.e., slaves to sin. And with this, wickedness followed throughout mankind's history.

Also, for the woman, she inherited painful childbirth and 'a desire for her husband'. This doesn't mean she simply desires him. No. When we examine the Hebrew text, it means that she would desire *to rule over him,* but that he would rule over her. In other words, there would now be an inherent struggle between the man and woman; harmony would be difficult to achieve. It meant the battle of the sexes had begun.

This power struggle began in Eden as soon as Adam blamingly stated:

> *"The woman you put here with me—she gave me some fruit from the tree, and I ate it." ~ Genesis 3:12 (NIV)*

But the marital relationship wasn't the only one that would suffer from this. All of man's relationships would ultimately suffer—our relationship with God and our relationship with one another.

4. Painful toil and sweat became our lot. Initially, Adam had been placed in the garden (in Genesis 2:15) *"to work it and take care of it"* (NIV). This was pretty much your typical dream job. There was no painful toil and sweat. It was a perfectly tailored and pleasant work. It kept Adam busy and gave him purpose as a regent of God's creation. He was literally working as a glorified gardener and keeper of an earthly paradise!

However, when he fell from dominion, he was now going to work hard in this newly fallen and bruised creation.

We have an expression in French about hard work that goes like this, *"I do not work for the devil, I work for his brother."* This is to say that hard work sometimes feels like working for the devil's brother—which is pretty close to the devil himself.

Well, after the fall, and with Satan taking rulership away from man, that's how it's been ever since.

Genesis 3:17-19 (NIV) puts it this way:

> *To Adam he said, "Because you listened to your wife and ate fruit from the tree about which I commanded you, 'You must not eat from it,'*
>
> *"Cursed is the ground because of you; through painful toil you will eat food from it all the days of your life. It will produce thorns and thistles for you, and you will eat the plants of the field. By the sweat of your brow you will eat your food until you return to the ground, since from it you were taken; for dust you are and to dust you will return."*

So, since that day, we have been under a cursed earth system that causes us to painfully toil and sweat to obtain our sustenance.

By living under Satan's rule for many generations, we have been conditioned to painfully toil, sweat, fret, and stress over money, food, clothing, and shelter. This is *the cursed earth system* that Satan rules. Sometimes, I call it *the Beast System.*

Under this broken system, very few manage to do enough, run fast enough, gather enough, and make enough money to get ahead.

A well-known Montreal talk-radio show host I used to listen to once said to a female listener calling in one day:

> *"Lady, you'll notice that we are often told in high-performance seminars these days: 'Go for it! You can do it!'*

The only problem I've seen from this seemingly encouraging statement is that it doesn't take into account that only one in every thousand people can actually 'Go for it and do it!'"

Nonetheless, as we will see later in much detail, Jesus came to set the captives free and to give GOOD News to the poor (Luke 4:18).

Living as citizens of the Kingdom of God, and knowing what this actually means, is the only way to be freed from the present cursed earth system of painful toil and sweat. We'll dive into more of this in latter chapters.

5. All of creation fell along with man. When man fell, the whole earth realm fell with him. If the pinnacle of creation falls (man), it is only normal that the rest follows. And thus began the whole hierarchical food chain and survival of the fittest, spilling of blood, illness, predator and prey, death and life cycles, etc.

Romans 8:19 (NIV) says:

"For the creation waits in eager expectation for the children of God to be revealed."

And Romans 8:22-24 (NIV) says:

"We know that the whole creation has been groaning as in the pains of childbirth right up to the present time. Not only so, but we ourselves, who have the firstfruits of the Spirit, groan inwardly as we wait eagerly for our adoption to sonship, the redemption of our bodies. For in this hope we were saved."

This earth realm is suffering, just as we have been since the fall. It is waiting eagerly for our manifestation because we are the rightful heirs of dominion here.

So, while we are able to take back territory from the enemy right now (more on that later), our full manifestation will only be completed at the second coming of Messiah.

6. Unwittingly, man kicked God out. When the woman chose to obey the voice of the Serpent and man followed, they transferred dominion of the earth realm over to Satan. They kicked God out when they opened the door to Satan. The words we heed rule over us. In this case, man gave credence to the devil's word instead of the Word of the King (God).

Now, when man was in charge, he welcomed God in the earth realm. It was a partnership.

But with Satan now legally in charge through our disobedience. Man found himself living under the legal jurisdiction of a new authority of the earth realm.

> The words we heed rule over us.

God found Himself on the outside looking in… *fully capable to intervene*, but bound by His own word, and now in the execution mode of His plan to rescue mankind from this mess.

Oh, and for the record: this was all scripted and part of the plan of the ages for the Almighty. God wasn't taken aback, surprised, or worried by the turn of events.

This, and so much more, is why we desperately needed God's redemptive plan.

7. God's mercy and grace became a necessity for man.

Obviously, all this drama caused by man's disobedience could have ended right there if God had not chosen to establish a redeeming plan for man. And this plan was made evident through two instances in Genesis.

a) First, when he prevented man from having access to the tree of life. This is very mysterious, but it can be understood.

As strange as this may seem, death was God's failsafe when He put man in charge of the earth realm. But while death was a possibility, it lay dormant, inactive. When man sinned, he activated death within himself. Romans 5:12 (NIV) says:

> *"Therefore, just as sin entered the world through one man, and death through sin, and <u>in this way death came to all people, because all sinned</u>."*

God said of the tree:

> *"but you must not eat from the tree of the knowledge of good and evil, for <u>when you eat from it you will certainly die</u>." ~ Genesis 2:17 (NIV)*

Death was dormant in man and would have remained dormant within man forever if he had not sinned. When man sinned, God's failsafe, a.k.a. death, was activated within man.

Why is that?

Death, although seen as a curse, was necessary to give man a chance at redemption.

So, it was a crucial provision when God also said, in Genesis 3:22-23 (NIV):

> *"The man has now become like one of us, knowing good and evil. <u>He must not be allowed to reach out his hand and take also from the tree of life and eat, and live forever</u>." So the Lord God banished him from the Garden of Eden to work the ground from which he had been taken. After he drove the man out, he placed on the east side of the Garden of Eden cherubim and a flaming sword flashing back and forth to guard the way to the tree of life.*

This banishment from the garden and the access to the tree of life protected man from his own demise and from permanently being in rebellion against God. Basically, mortality gave man a possibility of parole from the sentence of sin through Christ.

By becoming mortal, man also became redeemable, provided

> Mortality gave man a possibility of parole from the sentence of sin through Christ.

he seeks God while in mortal form. Also, being mortal and aware of our own mortality makes us seek life eternal, which is found in Jesus Christ alone.

Here is how this works...

If man had been made to live forever in a sinful, fallen state, he would have been stuck there, which is not a good place to be. God, in His mercy, would not allow man to live eternally in such a miserable sin-laden state. Indeed, it would have been nothing short of a nightmare to live eternally in this fallen state.

If he had remained immortal, he would have been just like the angels when they sinned and rebelled. The angels who sinned cannot be redeemed. They did not have the failsafe of death within them and thus, became irredeemable when they sinned. It says in Revelation that the eternal fire was prepared for the devil and his angels. If we had eaten from the tree of life after the fall, we would have been stuck in this fallen state forever.

Death makes our present sinful and fallen state temporary, not permanent. Death acts as a portal that makes us transfer realms and thus changes our reality and our state of being. We pass from souls in a physical body to a spiritual body.

So, being mortal grants us limited time in this earth realm, and this limited time is allotted to all of us unto the possibility of salvation.

b) Secondly, the prophecy concerning the Messiah. God showed Satan He wouldn't have the last word when He prophesied in Genesis 3:15 (NKJV): *"And I will put enmity Between you and the woman, And between your seed and her Seed; He shall bruise your head, And you shall bruise His heel."*

This was God saying to the Devil: *"I have made a way to someday re-establish the proper dominion in this realm that you have stolen by your craftiness. This is far from over. You will lose because I always win."*

God's Process of Re-Entry

In warfare, when the enemy takes territory from you, a plan needs to be devised to take it back.

When the earth realm was usurped by the devil in his clever Genesis scheme, it became legally his.

Even Jesus did not dispute the devil's claim. In Luke chapter 4:6-7 (NIV), when Satan tempted Him, the devil said:

"To you I will give all this authority and their glory, for it has been delivered to me, and I give it to whom I will. If you, then, will worship me, it will all be yours."

But Jesus came in the flesh to bind the strong man (Satan) with the power of God and to take back what he stole.

He explained this Himself in Luke 11:21-22 (NIV):

"When a strong man, fully armed, guards his own house, his possessions are safe. 22 But when someone stronger attacks and overpowers him, he takes away the armor in which the man trusted and divides up his plunder."

The Son needed to come *in the flesh* to have legality in the earth realm. And for this to happen, God needed to establish a covenant with man—*in the flesh*. He couldn't just barge into the house (the physical earth realm where He had given man dominion) uninvited.

This is why God made the covenant with Abraham *in the flesh*. God wanted to make sure that He would have access to the earth realm *through the flesh* in future generations. He bound Himself to Abraham through this covenant in the flesh in Genesis 17:1-14.

This was God's plan to redeem mankind lawfully and victoriously. It was to be done in the flesh and in full agreement with God.

As a side note, this is why no evil entity can verbally recognize Jesus coming *in the flesh*. John 4:2 (ESV) says:

> "By this you know the Spirit of God: every spirit that confesses that Jesus Christ has come in the flesh is from God." And this fact is reiterated in 2 John 1:7 (NIV): "I say this because many deceivers, who do not acknowledge Jesus Christ as coming in the flesh, have gone out into the world. Any such person is the deceiver and the antichrist."

A Physical Realm Requires a Physical Body

Here is something you need to understand: to have legality in the earth realm, you need a physical body.

Every living creature on the earth has a physical body, from the smallest cell to the biggest whale; from the smallest mouse to the giant Sequoia tree. God decreed it this way.

This is why, when you die, you have to leave the earth realm. When you die and don't have a body anymore, you basically become illegal here on earth.

This also explains why demons (who are the spirits of the deceased Nephilim of Genesis 6) want to inhabit human bodies all the time. This is their pathetic attempt at becoming legal in the earth realm once more. Ever since the flood, they have been wandering the earth looking for rest (i.e., a human body; Matthew 12:43). They are illegal here; in limbo, awaiting judgement, and they know it.

This also is why God became incarnate (in the flesh) in the person of Jesus. It was the best way for Him to enter the earth realm *fully and legally* to take back what the enemy had stolen.

But let's not get ahead of ourselves here. We'll definitely talk about the work of Christ later, as it is fundamental to explain *The Kingdom of God.*

Before God could come into the earth realm in the person of Jesus Christ, He had to set some wheels in motion. Remember, the Bible tells us in Galatians 4:4 that God sent His son *'In the fullness of time.'*

What does this mean? Well, the expression *'fullness of time'* can also mean: After a due length of time has elapsed; eventually.

Other synonyms may include *in due course, when the time is ripe, at a later date, one day, someday, in a while, etc.*

God first had to re-establish His covenant with man. Through disobedience (sin), man had a broken relationship with God which needed mending, a broken state, and even a broken realm.

To put it lightly, they were not on very good terms with the Almighty. As Paul put it, we were *children of disobedience.*

So, it was necessary for God to be in covenant with a few good men in the earth realm to, over time, make His big move in the person of Jesus Christ, entering the earth realm in the flesh and restoring all things.

That's where God's various covenants, or partnerships, came into play. And bear with me as I am not here reiterating exact theological concepts of dispensationalism. There are variances between proper dispensationalism doctrine and what I am explaining here for the sake of understanding how God partnered with man in the earth realm.

1. First, He chose Noah to re-establish His Law of intent:

Genesis chapter 9 is a reiteration of God's desire for man found first in Genesis 1. It is called the 'Noahic Covenant.' It reads:

> *"Then God blessed Noah and his sons, saying to them, "Be fruitful and increase in number and fill the earth. The fear*

and dread of you will fall on all the beasts of the earth, and on all the birds in the sky, on every creature that moves along the ground, and on all the fish in the sea; they are given into your hands. Everything that lives and moves about will be food for you. Just as I gave you the green plants, I now give you everything." ~ Genesis 9:1-3 (NIV)

This sounds a lot like the *'Be fruitful and multiply from Genesis.'* However, you will notice two major differences with Genesis 1:26-28:

The word 'dominion' is now interestingly, or should I say conspicuously, absent.

Man is now told that he can eat animals, as opposed to before.

So, after the flood, mankind got a reset of sorts, but not a full one.

Satan retained his usurped power over the realm. Therefore, man still had to work in a fallen creation with the Devil still operating as 'the prince of this world'. So, while man still retained some dominance in the earth realm, especially over nature, he had lost much of his original *spiritual authority*, his original dominion—which was now in the devil's grip.

Also, under this covenant, God gave the rainbow as a reminder that He would never again flood the whole earth on account of sin.

But the Kingdom of God was yet to come...

2. Second, He chose Abram (Abraham) to begin His Master Plan of re-entry and conquest.

The word *covenant* has the following synonyms: contract, compact, treaty, pact, accord, deal, bargain, settlement, agreement, arrangement, understanding, pledge, promise, bond, guarantee, etc.

I explained earlier how, in order to have legality in the earth realm, God needs able-bodied men who are in agreement, or in covenant, with Him and His word, to have full access.

Biological bodies are needed in this realm to be legal and able. This is why God made a covenant with Abraham.

The covenant with Abraham, when he came in agreement with God and obeyed Him, was the equivalent of God creating a beachhead in the earth realm through men's flesh and with their accord. This was very significant. In fact, this covenant in the flesh through the promise of many descendants was so important that God ordered Abraham to mark it on all of his descendants. This is why He ordained circumcision (Genesis 17:9-14). It was meant to be the symbol, or mark, of the covenant in the flesh through many offspring and generations until the arrival of Christ in the flesh (i.e., reproduction, hence on the genitals).

But let's get back to this covenant acting as a beachhead in the earth realm. In military terms, a beachhead is *a defended position on a beach taken from the enemy by landing forces, from which an attack can be launched. It is the first parcel of land that is officially conquered by an invading army.*

The Abrahamic Covenant is composed of three main things:

1. **The Promised Land of Canaan:** (Gen. 12:1; NIV) *"Go from your country, your people and your father's household to the land I will show you."*

2. **The Promise of Numerous Offspring:** (Gen. 15:5; NIV) *"He took him outside and said, 'Look up at the sky and count the stars—if indeed you can count them.' Then he said to him, 'So shall your offspring be.'"*

3. **The Promise of Blessings unto the World:** (Gen. 12:2-3; NKJV) *"I will make you a great nation; I will bless you And make your name great; And you shall be a blessing... And in you all the families of the earth shall be blessed."*

These three promises definitely indicate a re-taking of territory. The first has to do with land; the second has to do with growth in numbers. And finally, the third has to do with positive influence and expansion.

This is fascinating. The whole idea of creating the earth realm was for God to create a colony of heaven in a different realm.

You could compare it to the British commonwealth. Every country in the commonwealth is a colony of Great Britain. The commonwealth was Great Britain spreading its influence abroad. I live in Canada. On our money, we still have the picture of the queen of England. We are, in essence, a colony of Great Britain.

And here is an interesting side note: In Hebrew, the word *brit* literally means *covenant*. It comes from the word meaning '*to cut*,' i.e., *to cut a covenant*. Furthermore, the suffix '*ish*'– as in Brit-*ish*, means *man*. Therefore, in Hebrew, *Brit-ish* means '*covenant man*.' But I digress...

Earth is a colony of the Kingdom of God. We were colonized with the rulership of heaven. This is why in the Lord's prayer, we say:

'Thy Kingdom come, thy will be done on earth as it is in heaven.'

After the Abrahamic covenant, men who were born as his descendants and who followed the faith of Abraham (i.e., the Covenant) began calling themselves *sons of Abraham*. This is to say, 'we are sons of the promise.' But what promise? Ultimately, this promise had to do with Kingdom expansion through territory, descendants, and influence. The covenant of God with Abraham was crucial in ushering in God's lengthy redemptive plan and eventually make Jesus come in the flesh.

But the Kingdom of God was yet to come...

3. Thirdly, He built up the pillars of the Kingdom by establishing Jacob (Israel) and his sons (the 12 tribes)

Then came Jacob, who was renamed Israel, through whom God established the twelve tribes of Israel and the nation itself—in the flesh, as a people consecrated to Him.

God was solidifying his re-taking of territory by establishing twelve tribes named after Jacob's sons.

The promise to Jacob reads like this in Genesis 35:10-15 (NKJV):

> *"And God said to him, 'Your name is Jacob; your name shall not be called Jacob anymore, but Israel shall be your name.' So He called his name Israel. Also God said to him: 'I am God Almighty. Be fruitful and multiply; a nation and a company of nations shall proceed from you, and kings shall come from your body. The land which I gave Abraham and Isaac I give to you; and to your descendants after you I give this land.' Then God went up from him in the place where He talked with him. So Jacob set up a pillar in the place where He talked with him, a pillar of stone; and he poured a drink offering on it, and he poured oil on it. And Jacob called the name of the place where God spoke with him, Bethel.*

So, God here reiterates His desire for His people to *be fruitful and multiply*, but He also mentions kings and nations (plural). Yes, kings and nations! Interesting, isn't it? The plan was moving along more and more towards Kingdom vernacular.

But the Kingdom of God was yet to come…

4. Fourthly, He officially brought man back under His rulership by setting down His law through Moses. Any kingdom needs laws to operate properly. Laws set the standard for the quality of life in each society. They serve as guides and establish proper conduct.

After God freed His people from Egypt, He gave Moses His law. This law was to make Israel the most perfectly ruled earthly society ever and to glorify Him as King in the process. It was not meant to be a democracy or a monarchy but a theocracy.

Unlike those claimed by the Vatican or Iran today, this particular theocracy was perfect and made to bring about the closest thing to a utopian society ever devised by man. This is because it was not devised by man but by God.

The only thing that prevented this ideal from being achieved was that people were still sinners...unable to keep the law as intended.

Just as Paul said in Roman 7:7-12 (NKJV):

> *"What shall we say then? Is the law sin? Certainly not! On the contrary, I would not have known sin except through the law. For I would not have known covetousness unless the law had said, "You shall not covet." But sin, taking opportunity by the commandment, produced in me all manner of evil desire. For apart from the law sin was dead. I was alive once without the law, but when the commandment came, sin revived and I died. And the commandment, which was to bring life, I found to bring death. For sin, taking occasion by the commandment, deceived me, and by it killed me.* <u>*Therefore the law is holy, and the commandment holy and just and good.*</u>*"*

There are many mountains mentioned in the Bible, some even by name. We know of the mountains of Ararat, Carmel, and the mount of Olives, to name a few. But the two main mountains mentioned in the Bible are Mount Sinai and Mount Zion. The first one is where God gave man His laws; the second one is where God fulfilled His law and gave us grace, revelation, blessing, and ultimate glory.

Hebrews 12:18-24 (ESV) reads:

> *"For you have not come to what may be touched, a blazing fire and darkness and gloom and a tempest and the sound of a trumpet and a voice whose words made the hearers beg that no further messages be spoken to them [Sinai]. For they could not endure the order that was given, "If even a beast touches the mountain, it shall be stoned." Indeed, so terrifying was the sight that Moses said, "I tremble with fear." But you have come to Mount Zion and to the city of the living God, the heavenly Jerusalem, and to innumerable angels in festal gathering, and to the assembly of the firstborn*

who are enrolled in heaven, and to God, the judge of all, and to the spirits of the righteous made perfect, and to Jesus, the mediator of a new covenant, and to the sprinkled blood that speaks a better word than the blood of Abel."

But here is the kicker: There cannot be a Zion (glory) except through Sinai (the law).

Man could only experience Zion by realizing his failure at Sinai. Through Moses came the law, but also a glimpse of the Shekinah (Glory). Moses gave the people God's law, but when he came back down from Sinai, he also carried with Him God's glory (the Shekinah glory), which made his face shine (Exodus 34:29-35). So, from Sinai, the people could see the glory of Zion, but they couldn't quite reach it. So, the law was to serve God's purpose on two fronts:

To give men a standard of righteousness to abide by for a just society and as a testimony of God's provision, protection, righteousness, and glory. At the time, the law, if obeyed perfectly by all in Israel, would have made for a utopian society. This is why David said the *law is perfect* (Psalm 19:7).

To make man realize his own depravity and his need for a Savior, who brought the greater glory, and a New Covenant. In this way, it pointed to a better covenant, the New one brought by Jesus Christ.

The law was also meant *to keep mankind accountable in their covenant relationship with God, their ultimate King,* through obedience. It comprised a more detailed list of His expectations until Messiah would come. It served as a strict, beneficial, and albeit temporary tutor. As you know, a tutor is a rigid stick used to help a plant, tree, or shrub grow straight. Eventually, when the plant stands strong, it is removed.

But the Kingdom of God was yet to come...

5. Fifthly, He prepared His people for worship by emphasizing His Holiness through the Levitical priesthood. In his fallen state, man desperately needed to understand the kind of gap that separated him from the Most High and Holy God. It was a BIG gap.

While the prophets represent God to the people, priests play the opposite role: they represent the people to God.

God is Holy. Holiness means *separate* or *set apartness*. God, because He is Holy, is apart from us. This required someone to bridge the gigantic gap between us sinners and a Holy God. Priests were, therefore, established to represent the people to God, and through all their required ceremonies and sacrifices, they served to keep the sinful people in relationship to their Holy God. The Levitical priesthood was a temporary institution. It was an image and a precursor of the role Christ would eventually come to play (Hebrews 4:15). It was a precursor of the universal priesthood of all believers as well (Revelation 1:6; 1 Peter 2:9).

The Levitical priesthood served to show God's people two major things: a) He is Holy, and b) we are not.

The priesthood was God's temporary plaster on mankind's biggest wound: separation through sin. The priesthood's intricate, strict, repetitive, and orderly functioning showed God's people just how much is needed to be done in order for us to be in a relationship with Him.

But the Kingdom of God was yet to come...

6. Sixthly, He allowed His people to be made familiar with monarchy

When Israel begged God for a human king, God warned them through the prophet Samuel:

> *"But when they said, 'Give us a king to lead us,' this displeased Samuel; so he prayed to the Lord. And the Lord told him:*

'Listen to all that the people are saying to you; it is not you they have rejected, but they have rejected me as their king. As they have done from the day I brought them up out of Egypt until this day, forsaking me and serving other gods, so they are doing to you. Now listen to them; but warn them solemnly and let them know what the king who will reign over them will claim as his rights.'" ~ 1 Samuel 8:6-9 (NIV)

Despite Israel's rejection of Him as their King, God, nonetheless, made a covenant with Israel's great king, David. In 2 Samuel 7:12-16, God says this to King David:

"When your days are fulfilled and you rest with your fathers, I will set up your seed after you, who will come from your body, and I will establish his kingdom. He shall build a house for My name, and I will establish the throne of his kingdom forever. I will be his Father, and he shall be My son. If he commits iniquity, I will chasten him with the rod of men and with the blows of the sons of men. But My mercy shall not depart from him, as I took it from Saul, whom I removed from before you. And your house and your kingdom shall be established forever before you. Your throne shall be established forever.'" ~ 2 Samuel 7:12-16 (NKJV)

God allowed Israel to have an earthly king because even though they rejected Him in the process, He knew some good would come of it and that He could use this model to usher in His Kingdom. Monarchy was to serve as a practical lesson of how a kingdom operates. It was good for the people to be made familiar with imperfect kings and kingdoms before they would be given a perfect King and Kingdom. They would appreciate it more. And Jesus the Christ would be born from King David's lineage, and even call himself: *Son of David.*

But the Kingdom of God was yet to come...

A Better Covenant

Through His different covenants, God presented His many facets to men. He is the creator (Adam), judge (Noah), partner (Abraham), establisher (Jacob), lawgiver (Moses), Holy one (the priesthood), and King (the monarchy).

All of these different covenants made with men on the earth were preparatory wheels set in motion by God to come in the flesh in *'The fullness of time'* and re-establish His Perfect Kingdom—His government, His rulership. But in the New Covenant, it would now be established *in the hearts of men.*

As believers, we now have been living under the New Covenant… under the spiritual Kingship of Christ for the last 2000+ years.

When Christ came, He brought with Him permanent spiritual access to the throne and to the King. And not just the access, but the Kingdom itself in the hearts of men! Jesus said:

> *"Do not be afraid, little flock, for your Father has been pleased to give you the kingdom." ~ Luke 12:32*

This NEW Covenant is described this way in the epistle to the Hebrews:

> *"But now He has obtained a more excellent ministry, inasmuch as He is also Mediator of a better covenant, which was established on better promises […] For this is the covenant that I will make with the house of Israel after those days, says the Lord: I will put My laws in their mind and write them on their hearts; and I will be their God, and they shall be My people. None of them shall teach his neighbor, and none his brother, saying, 'Know the Lord,' for all shall know Me, from the least of them to the greatest of them. For I will be merciful to their unrighteousness, and their sins and their lawless deeds I will remember no more." ~ Hebrews 8:6, 10-12 (NKJV)*

Kingdom Now *or* Not Yet?

If you have studied in any way "Kingdom theology," you've probably heard or read that the Kingdom of God is under the tension of two realities. The Kingdom of God is both *now* and *not yet* in its fulfillment.

We know the full and glorious establishment of His Kingdom will only be completed upon the return of the King. He will bring about its fulfillment.

On the other hand, we also know that much of the Kingdom became manifest at Pentecost. The outpouring of the Holy Spirit's power on believers has released much of the Kingdom's glory through men and women of faith across the centuries. Ever since Pentecost, believers have both prayed *"Thy Kingdom Come"* and *"Thy Will be done on earth as in heaven"*. As a result, we have seen much of its glory released through the faith of men and women of God since the Church began. Nevertheless, only Christ can bring its *full realization* at His second coming.

Furthermore, I am convinced that how much of the Kingdom we see now depends greatly on how much faith is exercised by the people of God in the process of time—that is, by you and me.

I really like the sober-minded view that pastor and theologian, Timothy Keller, expressed about the Kingdom's tension between the now and not yet:

> *"God's Kingdom is present in its beginnings, but still future in its fullness. This guards us from an under-realized eschatology (expecting no change now) and an over-realized eschatology (expecting all change now). In this stage, we embrace the reality that while we're not yet what we will be, we're also no longer what we used to be."*

And while this is true, it has engendered somewhat of a problem in the minds of believers. In the expectancy of Christ's return, many have, through complacency, under-realized their own inherent Kingdom potential.

> In the expectancy of Christ's return, many have, through complacency, under-realized their own inherent Kingdom potential.

Because we know that Jesus will set all things right when He returns, we have become lazy in fulfilling our own dominion and occupation mandate.

I have noticed that my own children are also like that. For example, if I assign a task for them to do and then leave, they seem to go back to doing their own thing rather than doing what I asked—and very quickly so.

While they have the capacity and potential to do what I want, they choose not to because they feel they have time before I come back to check up on them. That's how the Church is today. We are not expressing our full Kingdom potential because we feel we still have time or because we expect "Daddy," the Lord Jesus, to fix all things when He returns. In short, more often than not, *we're lazy and complacent.*

In the meantime, let us focus on Kingdom NOW.

Walter Rauschenbusch rightly observed when he said:

> *"It is for us to see the Kingdom of God as always coming, always pressing in on the present, always big with possibility, and always inviting immediate action."*

So, to understand what we are and what we have *now*, we need to understand the first coming of Christ better. If we fail to understand His first coming and what He brought with it, we will bear little fruit and fail to accelerate His second coming.

So, when Christ came, what happened? What changed? This is the focus of the next chapter.

4

THE MISUNDERSTOOD GOSPEL OF JESUS CHRIST

Rediscovering the Mission and Purpose of Jesus

"The primary reason Jesus came to earth was to inaugurate the Kingdom of God. Often, we hear that the reason Jesus came to the earth was to die on the Cross. Jesus did come to die on the Cross, but that death on the Cross was for the purpose of establishing the Kingdom of God." ~ John Eckhardt

Now, in this chapter, we finally get to talk about The Kingdom of God as we New Testament believers need to understand it.

So, as we will see in this chapter: *In Adam, we lost our Dominion and authority...*

In Jesus Christ, we got it back.

At the beginning of this book, I introduced you to the words of Myles Munroe, who said: *"The main mission of Jesus was to establish the Kingdom of God, in the hearts of men."*

As the founder of *Thriving on Purpose Ministries*, I take great pleasure in discussing the importance of *purpose* whenever I can. When we (my wife—Elisabeth and I) named the organization *Thriving on Purpose*, it indicated just how much we value people and their purpose here on earth.

Human beings are made in the image of God, and each individual has a specific assignment to accomplish here on earth. You have a very specific God-given mandate here on earth for such a time as this.

The definition of purpose is the following: *The reason for which something is done or created, or for which something exists.*

You, dear friend, are not here by mistake. You were not created and put on this earth, at this time, under those circumstances by happenstance. God has singled you out for a specific task that only you can accomplish at this time in history. You have a specific purpose and Kingdom mandate to fulfill.

When I heard this for the first time, I was 40 years old. It changed my whole life and perspective. *And I had been a born-again believer for 30 years!* Sad, isn't it?

Until then, I thought my sole purpose, once saved, was to evangelize. I failed to see the BIG picture for my own life. I failed to understand my specific assignment here and now on the earth. I was under the brainwash of religious thinking, and it greatly handicapped my life. It also made me very depressed and miserable.

Until then, I had been taught the religious fallacy that God made me for heaven. I believed that I was put on earth for the purpose of going to heaven. I had a bad case of wanting to retire in heaven on "Someday Isle." I was so heavenly-minded that I was of no earthly good. And when I evangelized, I taught others the same doctrine.

I am thankful that God has done a makeover on my understanding and mindset.

I now believe the greatest tragedy in life is someone who lives his whole life and then dies, without ever knowing what their true purpose here on earth was.

I believe this to be a great tragedy because of the crucial importance purpose holds in people's hearts. People who know God and their specific purpose, you will notice, are the ones who are the light of the world. The others, unfortunately, seem to live in darkness and offer only a spark.

Sadly, many spent 75+ years here on earth, and all they ever did was exist. They were living but never truly alive. As the saying goes, *"they die at 25, but are only buried at 75."*

This is not the limit of God's will for you! Your redemption was only the beginning.

> People who know God and their specific purpose, you will notice, are the ones who are the light of the world. The others, unfortunately, seem to live in darkness and offer only a spark.

Now, as I pondered these things, a question came to my mind, *"Since all humans have a very specific purpose for being born, what was the specific purpose of Jesus?"*

We know that God sent His Son *"in the fullness of time,"* as we saw in the previous chapter. So, the timing of His coming was perfectly aligned with the will of the Father, mankind's place in history, and everything set in place at that time.

Was Jesus' purpose to just die on the cross as I was taught all these years? While Christ did refer to His impending death as the purpose for this particular hour (John 12:27), it was just the tip of the iceberg concerning *His whole Purpose*—Capital 'P.'

The Purpose of Jesus

So, what exactly was the purpose of Jesus?

Unlike many of us here on the earth, Jesus knew His purpose from the very beginning. He wasn't confused about it.

Remember when Mary and Joseph lost Him in Jerusalem? He was only 12 years old then. And despite His young age, in Luke 2:46-50 (NKJV), we read this...

> *"Now so it was that after three days they found Him in the temple, sitting in the midst of the teachers, both listening to them and asking them questions. And all who heard*

113

Him were astonished at His understanding and answers. So when they saw Him, they were amazed; and His mother said to Him, 'Son, why have You done this to us? Look, Your father and I have sought You anxiously.'

And He said to them, 'Why did you seek Me? Did you not know that I must be about My Father's business?' But they did not understand the statement which He spoke to them."

So, even at that young age, Jesus knew His unique assignment. But the purpose of Jesus was further defined by Himself when He had come of age and began His ministry around age 30.

As an interesting side note, you may not know why Jesus' ministry began only at age 30. However, the Book of Hebrews tells us that Jesus is our High Priest. And, according to the Old Testament, priests were to begin serving in the temple when they were 30 years old (1 Chronicles 23:2-5; Numbers 4:1-3, 21-23, 29-30). That is why Christ began His ministry at 30 and not before. It was, just like the rest of His life, *to fulfill Scripture.*

So, Jesus began His ministry by being first baptized by John, confirmed by God in public, and filled with the Holy Spirit when it descended on Him like a dove.

He then went off into the desert, where He was tempted by Satan and won that battle.

So, right from the get-go, He succeeded where Adam had failed. This was a major turning point and it established Him. And then He began His work.

The Work of Jesus

He began His work, like all great endeavours, by first publicly stating *His mission statement.*

As most entrepreneurs know, a mission statement is defined as *"a formal summary of the aims and values of a company, organization, or individual."*

So, what was the *formal summary of the aims and values* of Jesus? The first official words preached by Jesus in public, as recorded in Matthew 4:17 (NLT), are:

> *"From that time on Jesus began to preach, 'Repent, for the kingdom of heaven has come near.'"*

"From that time on." Other versions say, *"From then on."* This is to mean: *from this moment and habitually after that.*

From there, Jesus' message was mostly about the Kingdom of God. All throughout the gospels, the Kingdom was the main message of Jesus.

He would say: *"The Kingdom of God is like," "To what shall I compare the Kingdom of God?" "The Kingdom of God is,"* etc. The gospels are saturated with Kingdom talk from Yahushua.

Check this out in the King James Version Bible:

- ♔ The Kingdom of God appears 15 times in Mark.
- ♔ The Kingdom of God appears 31 times in Luke.
- ♔ The Kingdom of God appears twice in John.
- ♔ The Kingdom of God appears seven times in Acts.
- ♔ The Kingdom of God appears eight times in the rest of the New Testament.

Now, you may ask, *"What about the Gospel of Matthew?"*

Well, instead of *'Kingdom of God,'* Matthew used the term *'Kingdom of Heaven'?*

The *Kingdom of Heaven* appears a whopping 32 times in Matthew! Matthew chose to use the term *'Kingdom of Heaven'* rather than *'Kingdom of God'* in order to avoid offending his target audience, who were mostly Hebrews. They have long preferred not to name or use the name of God. They did so to avoid breaking the third commandment, which says, *"Thou shalt not take the name of the Lord thy God in vain."*

So, it is evident from the gospels that Jesus' main teaching and mission was to proclaim this *"Good News of the Kingdom."*

> It is evident from the gospels that Jesus' main teaching and mission was to proclaim this "Good News of the Kingdom."

In fact, He said it Himself in Luke 4:42-44 (NIV):

"At daybreak, Jesus went out to a solitary place. The people were looking for him and when they came to where he was, they tried to keep him from leaving them. But he said, 'I must proclaim the good news of the kingdom of God to the other towns also, because that is why I was sent.' And he kept on preaching in the synagogues of Judea."

In the New American Standard Version (NASB), it reads:

"But He said to them, 'I must preach the kingdom of God to the other cities also, for I was sent for this purpose.'"

So, Jesus said Himself that He was sent to *preach the Kingdom of God.* In His own words, this was His purpose.

Also, at the beginning of His ministry, we read in Mark 1:14-15:

"After John was put in prison, Jesus went into Galilee, proclaiming the good news of God. 'The time has come,' he said. 'The kingdom of God has come near. Repent and believe the good news!'"

Keep this in mind: *The Good News* is the translation of the word *'Gospel.'*

The Gospel According to Jesus

"The doctrine of the Kingdom of Heaven, which was the main teaching of Jesus, is certainly one of the most revolutionary doctrines that ever stirred and changed human thought."
~ H. G. Wells

The gospel means *Good News.*

The gospel that Jesus taught seemed more closely linked to the Kingdom of God than His sacrificial death—which is where the buck stops for many evangelicals. In fact, when reading the gospels, the good news is clearly the fact that *"the Kingdom of God has come near."*

This was the Good News (Gospel) then... *and it still is!*

But before we investigate more of what the Good News means, let's correct a few things first.

In religion, we were mostly taught *a part* of the good news, or some good news—*but not THE Good News of the Kingdom.*

We were mostly taught that the good news was about God forgiving our sins once we believe in Jesus. In fact, we were taught that this is the good news: forgiveness of sins through Jesus and going to heaven... *when we die.* This, dear friend, is the Gospel of Salvation, but not the Gospel of the Kingdom. While it is good news for sure, it is not *the good news of the Kingdom.*

> Jesus simply taught this: "The Kingdom of God has come to earth. Let all who will, repent, enter in, and partake of its grace, majesty, and power."

While the gospel of salvation is indeed good news... it is not *THE FULL GOSPEL*, or Good News.

So then, *what did Jesus really teach?*

Jesus simply taught this:

"The Kingdom of God has come to earth. Let all who will, repent, enter in, and partake of its grace, majesty, and power."

The Kingdom of God coming back to earth in the hearts of men and with full spiritual authority is THE GOOD NEWS. Jesus came to restore that which was lost in Adam. Dominion and authority were lost in Adam.

The Gospel vs. The *FULL* Gospel

Back in the 70s and 80s, there was a term used for churches that believed in tongues, miracles, healings, and casting out demons. Aside from familiar labels like *Charismatic*, *Pentecostal*, or *Assemblies of God*, these were also called: *Full Gospel churches.*

According to Wikipedia, the term 'Full Gospel' refers to Romans 15:18-19, where Paul says: *"... to make the Gentiles obedient, by word and deed, through mighty signs and wonders, by the power of the Spirit of God; so that from Jerusalem, and round about unto Illyricum, I have fully preached the gospel of Christ."*

Paul says here that the gospel he preached came with words *and deeds.* He says it was accompanied by many signs and wonders *"so that"* he *fully* preached the gospel of Christ.

The term *'so that'* here means *'in order to,'* implying that the full gospel would not have been preached without these signs and wonders. This means that if he had preached in word only, the gospel message would have been shortchanged.

Many churches and denominations have embraced an incomplete version of the gospel that is limited to the message of salvation. It is taught *in word only.* Therefore, their message often lacks the signs, wonders, and power that confirms its vital truth.

Changing Kingdoms

When we talk of conversion, we often say a man must be *born again.* This is taken from the Gospel of John (chapter 3 verse 3), where Jesus says to Nicodemus: *"Most assuredly, I say to you, unless one is born again, he cannot see the kingdom of God."* (NKJV)

The term 'born again' is adapted from the Greek Word *anōthen,* which means *from above.* In order to be admitted into the Kingdom, we must be *born from above.*

We know that we acquire citizenship of a country by birth. I was born in Canada; therefore, I am a Canadian citizen. If someone is born in China, he is Chinese by birth—a Chinese citizen.

The invitation to be born again is an invitation to acquire new, imperishable citizenship from the Kingdom of heaven *by being born into it* (born again)—not in the flesh but in the spirit.

When a man (or woman) receives salvation, he moves from being under the rulership of the kingdom of this world (Satan's authority, rules, and laws) to being under the jurisdiction and laws of God's Kingdom. He now has new citizenship with new rights and privileges stemming from a different Kingdom and a different ruler (God as King).

In Colossians 1:13 (NLT), Paul tells us:

> *"For he has rescued us from the kingdom of darkness and transferred us into the Kingdom of his dear Son."*

And Peter also makes a point of our new Kingdom identity when he says:

> *"But you are a chosen race, a royal priesthood, a holy nation, a people for his own possession, that you may proclaim the excellencies of him who called you out of darkness into his marvelous light." ~ 1 Peter 2:9 (ESV)*

This means that everyone in the Kingdom of God has dual citizenship. We all are citizens of our own country, but most importantly, we are citizens of the Kingdom of God.

How the Church Got Sidetracked

The gospel of salvation that the Church has been focused on for the most part of its history, while a very good and needed thing, should never have replaced *the Gospel of the Kingdom* Jesus charged His disciples to preach, even after He rose again (Acts 1:3).

Someone once said that the best foundation for deception is truth. The Devil, the Father of lies, knows this all too well. Throughout history, Satan has kept the Church sidetracked with many truths and many good things. He even made us teach these good things as if it were the full gospel itself. These good things are all an intrinsic part of what we are told is 'The Gospel' today:

- The cross and the atonement
- Evangelism through the Great Commission
- Being born again
- Eternal life
- Going to heaven when we die

These are all part of our 'evangelical' message. And for sure, there is no denying that these are all *good and biblical things*. No one can argue the importance of these foundational truths.

But the one thing Satan wanted to make sure that we wouldn't preach is this: the restoration of God's Kingdom on the earth, a.k.a., the good news of the Kingdom of God in the hearts of men... *and the power, authority, and restored dominion that comes with that.*

It was in Satan's best interest that he led us away from the Kingdom's full message.

The Devil will get you talking about heaven until

> The Devil will get you talking about heaven until you are out of breath, but what he really doesn't want you talking about is The Kingdom of God and its power here and now on the earth.

you are out of breath, but what he really doesn't want you talking about is *The Kingdom of God* and its power here and now on the earth.

He doesn't want believers to know of their authority and power here and now… on earth. He doesn't want them to know about the full restoration of their dominion.

Let's now look at the Great Commission sayings of Jesus. We are all familiar with Matthew 28:19-20 (NIV):

> *"Therefore go and <u>make disciples of all nations</u>, baptizing them in the name of the Father and of the Son and of the Holy Spirit, and teaching them to obey everything I have commanded you. And surely I am with you always, to the very end of the age."*

But let's look at the other Great Commission passages:

Mark 16:15 (NIV) says:

> *"He said to them, 'Go into all the world and preach the gospel (good news) <u>to all creation.</u>'"*

And Matthew 24:14 (NIV) says this:

> *"And this gospel (Good News) of the kingdom will be preached <u>in the whole world</u> as a testimony to all nations, and then the end will come."*

So, it is clear from these that the Gospel of the Kingdom of God is to be spread upon the whole earth. As a side note, it seems to me a scary prospect that since the Church isn't busy preaching 'The Good News of the Kingdom,' we might thus be postponing His second coming. Think about that! Furthermore, Satan relishes in this because as long as we don't preach the gospel of the Kingdom to the whole world, it buys him more time.

The late Dr. Myles Munroe said this in his excellent book, *Rediscovering the Kingdom*:

"We have gotten so sidetracked on secondary and peripheral issues. It seems that the message of the Kingdom has all but disappeared. There is no doubt that Jesus Christ died on the cross that we might be forgiven of our sins and find eternal life in Him. There is also no doubt that we need to tell people that He is the way, the Truth, and the Life, and that He is the only way to eternal life. All of this is part of the message of the Kingdom, but it is not all of the message. The cross of Christ is the beginning point of life in The Kingdom of God, not the ending point. There is no ending point because life in the Kingdom has no end."

Then he added this:

"Our problem is that we spend so much time telling people how to get into the Kingdom that we rarely teach them what to do once they get inside. Often, we don't know ourselves because no one has ever taught us, either. We spend so much time preaching about the door (Jesus, the cross, and repentance) that we forget all about the palace inside."

This reminds me of a saying I once heard which said: *"Christianity is the best religion in the world. What a shame that it has never been truly practiced."*

The Kingdom of God in the Kolbrin

The Kolbrin is an ancient collection of writings from the Egyptians and the Celts.

On Amazon, it is described as:

"a compilation of ancient writings dating back 3,600 years. This two-part, 11-book secular anthology is nearly as large as the King James Bible. The first six books are called the 'Egyptian texts' and were penned by Egyptian academicians following the Hebrew Exodus. The last five books are called

the 'Celtic texts' and were penned by Celtic priests following the death of Jesus."

As you have guessed, the book is an interesting read, to say the least.

There are passages in the Kolbrin that are attributed to Jesus Himself and some of His teachings. While some of these do align with the Bible, some others clearly don't.

Nevertheless, there is a passage in the writings of the Kolbrin that really caught my attention. I believe it to be genuine. It makes me think Jesus knew the Church would get sidetracked from preaching the Gospel of the Kingdom. While the Kolbrin comprises writings outside of the Bible and is not to be put on equal footing with the scriptures, I believe this insightful passage is deserving of our careful attention:

> *"Jesus said, 'The Kingdom of Heaven is like a woman carrying a jar of good wine. Being careless she puts the jar down heavily and crashes it, and when she resumes her way the wine spills out behind her on the road, but she blithely continues on her way unaware of the spillage. When she enters the house, the master takes the wine jar and finds it empty'. The disciples asked what this could mean, and Jesus replied, 'When you possess the good things of the Kingdom of Heaven, do not let them slip away.'"* ~ The Kobrin, The Britain Book, Chapter 3

In all honesty, when I first read this passage, I didn't know what to make of it. I had no understanding of its meaning whatsoever. But, later that day, as I was pondering this analogy, the Holy Spirit gave me its interpretation. As a result, I now believe this short extra-biblical parable really came from our Lord. This, however, is by no means a full endorsement of the Kolbrin. I always urge my readers to chew the grass and spit out the hay when they do research outside of the accepted Scriptures.

As for the interpretation of the parable, here goes...

I believe the woman in this passage is the Church, the Bride of Christ. The wine she is carrying is *the Gospel of the Kingdom,* the central teachings of Jesus. Her crashing of the jar is her neglect of the centrality of the Kingdom message. Her travel is the way of the Church throughout history. When *'she enters the house'* is figurative of when the Church is reunited with the Bridegroom at the end of the Age and enters Heaven. The Master represents the Lord Jesus. When He finds the jar empty upon inspection, it echoes the rhetorical question of Jesus when He asked: *"When the Son of Man comes, will he find [the] faith on earth?"* (brackets mine)

> The Church dropped the ball early in its history, replacing the full Gospel of the Kingdom, which Jesus taught, with the gospel of salvation and eternal life of institutionalized Christianity.

As I said earlier in the book: The Church dropped the ball early in its history, replacing the full Gospel of the Kingdom, which Jesus taught, with the gospel of salvation and eternal life of institutionalized Christianity. We have been carrying a semi-empty jar for some time now, and it needs to change, lest we be judged unfavorably by the Master of the house.

Russian philosopher, Nikolai Berdyaev, was right when he said: *"The Church is simply the path of history and not the actual kingdom of God."*

What Makes the Kingdom Such Good News?

We know that Jesus preached the Good News of the Kingdom during His ministry and even after His resurrection.

In Acts 1:3 (NIV), we read:

"After his suffering, he presented himself to them and gave many convincing proofs that he was alive. He appeared to them over a period of forty days <u>and spoke about the Kingdom of God.</u>"

Even after He rose again, for the ensuing 40 days, the Kingdom message was His priority.

So now, let's consider what Jesus' Kingdom message and mission entailed, so that we may understand just how Good the news is:

1. Firstly, Jesus Christ came in the flesh. I briefly mentioned in the previous chapter just how crucial this is. According to God's decree in Genesis 1:26-28, man was given authority and dominion to operate in the earth realm. So, we can only imagine the tremendous power God brought forth when Christ came in the flesh! He was the Son of God in a human body. Now, as The Word in human form, God had the full authority to act out His will on the earth. Heaven's will was brought forth with full force upon the earth in the form of a man—*a Kinsman redeemer!*

The Enemy had been foretold of this plan of God in Genesis 3:15. So, forewarned, he repeatedly tried to block this from ever happening. He feared this day. This is why we read in the Scripture of how he…

Tried to infiltrate the seed line of man (and even animals) by hybridizing mankind with, among other ways, fallen angels (Genesis 6:1-4).

Corrupting the seed line of man was a sure way to make human beings into something abominable, corrupt, and more importantly, not 100% human and therefore: unredeemable.

This is why God chose Noah for His initial great reset with humanity. In Genesis 6:9 (NKJV), it is written: *"Noah was a just man, perfect in his generations."*

Perfect in his generations implies that his seed line had not been corrupted through hybridization. Noah was one of the only remaining 100% humans at the time. Also, in verse 12 (NKJV), we read: *"God looked upon the earth, and indeed it was corrupt; for all flesh had corrupted their way on the earth."*

125

The term, *all flesh had corrupted their way* implies more than mere moral corruption; it was also physical.

Raised enemies and temptations against Israel all throughout the Old Testament to try and destroy them.

Time and again, in the Old Testament, the people of Israel were told by God *not to intermarry* with the people of surrounding nations. These other nations had corrupted their seed line after the Flood. This, again, was to keep the seed line untainted for the coming of the Messiah.

Furthermore, they were surrounded by enemies constantly. If Satan could not infiltrate their gene pool, he resorted to attempting genocide against God's people. Just think of all the *'ites'* in the Bible that Israel had to wage war against: The *Hittites*, the *Girgashites*, the *Amorites*, the *Canaanites*, the *Perizzites*, the *Hivites*, and the *Jebusites* (Joshua 3:10). And let's not forget the *Philistines!*

Committed the cruel murder of the firstborn. Through King Herod, the devil tried to put baby Jesus to death prematurely. He wanted to abort God's plan, pun intended.

In Matthew 2:16-18 (ESV), we read of this horrid event:

> *"Then Herod, when he saw that he had been tricked by the wise men, became furious, and he sent and killed all the male children in Bethlehem and in all that region who were two years old or under, according to the time that he had ascertained from the wise men. Then was fulfilled what was spoken by the prophet Jeremiah: 'A voice was heard in Ramah, weeping and loud lamentation, Rachel weeping for her children; she refused to be comforted, because they are no more.'"*

This, of course, was the last resort, and it still failed. Despite centuries of attempts to thwart God's plan, in the fullness of time, Jesus Christ came in the flesh and:

"Grew in wisdom and stature, and in favor with God and man." ~ Luke 2:52 (NIV)

The full force and authority of the Kingdom of God came in a human body (Jesus Christ), with human DNA, with full legality, and therefore was able to make everything that was wrong right again. To redeem mankind, God needed to be fully (and purely) human. This was the kickoff of God to usher in the Kingdom of God: He needed to be made manifest in the flesh to retake all authority from the Enemy. He made Himself into a perfect *Kinsman redeemer*. The devil and the hordes of hell scream at this very truth because it is what spelled their ultimate defeat.

> The full force and authority of the Kingdom of God came in a human body (Jesus Christ), with human DNA, with full legality, and therefore was able to make everything that was wrong right again.

1 John 4:2-3 (NKJV) says:

> *"By this you know the Spirit of God: Every spirit that confesses that Jesus Christ has come in the flesh is of God, and every spirit that does not confess that Jesus Christ has come in the flesh is not of God. And this is the spirit of the Antichrist, which you have heard was coming, and is now already in the world."*

Hebrews 2:17-18 (NKJV) says:

> *"Therefore, in all things He had to be made like His brethren, that He might be a merciful and faithful High Priest in things pertaining to God, to make propitiation for the sins of the people. For in that He Himself has suffered, being tempted, He is able to aid those who are tempted."*

And Hebrews 4:15 (NKJV), we read:

> *"For we do not have a High Priest who cannot sympathize with our weaknesses, but was in all points tempted as we are, yet without sin."*

The second component of the Good News of the Kingdom is: Man has been brought back into full communion and relationship with God through salvation.

What used to be something temporary done through the sacrifices of the Old Mosaic covenant is now a permanent fixture and privilege in Christ Jesus.

In Jesus, we are fully reconciled to God. In 1 Corinthians 5:17-21 (NIV), we read:

> *"Therefore, if anyone is in Christ, the new creation has come: The old has gone, the new is here! All this is from God, who reconciled us to himself through Christ and gave us the ministry of reconciliation: that God was reconciling the world to himself in Christ, not counting people's sins against them. And he has committed to us the message of reconciliation. We are therefore Christ's ambassadors, as though God were making his appeal through us. We implore you on Christ's behalf: Be reconciled to God. God made him who had no sin to be sin for us, so that in him we might become the righteousness of God."*

So, since Jesus came, nothing separates us from God—except, of course, our own sin and stubbornness when we dare not come to Him humbly.

The third component of the Good News of the Kingdom is: It restored man to His rightful place of authority and dominion.

Through Christ, God wanted to restore that which was lost in Adam. We learned that man lost his spiritual dominion (authority) on the earth when he fell. Well, Jesus brought it back.

Just before He gave His Great Commission in Matthew 28:18, He said: *"All authority has been given to Me in heaven and on earth. Go therefore..."* And, in Matthew 16:19 (NIV), we read:

"I will give you the keys of the kingdom of heaven; whatever you bind on earth will be bound in heaven, and whatever you loose on earth will be loosed in heaven."

Again, we see that man was given back authority on earth: Whatever you bind on earth and whatever you loose on earth will be loosed or bound in Heaven. Jesus gave us the keys.

Jesus said, in Luke 11:17-22 (NIV), answering those who accused Him of casting out demons by the power of Beelzebul:

"Any kingdom divided against itself will be ruined, and a house divided against itself will fall. If Satan is divided against himself, how can his kingdom stand? I say this because you claim that I drive out demons by Beelzebul. Now if I drive out demons by Beelzebul, by whom do your followers drive them out? So then, they will be your judges. But if I drive out demons by the finger of God, then the kingdom of God has come upon you.

"When a strong man, fully armed, guards his own house, his possessions are safe. But when someone stronger attacks and overpowers him, he takes away the armor in which the man trusted and divides up his plunder."

In this illustration, Jesus is that *someone stronger* who attacked the strong man of the house and bound him (that is Satan). He took his possessions away, which are the sons of men living under his jurisdiction since the fall. And, after all this, He gave us back the house—which is the full authority in the earth realm.

And finally, everything has been restored unto us. In Ephesians 1:22-23 (NIV), we read:

"God placed all things under his feet and appointed him to be head over everything for the church, which is his body, the fullness of him who fills everything in every way."

One pastor put it this way, *"Everything is under His feet...and His feet are His body...and we the Church are the body."*

The fourth component of the Good News of the Kingdom is: He has given us true and permanent *POWER*.

Friends, we are not powerless anymore! We have the Holy Spirit in permanence!

Before Christ came, in the Old Testament, the Holy Spirit wasn't a widespread or permanent gift. Scholars' views vary on whether it only resided in a select few or whether it just didn't remain in permanence within men. But suffice it to say that the Spirit of God made Himself a lot scarcer than it is now.

It is such a tragedy that the Church today does not claim the full power given to us through whom author and pastor Francis Chan has nicknamed *'The Forgotten God.'*

The failure of today's believers to fully tap into the power of the Holy Spirit is what makes the Church appear like just any other religion: ritualistic, dogmatic, and yes, dare I say it: *powerless.*

> The failure of today's believers to fully tap into the power of the Holy Spirit is what makes the Church appear like just any other religion: ritualistic, dogmatic, and yes, dare I say it: powerless.

Therefore, in the eyes of many, Christianity, or perhaps I should say, *churchianity*, is unappealing.

Remember, when prompted by the religious leaders, Jesus said this about the Kingdom of God in Luke 17:21 (NKJV):

> *"Now when He was asked by the Pharisees when the kingdom of God would come, He answered them and said, 'The kingdom of God does not come with observation; nor will they say, 'See here!' or 'See there!' For indeed, the kingdom of God is within you.'"*

And that Kingdom within is manifested through the POWER of the Holy Spirit.

John the Baptist foretold in Matthew 3:11 (NASB) of how we would inherit the baptism of the Holy Spirit:

> *"As for me, I baptize you with water for repentance, but He who is coming after me is mightier than I, and I am not fit to remove His sandals; He will baptize you with the Holy Spirit and fire."*

And later, this was fulfilled in Acts 1:4-8 (NKJV),

> *"And being assembled together with them, He commanded them not to depart from Jerusalem, but to wait for the Promise of the Father, 'which,' He said, 'you have heard from Me; for John truly baptized with water, but you shall be baptized with the Holy Spirit not many days from now.' Therefore, when they had come together, they asked Him, saying, 'Lord, will You at this time restore the kingdom to Israel?' And He said to them, 'It is not for you to know times or seasons which the Father has put in His own authority. But you shall receive power when the Holy Spirit has come upon you; and you shall be witnesses to Me in Jerusalem, and in all Judea and Samaria, and to the end of the earth.'"*

You shall receive what? ... *POWER!*

The word *power* here is from the Greek: *Dunamis.* This is the same word from whence we derived *dynamite.* It means *physical power, force, might, ability, efficacy, energy.*

And here is what Jesus meant by this:

> *"He said to them, 'Go into all the world and preach the gospel to all creation. Whoever believes and is baptized will be saved, but whoever does not believe will be condemned. And these signs will accompany those who believe: In my name they will drive out demons; they will speak in new*

tongues; they will pick up snakes with their hands; and when they drink deadly poison, it will not hurt them at all; they will place their hands on sick people, and they will get well.'" ~ Mark 16:15-18 (NIV)

And in Matthew 17:20 (NIV), He said: "

Truly I tell you, if you have faith as small as a mustard seed, you can say to this mountain, 'Move from here to there,' and it will move. Nothing will be impossible for you."

In John 14:12-14 (NIV):

"Very truly I tell you, whoever believes in me will do the works I have been doing, and they will do even greater things than these, because I am going to the Father. And I will do whatever you ask in my name, so that the Father may be glorified in the Son. You may ask me for anything in my name, and I will do it."

And Paul reminded his young apprentice in 2 Timothy 1:7 (NIV):

"For God has not given us a spirit of fear, but of power and of love and of a sound mind."

The reason most believers do not experience these things is because of a very destructive doctrine taught by many prominent evangelical leaders called: *cessationism.*

Cessationism is the (false and destructive) doctrine that spiritual gifts such as speaking in tongues, prophecy, healing, and miracles *ceased* with the apostolic age. This is not only gravely erroneous and unbiblical, but it renders believers impotent in the Kingdom of God, and therefore, makes them seem like everyone else. It makes the Kingdom of God appear bland and powerless. In turn, it makes those who might have otherwise sought the Kingdom, uninterested.

And the worst part is that these churches teach that this is completely normal. They teach that the miraculous signs were for a season only—for the beginnings of the Church.

Cessationism, in my opinion, is one of the most destructive doctrines in churches today. And dare I say it, I believe it is a doctrine of demons as it does serve their purposes so well by enforcing religion over Kingdom.

Cessationism breeds:

- ♛ **Religiosity**
- ♛ **Backslidden believers**
- ♛ **An orphan spirit**
- ♛ **Atheism and agnosticism**
- ♛ **Having a form of godliness but denying its power (2 Timothy 3:5)**

I have often taught people that if their church teaches cessationism, they need to drop it like a bad habit. They need to get out of there—fast! I'm sorry if that applies to you, but it's true.

Most cessationist churches do not experience the full power of God because they do not believe in the full power of God. It's that simple.

Jesus told the blind men, *"It will be done to you according to your faith"* (Matthew 9:29). If you do not believe the Word of God concerning what you were given through the Holy Spirit, you will not experience it.

The fifth component of the Good News of the Kingdom is: It has given us access to God's infinite riches... *both spiritual and physical!*

In Luke 4:18 and Matthew 11:4, Jesus said He was *'anointed to preach the good news to the poor'*. Although in some places the word 'poor' may refer to the *poor in spirit*, such as in the sermon on the mount, His Good News was also for the physically and financially poor. He confirmed this when He multiplied bread for the masses (more than once). This was a symbol of the good news for the poor.

So, the good news of the Kingdom was first preached to the poor. Why is that? Because it is *great news* for the poor.

In the Sermon on the Mount, Jesus told believers that the way to obtain their necessities was to be different under Kingdom jurisdiction. In Matthew chapter 6:31-33 (NIV), we read:

> *"Therefore do not worry, saying, 'What shall we eat?' or 'What shall we drink?' or 'What shall we wear?' For after all these things the Gentiles seek. For your heavenly Father knows that you need all these things. But <u>seek first the kingdom of God and His righteousness, and all these things shall be added to you</u>."*

And in Philippians 4:19 (NKJV), a favourite verse of many, including myself, we read:

> *"My God shall supply all your need according to His riches in glory by Christ Jesus."*

So, as Kingdom citizens, we have access to Kingdom provision, blessings, and an inheritance of our God and Father—the King of heaven and earth.

The God who told the Israelites in Deuteronomy 15 that:

> *"There should be no poor among you (V.4)*

And also promised that:

> *"His divine power has granted to us <u>all things that pertain to life</u> and godliness." ~ 2 Peter 1:3 (ESV)*

The Word says *all things*. All we have to do is ask, seek, and knock.

Remember, Jesus said in John 16:23-24 (NIV):

> *"Very truly I tell you, my Father will give you whatever you ask in my name. Until now you have not asked for anything in my name. Ask and you will receive, and your joy will be complete."*

God, whose riches are unlimited, will not withhold anything good from His children, provided we ask in faith and according to His will.

So, when I said that Christ restored the Kingdom unto us and it changed everything, I meant it.

Now, for most of you, there is only one thing standing in the way of all that the Father has in store for You.

And that, dear reader, is yourself.

All the deliverance and providence that God has re-established is now available to those who believe. The problem is... *most do not believe.* Many of us lack faith one way or another.

> All the deliverance and providence that God has re-established is now available to those who believe. The problem is... most do not believe.

We call ourselves *believers...* but what do we believe?

- ♔ Do we *believe* in the promises of God?
- ♔ Do we *believe* in the Word of God? And most of all...
- ♔ Do we *believe* that God is good?

This, friends, will be the subject of our next chapter, as we explore the biggest obstacle to our living the abundant life of the Kingdom: our corrupt thinking, our lack of faith, and our twisted beliefs about our God and King.

5

GOD IS GOOD... ALL THE TIME!

Reconnecting with the Father's Unfailing Love

"If you can really make a man believe you love him, you have won him; and if I could only make people really believe that God loves them, what a rush we would see for the kingdom of God!" ~ Dwight L. Moody

There is a reason I opted to put this chapter close to the middle of this book. It's because God's love and goodness is central to His Kingdom. It is the fundamental of fundamentals.

> God's love and goodness is central to His Kingdom. It is the fundamental of fundamentals.

In the last chapter, we learned that the true Gospel of Jesus Christ, the REAL good news, was that God brought the power and influence of the Kingdom of Heaven back to earth... in men's hearts and through the power of The Holy Ghost.

We also learned that through this New Covenant, we have access through Jesus Christ to God's favor, blessings, and yes... riches— *here and now.*

We learned that painful toil and sweat (and worry) to obtain sustenance is the way of the pagans (or unbelievers) according to Jesus in Matthew chapter 6:31-33 (NIV), when He said:

> *"Do not worry, saying, 'What shall we eat?' or 'What shall we drink?' or 'What shall we wear?' For the pagans run after*

*all these things, and your heavenly Father knows that you
need them. But seek first his kingdom and his righteousness,
and all these things will be given to you as well."*

Indeed, the coming of Jesus changed everything—*for those
who believe.*

Now, you might be thinking, *'If that's true, how come there is so
much suffering on earth? And most of all… how come this hasn't been
true in my life?'*

In this chapter, we will tackle why few believers actually tap into
the blessed and abundant life that Jesus promised.

And… as you will see, *it isn't God's fault!*

The Renewing of the Mind

In his epistle to the Romans, Paul admonishes us:

> *"Do not conform to the pattern of this world, <u>but be
> transformed by the renewing of your mind.</u> Then you will
> be able to test and approve what God's will is—his good,
> pleasing and perfect will." ~ Romans 12:2 (NIV)*

As believers, we are not to be conformed to what Paul calls *the
pattern of this world.* We are not to think like the world thinks, see
like the world sees, understand like the world understands, live like
the world lives, and most of all, believe what the world believes.

The world, or unbelievers, believe through their senses—what
they can see, touch, hear, or smell, etc.

As believers, we are called to a renewing of our minds which
leads us into transformation.

In the gospel, there is an instance when Jesus gets somewhat
impatient with our conformity with the world. This interesting
narrative is found in Matthew 17:14-18 (NIV):

> *"When they came to the crowd, a man approached Jesus and knelt before him. 'Lord, have mercy on my son,' he said. 'He has seizures and is suffering greatly. He often falls into the fire or into the water. I brought him to your disciples, but they could not heal him.' <u>'You unbelieving and perverse generation,' Jesus replied, 'how long shall I stay with you? How long shall I put up with you?</u> Bring the boy here to me.' Jesus rebuked the demon, and it came out of the boy, and he was healed at that moment."*

Jesus said, *"You unbelieving and perverse generation."* These words sound harsh, but what did He mean exactly?

Well, if we read the end of the story, we realize that Jesus equated *'perverse thinking'* with unbelief.

When His disciples asked why they couldn't cast out the demon, He answered them:

"Because you have so little faith. Truly I tell you, if you have faith as small as a mustard seed, you can say to this mountain, 'Move from here to there,' and it will move. Nothing will be impossible for you." ~ Matthew 17:20 (NIV)

Perverse Thinking

Merriam-Webster defines perverse this way:

a: Turned away from what is right or good: Corrupt

b: Improper, Incorrect

Also: obstinate in opposing what is right, reasonable, or accepted: Wrongheaded

So, *perverse* in the context means *wrongheaded*, which is to say: *having or showing bad judgment; misguided.*

It is clear that the disciples could not cast out the demon because they had too little faith and wrong thinking. The two are inextricably linked.

When we fail to move mountains in our own lives, it is not because God has failed us; it is because we have failed God...through our own lack of faith. We cannot have what heaven has unless we think like heaven thinks.

> We cannot have what heaven has unless we think like heaven thinks.

We need to repent from our *perverse thinking* and replace it with *right thinking*. Only right thinking can bring right believing. And only right believing can make us say to mountains: move out of the way.

Acts of God

The first and most important corrective measure believers need to bring to their understanding in order to have mustard seed faith is that God is good... *all the time.*

We say it—*all the time*, but do we believe it?

Consider this...

In our insurance policies, we have what is termed to be *"Acts of God."* These are natural disasters like earthquakes, volcanoes, tornadoes, and hurricanes, which can take the lives and possessions of many people. That is in our everyday business vernacular. So, we basically equate the massive loss of life and destruction with God's will.

And then we kid ourselves in trying to reconcile such things with our supposed belief that *God is good.*

So, according to this train of thought, God brings death and destruction, but we say He is good? Um, really?

Now, don't get me wrong... I am not in actuality agreeing with insurance companies that God causes these natural catastrophes. No. What I am saying is that we ascribe these destructive natural events *to Him alone*. And yet, in the Bible, these were caused by God in certain unique instances only. The flood, Sodom and Gomorrah, the plagues of Egypt, and the tribulation in Revelation are unique instances where God brings judgement on people who oppose Him on a grand scale. But can we say that every storm, tornado, and earthquake are sent by Him? Of course not. In the Book of Job, Satan himself was able to control weather patterns to bring about destruction (Job 1:16-19).

I believe that when God created wind currents, weather patterns, and seasons, He gave them something similar to human free will to go to and fro and accomplish their purpose on the earth—within certain limitations (Job chapter 38). Nature was meant to be, to a large extent, self-regulating. I also believe that at certain times, God may take hold of these wind currents and weather patterns to bring them the way He wants and to fulfill His purposes. He can also assign this task to mighty angels. But I believe this is the exception and not the rule.

Now, this is just my opinion, and you may disagree theologically. That's okay.

Testimony of an Avowed Agnostic

Bart D. Ehrman is one of the most distinguished New Testament scholars in the world. I have two of his books in my personal library. His writings and publicized debates have helped me to better understand the origins and makings of our beloved New Testament. His works are scholarly, insightful, and very well-researched.

However, and this may come as a shock to some of you, Mr. Ehrman is a self-avowed *agnostic*. Yes, you read that right. Although he is a gifted Bible scholar, *he is not a believer*. He used to be, as a youth, but along the way, his convictions changed.

The most interesting thing about his lack of faith in the God of the Bible is the reason behind it. Here is *why* one of the most respected Bible scholars of this generation is not a believer… in his own words and from his own blog titled *Leaving the Faith* (https://ehrmanblog.org/leaving-the-faith/):

> *"As a Christian—from the time I was able to think, through my teenage and early-twenties fundamentalist period, up to my more mature adult liberal phase—I had believed in some form of the traditional, biblical God. This was a God who was not some kind of remote designer of the universe who had gotten the ball rolling and then stood aloof from everything he had created. This was a God who was active in the world. He loved people and was intent on showering his love on them. He helped them when they were in need. He answered their prayers. He intervened in this world when it was necessary and important to do so.*
>
> *But I had come very much to doubt that any such God existed. And it was the problem of suffering that had created these doubts and that eventually led me to doubt it so much that I simply no longer believed it. If God helps his people— why doesn't he help his people? If he answers prayer, why doesn't he answer prayer? If he intervenes, why doesn't he intervene?*
>
> *It was innocent suffering that made me think there is no such God. People who are faithful to God, who devote their lives to him, who pray to him suffer no less than those who are indifferent to God or even scornful toward his existence."*

So, Mr. Ehrman said in his blog that he lost faith in the God of the Bible because there is too much suffering in the world, and he believes it is because of God, or rather God's lack of involvement. In fact, I had the opportunity to hear a few debates featuring Bart Ehrman, and he was very open about this.

Bart Ehrman stopped believing in the God of the Bible because he thought that an all-powerful and sovereign God who allowed this much suffering in the world didn't make any sense. This is a very common complaint among unbelievers. You've probably heard many friends, family members, and acquaintances express the same grievances when you shared your faith with them, right? I know I have—countless times!

Now, we saw in earlier chapters why that is. It is because God gave dominion to man, and He cannot violate His own word.

However, most are unaware of this fact, even among believers. So, Bart Ehrman is not alone. Far from it. The perverse belief that God causes or allows all the suffering in the world has made hundreds of thousands, perhaps even millions of atheists and agnostics worldwide and throughout history.

But that's not all. The worse part is that many professing Christians believe this as well!

> The perverse belief that God causes or allows all the suffering in the world has made hundreds of thousands, perhaps even millions of atheists and agnostics worldwide and throughout history.

This is nothing less than *perverse thinking*. It is the result of perverse thinking and a misunderstanding of the God of the Bible.

In previous chapters, we saw how God relinquished dominion of the earth realm to man in Genesis. We have also seen how it is man who made a mess of things.

Most of all, we have seen how God, because of His word to us in Genesis, and in order to intervene in the earth realm, requires man to be in covenant and relationship with Him.

Therefore, the responsibility for pain, suffering, and death on the earth is not the will of God or the results of God's actions. He says it Himself in the Book of Ezekiel:

> *"I have no pleasure in the death of anyone, declares the Lord God." ~ Ezekiel 18:32 (ESV)*

And,

> *"'As surely as I live, declares the Sovereign Lord, I take no pleasure in the death of the wicked, but rather that they turn from their ways and live. Turn! Turn from your evil ways! Why will you die, people of Israel?'" ~ Ezekiel 33:11 (NIV)*

The Reasons for Pain, Suffering, and Death

There are three main reasons for pain, death, and suffering in the world, and they are: this fallen world, our wayward flesh, and the devil.

- ♕ **The World:** We live in a fallen world. This world has not yet been restored to its original glory. We still have to contend with sickness, disease, brokenness, natural disasters, and death. Romans 8:19-22 (NIV) says: "For the *creation waits in eager expectation for the children of God to be revealed. For the creation was subjected to frustration, not by its own choice, but by the will of the one who subjected it, in hope that the creation itself will be liberated from its bondage to decay and brought into the freedom and glory of the children of God. We know that the whole creation has been groaning as in the pains of childbirth right up to the present time."*

- ♕ **The Flesh:** Jesus said to His disciples: *"The spirit is willing, but the flesh is weak"* (Matthew 26:41). The weakness of our flesh is not just found in our inability to do good consistently, like Paul decried in Romans 7. It is also found in our incomplete knowledge and failure to do things perfectly. It is found in man's inadequate exercise of control and dominion. Our sinful and imperfect nature and intelligence have led to faulty buildings and constructions, which engender deaths; manufacturing of weapons and wars, which engender death; evil in our hearts, which engenders death. We also see it in our lusts and love of money, which engenders doing evil things and making others suffer.

👑 **The Devil:** Obviously, we cannot forget the deadly enemy of our souls. Satan loves to steal, kill, and destroy. In fact, it is his mission statement. It is what he's best known for. In John 8:44, Jesus reminds us that Satan was a murderer from the beginning. I haven't taken the time to talk about it, but Satan also rules a kingdom in this fallen world: The kingdom of darkness. His kingdom, like God's, has citizens, principalities, powers, departments, ambassadors, and all the other kingdom constituents and organizational hierarchies we explored in chapter one. The reason is simple: He learned Kingdom hierarchical organization back when he was in heaven as Lucifer. He knows just how efficient it can be, and he learned from the best (God).

The "god of this age," the "prince of this world" is highly organized, and he never rests *"because he knows his time is short"* (Rev. 12:2), especially now. His servants, angels, demons, humans, and otherwise, are highly dedicated to his agenda. Their goal is the total control of the earth realm and the annihilation of the servants of the King of kings. Make no mistake about it: if the devil can get any legal right to make you ill or kill you, he will. Period. This is why you need to:

> *"Be sober, be vigilant; because your adversary the devil walks about like a roaring lion, seeking whom he may devour"* (1 Peter 5:8).

Now, let's get back to the issue at hand: perverse thinking.

Before we point accusing fingers towards people like Bart Ehrman or even Richard Dawkins (the world-famous atheist and author of *The God Delusion*) for defective or perverse thinking, let's consider our own thinking towards God—as believers.

We, as believers, exercise perverse thinking in many instances; we just don't realize it. We disguise it as being *spiritual* (ahem… *deep*), or *theological* (ahem… *smart*), or even *humble* (ahem… *holy*). Well, demons are "spiritual" too, so perhaps we should take heed where we're going with this.

Remember, judgment always begins with the house of God (1 Peter 4:17). This is because we are supposed to be the light of the world. We are the ones who should shed light for the peoples and nations of the world who are walking in darkness—the light of the Kingdom and its King.

But in order to be lights, we must first be enlightened ourselves.

> **In order to be lights, we must first be enlightened ourselves.**

Our understanding, how we receive His light, must be perfected. As Jesus said:

"The eye is the lamp of the body. If your eyes are healthy, your whole body will be full of light. But if your eyes are unhealthy, your whole body will be full of darkness. If then the light within you is darkness, how great is that darkness!"
~ Matthew 6:22-23 (NIV)

God Did it. Or Did He?

When we adhere to perverse thinking, we often equate life's hardships like cancer, illness, loss (of a job, house, or loved one), or poverty with being *the will of God*.

We wrongly interpret life's calamities as either coming directly from the hand of God, perhaps in judgement, or as the result of God "allowing it" in our lives—to discipline or sanctify us. Either way we spin it, we depict Him as always having the final say in the matter.

For example, to someone who just lost a child, we might say trite things such as:

"God took your little one because He needed another angel in heaven." To that, some could reply, "Wow! Really? Was He that desperate and resourceless?"

This example brings me to share a very personal story.

Back in 2006, Elisabeth and I were excited to become first-time parents. The twenty-week ultrasound scan showed us that we were expecting a little girl. We already knew her name would be Jennifer.

On the day of her delivery, however, things didn't go as planned. I will not go into all the details here because that, in itself, could be made into a book, but unbeknownst to us and the doctors, Jennifer had *pulmonary hypoplasia*, which is a fancy way of saying she had *underdeveloped lungs*.

So, when she was born and they proceeded to cut the umbilical cord, she was unable to breathe by herself. As a result, she survived mere minutes.

To say we were devastated would be an understatement.

What followed was a tsunami of emotional and spiritual upheaval, the likes of which I wouldn't wish on my worse enemy. We felt like our lives had just been shattered. And, as is the case in any such trials, one question was on our befuddled minds and hearts: *Why?*

- **Why did God allow this?**
- **Why did God not prevent this?**
- **Why did God do this? Or did He? Oh, why?! Why?!!!**

And when the answers weren't forthcoming, we began forging our own.

At the time, with the understanding I had, I believed that God, in His sovereignty, had *allowed* this tragic death to befall our family. And I might have just said that I believed He killed Jennifer (and I sometimes wondered about that). Because, after all, if He allowed it, this meant He could have done something about it, but chose not to, right?

I also went through the whole guilt-ride roller-coaster of *"what sin in my (our) lives is God punishing me (us) for?"* Oh, and just for the record... this definitely didn't help my faith, inner healing, or outlook.

Even after a few years, I still maintained that He had *allowed it*, but that it was for our good, for us to learn and grow in sanctification from experience (sounds spiritual, doesn't it?). I often referred to Romans 8:28 (NIV) to justify my belief:

> *"And we know that in all things God works for the good of those who love him, who have been called according to his purpose."*

Note how the verse doesn't say, *"And we know that in all things that God causes or allows..."* Rather, it implies that in all things (that befall us in this fallen world), God works for the good of His children. This means that after trials and tribulations come our way, God, in His love, picks up the fragments of our shattered lives to make something good out of them. He works on our behalf to use even the bad stuff that hurt us to make us and our lives better and improved.

These failed attempts at reasoning away the cause of pain and suffering make God seem like, yes, a self-centred monster. But then, we try to rationalize it by adding insult to injury, saying things like: *"We do not always understand why God does or allows such things because His thoughts are above our thoughts and His ways are above our ways"* (trying to quote from Isaiah 55:9, and out of context).

> We often make the grave theological mistake of equating the sovereignty of God and everything happening in the earth realm as being 'His Will.'

We often make the

grave theological mistake of equating the sovereignty of God and everything happening in the earth realm as being 'His Will.'

And yet, in the Lord's prayer, we say: *"Your will be done on earth as it is in heaven,"* intrinsically stating that *it isn't being done*. This, friends, is part of our *perverse thinking*.

God's Discipline

We often talk as if God's will is to cause us intense pain in order to somehow, through it, bring about good things. Now, don't get me wrong: God does *use* our pain and turns it to good, just as Romans 8:28 says. But *He doesn't will the ill*, and only very rarely, if ever, would He cause it for the sake of disciplining you.

Now, does God discipline us? Of course, He does. In fact, there are many accounts of this in Scripture. Is His discipline sometimes painful? Yep, you better believe it. A funny Christian lady, Barbara Johnson, once wrote: *"There's nothing worse than a whooping from the Lord."* She was right.

Like any good, good father, God does indeed discipline His children. There are even some biblical accounts that make us tremble in fear. Just think of God's dealings with David's baby boy after his affair with Bathsheba, or His dealings with Ananias and Sapphira after their mutual lie. Nevertheless, there are some distinct ramifications to these particular examples (and to others) that would take too long to get into here. Suffice it to say that such extreme examples of God's discipline are the definite exception, and not the rule.

Think about it... Would you kill your child's pet hamster to teach him a lesson? Only in extreme cases (if ever) would a parent resort to such psychologically torturous measures, right?

Well, it's the same with our Father in heaven. His discipline of

His children is more along the lines of a time-out, skip supper, go-to-your-room kind of discipline. And yes, sometimes, when we're really rebellious, He spanks us—and rightfully so.

God Doesn't Will the Ill in Your Life

James 1:13 (NIV) says:

> *"When tempted, no one should say, 'God is tempting me.' For God cannot be tempted by evil, nor does he tempt anyone."*

When it comes to our view of God's involvement in our suffering, our thinking is partly based on verses like Job 5:18 (NIV), where we read the words of Job's friend, Eliphaz, who says, *"For he wounds, but he also binds up; he injures, but his hands also heal."*

At first glance, this seems to make sense. It sums up many churchgoers' beliefs.

However, we forget the rebuke of the Lord on Eliphaz at the end of the book, where He accuses Eliphaz of having spoken wrongly of Him! At the end of the book, God basically accused Eliphaz of slander!

God says to Eliphaz, in Job 42:7-9 (NIV):

> *"'I am angry with you and your two friends, because you have not spoken the truth about me, as my servant Job has. So now take seven bulls and seven rams and go to my servant Job and sacrifice a burnt offering for yourselves. My servant Job will pray for you, and I will accept his prayer and not deal with you according to your folly. You have not spoken the truth about me, as my servant Job has.' So Eliphaz the Temanite, Bildad the Shuhite and Zophar the Naamathite did what the Lord told them; and the Lord accepted Job's prayer."*

So, the lesson is this: we must always keep the Bible in context, lest we find ourselves guilty of assigning things to God which are not true.

Remember: *God is good... all the time!*

The Tale of a Tower

In Luke chapter 13, there is another good illustration about attributing deeds wrongfully to God.

There was a tower in the town of Siloam that fell and killed 18 people in the process. As you can imagine, it made the local news that day. Our usual line of thinking (and our insurance policies) when something like this happens is: *Act of God.*

The average Christian might think along the lines of: *"He did this for reasons unknown to us. Perhaps they were judged."* And yet, what did Jesus say? He said this:

> *"Or those eighteen on whom the tower in Siloam fell and killed them, do you think that they were worse sinners than all other men who dwelt in Jerusalem? I tell you, no; but <u>unless you repent you will all likewise perish</u>." ~ Luke 13:4-5 (NKJV)*

So, in this intriguing passage, we learn the following:

- ♛ Contrary to what most people thought, the tower didn't fall as a result of God's judgement. It was probably too old or due to faulty construct.

- ♛ The people who died in the accident were not worse than any of the others in the city.

- ♛ Finally, we need to repent so we can be saved because we know not how our end will come in this fallen, broken, and unpredictable world.

So, here is what I'm trying to tell you:

God is good, and He doesn't want any harm, or ill, or pain, or suffering, or even death for any human being made in His image. This was not His plan from the beginning.

In Ezekiel 18:23 (NIV), we read:

> *"Do I take any pleasure in the death of the wicked? declares*

151

the Sovereign Lord. Rather, am I not pleased when they turn
from their ways and live?"

Keep in mind this is concerning the wicked, not the redeemed. He doesn't take pleasure in it for the *wicked*...how much less for us, His redeemed children!!

And in verses 30-32 (NIV), we read:

> *"Repent! Turn away from all your offenses; then sin will not*
> *be your downfall. Rid yourselves of all the offenses you have*
> *committed, and get a new heart and a new spirit. Why will*
> *you die, people of Israel? For I take no pleasure in the death*
> *of anyone, declares the Sovereign Lord. Repent and live!"*

As for His Children, here is what Jesus had to say about God's will towards us, under the New Covenant:

> *"Which of you, if your son asks for bread, will give him a*
> *stone? Or if he asks for a fish, will give him a snake? If you,*
> *then, though you are evil, know how to give good gifts to your*
> *children, how much more will your Father in heaven give*
> *good gifts to those who ask him!"* ~ *Matthew 7:9-11 (NIV)*

In this passage, Jesus is correcting our perverse thinking.

The point Jesus is making is this: God would never, ever do worse things to us than we do to our own children. And whatever good we would do for our children, us being evil, imagine how much better the Father would do for us!

So, with this in mind, let's suppose a little...

- ♛ If your child had cancer, and you had the power to heal him, wouldn't you?
- ♛ If your child needed money, and you were a king, wouldn't you provide him more than enough?
- ♛ If your child lost his job, and you owned a large and wealthy

company, wouldn't you employ him at your company? Wouldn't you give him a job?

👑 If your child asked you for some ice cream on a hot summer day... you would give him some, right?

Okay, so that's settled. You would do all these things if you could, *even though the Word of God says you are evil.*

How is it then, that even knowing that God is good and perfect in His love for us, we still think that our hurts, pains, and trials are His will for us?

Shame on us. This is due to perverse thinking on our part.

Now, let's take it a step further.

What happens when we have perverse thinking and we pray? What happens when we have perverse thinking and we ask God for, well, anything?

This is what happens:

👑 If we are ill, we pray: *"God, if it be your will, please... heal me."*

👑 If we need a job and can't pay the rent, we pray: *"God, if it be your will, please help me to get a job so I can pay the rent."*

👑 If our spouse is dying, we pray, *"God, if it be your will, please... heal my spouse."*

Too often, we pray, *"If it be your will, Oh Lord."* We think of ourselves as spiritual and humble when we pray that way. *"After all,"* we reason, *"didn't Jesus pray this way in Gethsemane?"* So, you compare your need for, say, a better job with Jesus' Kingdom mandate of going to the cross to save humanity? Think about that for a moment.

The truth is, when we pray that way, we are only faithless in the Father's goodness. We pray that way to justify our lack of faith by giving our prayer a spiritual failsafe. If we do not get our prayer answered, we can then reason it away, saying, *"Well, I guess it wasn't God's will after all.*" Instead of owning up to our inherent lack of faith, we can then blame God for not responding favourably, which is far easier.

So, you see, our whole walk with God is hampered if we fail to fully grasp that *God is good... all the time.*

Of course, it is His will that you are healthy! Of course, it is His will that you have more than enough to live! Of course, it is His will that you live and not die (without fulfilling your purpose)!

I love how *The New Living translation* (NLT) of the Bible rendered Ephesians 3:18-19; which really expresses how important it is that we understand His great love for us. It reads:

> *"And may you have the power to understand, as all God's people should, how wide, how long, how high, and how deep his love is. May you experience the love of Christ, though it is too great to understand fully. Then you will be made complete with all the fullness of life and power that comes from God." (NLT)*

In other words, we cannot be made complete, full of life and power, unless we know, receive, and experience the love of God!

His Promises Are Always 'YES' and 'AMEN'

In 1 Corinthians 1:20 (NKJV), the apostle Paul reminds us that *"all the promises of God in Him are Yes, and in Him Amen, to the glory of God through us."*

In other words, all of the promises and expressions of His will in the Bible are a pre-approved YES for an answer.

- ♛ Does He want you healthy? YES!
- ♛ Does He want you to have a long life? YES!
- ♛ Does He want you to have children? YES!
- ♛ Does He want you to prosper? YES!
- ♛ Does He want you happy and blessed? YES!

It's not that God doesn't want to give us these good things. It's rather that we fail to believe that He does. And if you don't think He wants you to have a certain thing, you will not ask. So, the main problems with our poor living conditions are the following:

1. The Book of James says we have not because we ask not (James 4:2). It also says that we are unstable: *"If any of you lacks wisdom, let him ask of God, who gives to all liberally and without reproach, and it will be given to him. But let him ask in faith, with no doubting, for he who doubts is like a wave of the sea driven and tossed by the wind. For let not that man suppose that he will receive anything from the Lord; he is a double-minded man, unstable in all his ways." ~ James 1:5-8 (NKJV)*

2. And secondly, we have not because we have no faith. Remember the passage at the beginning where Jesus said: "Because of your lack of faith." Also, in Nazareth, His hometown, Jesus didn't do many miracles because of their unbelief.

   A mustard seed is all you need.

   Remember, a mustard seed is all you need.

3. And thirdly, we have no faith because we do not really believe that 'God is Good.' How can we expect anything good if we are not fully convinced of His goodness?

If we first fix our perverse thinking and BELIEVE that God is really good (not just in word), it will unlock our faith in Him. Now, dear friend, the assurance and perfect confidence that God is good is the main key to get our prayers being answered.

How can you possibly receive from God any good thing if you do not really believe it is His will to give you good things?

Jesus said in John 10:10:

"I have come that they may have life, and have it to the full."

Through everything He did, going to the cross, rising from the dead, and the subsequent outpouring of the Holy Spirit, He followed through. He delivered. He gave us, indeed, *"everything that pertains to life and godliness."*

So, let us reason together. Since Jesus is no liar... if we do not have *"Life to the full,"* it has to be on us, not on Him, right? His word is true. We then need to correct our perverse thinking.

It is, therefore, mostly because of our perverse thinking and lack of faith that we lack God's good gifts.

Just as James reminds us in James 1:17 (NIV), *"Every good and perfect gift is from above, coming down from the Father of the heavenly lights, who does not change like shifting shadows."*

Life to the full is given to us, provided we believe. Life... *to the MAX!* This is what Jesus came to give us.

So, moving mountains is possible if we believe *first* that God is good. It all starts with understanding that God really is good. Change this in your life, change this in your thinking, and your life will change right away. Do not be conformed but be transformed! The deep love of God and belief in His goodness are what transform us.

> It all starts with understanding that God really is good. Change this in your life, change this in your thinking, and your life will change right away.

What do other Bible passages tell us of God's goodness? Here are a few...

> *"For I know the plans I have for you," declares the Lord, "plans to prosper you and not to harm you, plans to give you hope and a future." ~ Jeremiah 29:11 (NIV)*

> *"Taste and see that the LORD is good; blessed is the one who takes refuge in him." ~ Psalm 34:8 (NIV)*

"For the LORD God is a sun and shield; the LORD bestows favor and honor; no good thing does he withhold from those whose walk is blameless." ~ Psalm 84:11 (NIV) (...and we are blameless in Christ.)

"You, Lord, are forgiving and good, abounding in love to all who call to you." ~ Psalm 86:5 (NIV)

"Give thanks to the LORD, for he is good; his love endures forever." ~ Psalm 107:1 (NIV)

"The LORD is good to all; he has compassion on all he has made." ~ Psalm 145:9 (NIV)

"As Jesus started on his way, a man ran up to him and fell on his knees before him. "Good teacher," he asked, "what must I do to inherit eternal life?" "Why do you call me good?" Jesus answered. "No one is good—except God alone." ~ Mark 10:17-18 (NIV)

"And without faith it is impossible to please God, because anyone who comes to him must believe that he exists and that he rewards those who earnestly seek him." ~ Hebrews 11:6 (NIV)

Dear friend, rewards are given to us *because He is good!*

Agreeing with Heaven

So, as we reach the end of this chapter on the goodness of God, one thing is clear:

In order to have what heaven has, we must agree with what heaven says.

Unfortunately, many equate God's care for them with what they see, feel, and experience day-to-day.

Addressing this, Chris Reed, a Spirit-filled pastor and revivalist, wrote the following insightful observation on social media:

*"There is a difference between our 'legal position' in Christ–
what we freely receive in The Spirit–and our 'living condition',
what we actually experience in our everyday lives. Our 'legal
position' is the way God sees us IN CHRIST and what is
freely ours in The Spirit. Our 'living condition' is what we
actually experience of that which is freely available. <u>The
whole goal of your walk with The Lord is to bring UP your
'living condition' to the same level as your 'legal position'.</u>*

So, unless we come in full agreement with what the Kingdom of
God is, says, and how it operates, we cannot possibly enjoy its fruit in
our lives. We must align our beliefs with what the King says. This is done
by faith, by believing the invisible over the visible.

> Unless we come in full agreement with what the Kingdom of God is, says, and how it operates, we cannot possibly enjoy its fruit in our lives.

There is *GREAT* power in agreeing with heaven!

Friend, He is so good. He is your Father, and He loves you. He is
the King; He is wealthy beyond limits, and His Kingdom, just like the
Bible says in Luke 12:32 (NIV), *is yours!*

"Do not be afraid, little flock, for your Father has been pleased to
give you the kingdom."

So, when your living condition doesn't align with this reality, it
shouldn't affect your faith in His character and heart for you. He is
for you, not against you. Hold to this truth, walk it out daily, worship
the King, and your living condition will rise up to meet your legal
position.

James 2:5 (NKJV) further encourages us with these words:

*"Listen, my beloved brethren: did not God choose the poor of
this world to be rich in faith and heirs of the kingdom which
He promised to those who love Him?"*

Our God is a Good, Good Father

I trust that your belief and outlook concerning God will be renewed and changed with what you learned in this chapter. And I trust that you will, with this renewed mind and understanding, and to paraphrase what Hebrews 4:16 (NIV) says:

> *"Let us then approach God's throne of grace with confidence, so that we may receive mercy and find grace to help us in our time of need."*

Singer and songwriter, Chris Tomlin, wrote a wonderful song titled "Good Good Father." It was a hit upon its release back in 2016. I believe the song espouses much of what was said in this chapter. I encourage you to find it on YouTube or better yet, buy the album. I believe the song's lyrics capture the full meaning of our Kingdom identity as children of the King, but most of all, the Father's heart. Here, as you end this chapter, are the powerful words of this uplifting song:

Oh, I've heard a thousand stories of what they think You're like
But I've heard the tender whisper of love in the dead of night
And You tell me that You're pleased and that I'm never alone

You're a good, good Father
It's who You are, it's who You are, it's who You are
And I'm loved by You
It's who I am, it's who I am, it's who I am

Oh and I've seen many searching for answers far and wide
But I know we're all searching for answers only You provide
'Cause You know just what we need before we say a word

You're a good, good Father
It's who You are, it's who You are, it's who You are
And I'm loved by You
It's who I am, it's who I am, it's who I am

Because You are perfect in all of Your ways

You are perfect in all of Your ways
You are perfect in all of Your ways to us
(Ohh) You are perfect in all of Your ways (all of Your ways)
Oh, You're perfect in all of Your ways (Your ways)
You are perfect in all of Your ways to us

Oh, it's love so undeniable I
I can hardly speak
Peace so unexplainable I
I can hardly think
As You call me deeper still
As You call me deeper still
As You call me deeper still into love, love, love

You're a good, good Father
It's who You are, it's who You are, it's who You are
And I'm loved by You
It's who I am, it's who I am, it's who I am
You're a good, good Father
It's who You are, it's who You are, it's who You are
And I'm loved by You
It's who I am, it's who I am, it's who I am

You're a good, good Father
It's who You are, it's who You are, it's who You are
And I'm loved by You
It's who I am, it's who I am, it's who I am
(You're a good, good Father)
You are perfect in all of Your ways
(it's who You are, it's who You are, it's who You are)
(And I'm loved by You)
You are perfect in all of Your ways
(it's who I am, it's who I am, it's who I am)

6

GOD'S RULES OF ENGAGEMENT

Considering God's Unique Ways in the Earth

"Without God, man cannot, without man, God will not."
~ Augustine

G od employs very strict and defined 'rules of engagement' when exercising His influence and accomplishing His sovereign will on the earth. Understanding these rules of engagement is crucial for you as a Kingdom citizen to understand your King better and exercise your role more efficiently on the earth.

Rules of engagement are defined in the dictionary as:

> *"A directive issued by a military authority specifying the circumstances and limitations under which forces will engage in combat with the enemy."*

As we saw throughout since the beginning of this book, God assigned rulership of the earth realm to man. He gave mankind *dominion* in the earth. Throughout this book, this truth is repeated because of its importance. Appropriating this truth for yourself will enable you to think differently and walk in Kingdom authority.

The Bible says:

"The highest heavens belong to the Lord, but the earth he has given to mankind." ~ Psalm 115:16 (NIV)

Indeed, He has given the earth to man, and although man failed and was overtaken by an enemy (Satan), God couldn't just barge in and impose Himself to fix things. As we saw, He adopted a process of re-entry in order to do it without breaking His Word, in order to do it lawfully.

We also saw how God bound Himself to His Word and that He will never break it. Therefore, He had to orchestrate a whole plan of re-entry into the earth realm after man had been deceived. This was His rescue operation, and He had to be in covenant with man for it to be 'legal.'

There are differing and specific circumstances that enable God to accomplish His will in the earth realm without overstepping the bounds He Himself set.

In order to understand this concept better, we need to understand *God's rules of engagement.*

Understanding God's Ways

I remember back in the day when Elisabeth and I were engaged to be married; we attended premarital class with our pastor at the time. He told me something I never forgot. He said:

"Sebastien, you have to see yourself as attending the University of Elisabeth now. You have to study her and her ways in everything she does. There is a certain way about each and everyone of us that makes us unique. The more you study her ways, the more you'll be able to please her, and the better your marriage will be."

Understanding God's rules of engagement is a lot like that. It is the study of God's ways of interacting with mankind. It is the scrutiny of the King's habits and methods—His ways. This, in large part, has to do with *seeking first the Kingdom of God.*

In the dictionary, *'ways'* are defined thusly:

"A method, style, or manner of doing something. One's characteristic or habitual manner of behavior or expression.

The typical manner in which something happens or in which someone or something behaves."

King David was one of those people who observed and pondered God's ways passionately. He was a man after God's own heart who delighted in knowing God more, but also in knowing more about God. In Psalm 25:4 (ESV), he wrote: *"Make me to know your ways, O Lord; teach me your paths."*

And in Psalm 86:11 (ESV), he wrote:

"Teach me your way, O Lord, that I may walk in your truth."

As much as our human hearts may long to learn His ways, and as much as we benefit from searching His ways, we cannot kid ourselves: God, our King, remains unfathomable to our limited understanding. There will always be things that we cannot grasp about the King, but it shouldn't deter us from doing like David and asking, *"Make me to know your ways, O Lord."*

> There will always be things that we cannot grasp about the King, but it shouldn't deter us from doing like David and asking, "Make me to know your ways, O Lord."

In this chapter, as I give my own two cents about God's ways, I am fully aware that some things are still far too great for me to understand. As I try to bless you with a better understanding, I myself am still baffled by many of His unsearchable ways and by the depth of His purposes. He says it Himself in Isaiah 55:8-9 (NKJV):

"My thoughts are not your thoughts, nor are your ways My ways," says the Lord. "For as the heavens are higher than the earth, so are My ways higher than your ways, and My thoughts than your thoughts."

A whole book could be written, or a whole series of books, about

God's ways, and it still wouldn't be enough to even scratch the surface of His purposes, will, thoughts, and intentions.

And yet, I believe He did reveal to me some mighty insights about His ways. This is why I feel compelled to share these treasured thoughts with you as you move further in this chapter.

There might be things that I share in this book and in this chapter that you will object to. In fact, I know there will be some. That's okay—I'm still learning. Like you, I too am at *"The University of The Lord."* I am still being schooled by His Holy Spirit, and, as you know, we only graduate upon death.

A Tale of Two Servants

My wife, Elisabeth, is a very gifted teacher with our children. One day, she wanted to teach them the principle of servanthood and serving one another in love.

She told them the following story:

> A certain king had two servants. They were both dedicated, and both did everything the king asked at all times. However, there was one critical difference. The first of the two servants did everything the king asked and nothing more. The second servant always tried to go the extra mile by studying the king's ways.
>
> This particular servant was very attentive to everything the king required but also tried to memorize all the ways of the king. He listened intently whenever the king spoke and tried to decipher any and every little detail of the king's mannerisms, body language, tone, preferences, etc.
>
> In doing so, he quickly became capable of anticipating the king's every desire before the king even asked! If the king asked for coffee, the servant knew exactly what temperature

the coffee should be and how many sugars and how much cream the king desired. He also knew what kind of cup the king preferred and even why.

But there was so much more! The servant knew every little detail of the king's daily routine, habits, and preferences. This way, the servant was always one step ahead of the king's wants, offering the king what he needed before he even knew to ask for it. This greatly pleased the king. It pleased him so much that he wanted this servant around as much as possible.

Now, one day, the king needed to appoint a new chamberlain. A chamberlain is a senior royal official in charge of managing a royal household. It is a highly esteemed position that comes with great honor. He had the choice to promote either of his two main servants to the distinguished position.

Elisabeth then looked at our kids and asked: "Which one of the two servants do you think the king will appoint as chamberlain? The one who did everything the king asked, or the one who studied, knew and did everything the king wanted?"

And, of course, all the children answered: "The second. The servant who knew the king and his ways."

I was glad they understood the lesson.

Indeed, the second servant made himself familiar with all of the king's ways, and in so doing, became very valuable to the king.

In the same manner, in the Kingdom, there are two types of believers. There are those who know the Word of God and try to do what it says, which is good. And there are those who know both the Word of God and the ways of God, because they know God, which is far better!

An Example from History

The following story illustrates well someone who understands his king's ways...

The Greek philosopher, Anaximenes, accompanied Alexander the Great on his expedition against the Persians in an advisory role. As a keen observer and thinker, he studied the ways of Alexander and became well acquainted with the monarch's thoughts, philosophy, and motivations.

In the course of the campaign, Alexander's forces captured Lampsacus, the birthplace of Anaximenes.

Anxious to save his native city from destruction, Anaximenes sought an audience with the king.

Alexander anticipated his plea: *"I swear by the Styx, I will not grant your request,"* he said.

"My Lord," calmly replied Anaximenes, *"I merely wanted to ask you to destroy Lampsacus."*

And so, *knowing his king's ways*, Anaximenes saved his native city.

Oh, that we would be so well acquainted with our King's ways!

Caretakers in His Kingdom

While the Bible tells us that God gave the earth to man (Psalm 115:16), we know that He is still the owner of it, for again, the Scripture tells us:

"The earth is the Lord's, and the fulness thereof; the world, and they that dwell therein." ~ Psalm 24:1 (KJV)

So, does God own the earth, or does man? How do we reconcile these seemingly opposing verses?

The best illustration I can give you to understand man's rulership under God's ownership is to compare it to renting a house.

Imagine that you just rented a beautiful property on a nice lot. For a certain monthly fee, the landlord allows you to live in it. You have all the rights and privileges of someone who owns a house:

- 👑 You can decorate it, for the most part, the way you like.
- 👑 You can have all the furniture you want in it.
- 👑 You enjoy all the house has to offer for your needs.
- 👑 You tend to it and keep it tidy.
- 👑 You decide how warm or cold to set the temperature day and night.

However, before you moved in, you had to sign a leasing agreement. In this agreement, there are certain things the landlord allows or forbids in the house or on his property. Normally, these agreements cover what is not tolerated by the landlord and what is expected of the tenants. These might include if pets are allowed, if smoking is allowed, or what colours he might tolerate on his walls. These are the laws (or, in the Scripture, the laws and commandments) of the landlord. If you abide by them, the landlord can never come into your house uninvited. So, while the house isn't yours, it is still your home, and a man's home is his castle, right?

The landlord also expects the tenants to keep the property clean, functional, and in order. That is the primary duty of the tenant as an occupier of the house—aside from paying his rent, that is.

Calling the Landlord

Back in Eden, we are told that God *"took the man and put him in the garden of Eden to work it and keep it."* ~ Genesis 2:15 (ESV)

This was the duty of man in the beginning, and in many ways, it still is. Back then, however, man didn't need to pray, *"Your will be done on earth as it is in heaven."* God's will was already being done on the earth at the time. Man only needed to maintain it and keep it going.

In fact, when man was given his initial rental agreement, everything was in perfect working order. Nothing was broken or in need of repair. It was meant to stay that way.

But after the fall, it became a different story. The property was now under a degenerative curse. There were now many things that weren't working properly. In the second generation only, the first murder occurred: Cain killed Abel. The realm was broken, but through sin, the people also were. The Bible tells us that when Seth was born (after Abel was killed), his generation began *"calling upon the name of the Lord"* (Genesis 4:26).

Similarly, when something is broken or is not functional in the house, the tenant is expected to advise the landlord so that measures can be taken to intervene and fix the issue.

For example, if the toilet is broken, it is not the responsibility of the tenant to fix it. Instead, the tenant will pick up the phone and call the landlord to tell him about it. Then, the landlord will intervene quickly to resolve the issue, either himself or by calling a plumber. This is the privilege of the tenant/landlord relationship.

But what happens if you break the rules written on the leasing agreement? What happens if you paint the walls black? Or if you do not pay your rent? Or if you decide to create a meth lab in the basement? In those instances where the leasing agreement is broken, the landlord can intervene directly to warn the tenant to shape up, and if he doesn't, he can legally have him evicted to take back his property. In the Bible, we see these events take place time and again. We call them *judgments*.

Prayer: An Invitation to 'Fix' Things

The previous illustration about the tenant and homeowner is an excellent example of the dynamics that exist between God, man, and man's assigned dominion in the earth realm.

God knows that man cannot fix everything that goes wrong in the earth realm. While He has assigned man to be the caretaker of this planet, God knows that man has limitations. Therefore, He gave us prayer.

> *"Only God can move mountains, but faith and prayer can move God." ~ E.M. Bounds*

Prayer is what man does when the toilet breaks, so to speak. When something goes

> "Only God can move mountains, but faith and prayer can move God." ~ E.M. Bounds

wrong in our lives, we pick up the phone and tell God about it. By doing this, we invite God to come over to our house momentarily to fix things. Technically speaking, through our earthly dominion, we give God permission (for lack of a better word) to intervene. We invite heaven down to earth.

I like what pastor and author, Rich Nathan, said about prayer:

> *"Prayer is the bridge over which the Kingdom of God comes to the earth."*

And Myles Munroe packaged it in an even more shocking statement:

> *"What Is Prayer? Prayer is man giving God the legal right and permission to interfere in earth's affairs."*

As astounding and haughty as this statement may sound, this is exactly what we do when we pray. If you understand this, your prayer life will change dramatically.

Oftentimes, however, we use prayer as a last resort. If the "toilet" is broken, we prefer trying to fix it ourselves or call a friend to help. Too many tenants don't like 'bothering the landlord.'

The Privilege of Partnering with God

Any good landlord will appreciate us calling on him to get something fixed. After all, he wants his property looked after and taken care of, doesn't he? And God is not just a good landlord; He is a good, good Father who has His very children in agreement with Him and residing in the house.

Now, think about it…If you were a landlord and had your own children living in your property, wouldn't you want it looked after even better than if it were strangers?

It is the will of the Father that we ask Him for help in taking care of His business on earth. Jesus knew this at 12 years of age. He said to Mary and Joseph, after they had been frantically looking for Him for three days:

> *"Why did you seek Me? Did you not know that I must be about My Father's business?" ~ Luke 2:49 (NKJV)*

Likewise, we must be about our Father's business and not hesitate to call on Him when something needs fixing.

I like what Smith Wigglesworth said about prayer and its under-usage by man: *"God is more eager to answer than we are to ask."*

When God told us, as His servant/children, to *"engage in business until He comes"* (Luke 19:13), He left us a way to reach Him as an *"ever present helpline in times of trouble"* (Psalm 46:1, paraphrased).

> *"God is more eager to answer than we are to ask." ~ Smith Wigglesworth*

He wants to help. He delights when we call upon Him to 'fix things.' It's His pleasure to be invited to positively intervene in our earthly business of Kingdom expansion. Like any good landlord who respects the leasing agreement, however, God will not show up uninvited to our abode unless we ask Him. And when we ask God for help in looking after His business, He always responds favourably.

Notable Calls to the Landlord

"Whether we like it or not, asking is the rule of the kingdom. If you may have everything by asking in His Name, and nothing without asking, I beg you to see how absolutely vital prayer is." ~ Charles H. Spurgeon

The Bible is full of great examples of men and women who *"called the landlord to come and fix things,"* i.e., who prayed to the Lord earnestly to intervene in the earth realm. And intervene He did!

There are too many instances in the Bible to list them all here, but here are some of the most notable ones:

Abraham: The bold negotiating Abraham did with God on behalf of Sodom is one of the most astounding passages in the Bible. The whole story is found in Genesis 18:16-33. In the account, Abraham is trying to get God to spare the city if enough righteous people are found in it. He starts at 50 and works his way down to 10. God assured him that for just ten righteous people, He would not strike down the city.

This story is a great reminder of how our prayers and intercession can move God in surprising ways. It is also a great reminder of our Landlord's incredible longsuffering and patience. He would have kept Sodom standing even for the sake of only ten righteous people. Ultimately though, there weren't even ten righteous in the whole city. The people in the city were just too corrupt and past the point of repentance or salvation. So, the Landlord had to destroy this run-down and irredeemable property (Sodom and Gomorrah)—with the tenants still in it!

Moses: After the golden calf fiasco, God had just had enough of the rebellious and unbelieving Hebrews. He wanted to exterminate them all and do a reset with Moses, just as He had done with Noah. He told Moses:

171

> *"I have seen these people," the Lord said to Moses, "and they are a stiff-necked people. Now leave me alone so that my anger may burn against them and that I may destroy them. Then I will make you into a great nation." ~ Exodus 32:9-10 (NIV)*

And Moses replied to the landlord (God), bringing Him back to the initial rental agreement (His covenant):

> *"But Moses sought the favor of the Lord his God. 'Lord,' he said, 'why should your anger burn against your people, whom you brought out of Egypt with great power and a mighty hand? Why should the Egyptians say, 'It was with evil intent that he brought them out, to kill them in the mountains and to wipe them off the face of the earth'? Turn from your fierce anger; relent and do not bring disaster on your people. Remember your servants Abraham, Isaac and Israel, to whom you swore by your own self: 'I will make your descendants as numerous as the stars in the sky and I will give your descendants all this land I promised them, and it will be their inheritance forever.'" Then the Lord relented and did not bring on his people the disaster he had threatened." ~ Exodus 32:11-14 (NIV)*

And, after God relented, Moses probably wiped the sweat off his brow and went, *"Phew!"*

Joshua: Probably the boldest prayer in the Old Testament and the most remarkable miracle in the whole Bible. Joshua ordered the sun and moon to stand still!

Joshua needed more daylight time to see what he was doing as he was warring against enemies. He boldly asked the King to keep the "big luminary" in place a little longer to get the job done. Amazingly, the Landlord agreed! The sun stood still! This phenomenal account is found in Joshua 10:12-14.

It says in verse 14 (ESV):

"There has been no day like it before or since, when the Lord heeded the voice of a man, for the Lord fought for Israel."

The other times we find such use of authority in the Scriptures is in the New Testament, in the life of Jesus and the disciples. The way Joshua prayed that day, you would think he was a modern-day charismatic. It was an authoritative New Testament prayer before its time.

In verses 12 and 13 (ESV), we read:

"At that time Joshua spoke to the Lord in the day when the Lord gave the Amorites over to the sons of Israel, and he said in the sight of Israel, 'Sun, stand still at Gibeon, and moon, in the Valley of Aijalon.' And the sun stood still, and the moon stopped, until the nation took vengeance on their enemies. Is this not written in the Book of Jashar? The sun stopped in the midst of heaven and did not hurry to set for about a whole day."

Elijah: In the New Testament, James reminds us of Elijah's intercession to the Landlord to *cut off the water in the neighbourhood*:

"The effective, fervent prayer of a righteous man avails much. Elijah was a man with a nature like ours, and he prayed earnestly that it would not rain; and it did not rain on the land for three years and six months. And he prayed again, and the heaven gave rain, and the earth produced its fruit." ~ James 5:17-18 (NASB)

The original account is found in 1 Kings 17:1.

Now, there was a guy who, as a tenant, understood what needed to get done and wasn't afraid to call on the Landlord to get it done! That day, Elijah displayed a tremendous amount of boldness and authority.

Jabez: I remember when Bruce Wilkinson wrote his tiny book, *The Prayer of Jabez*, back in 2000. I had bought a copy, and I was astounded at this gem of a prayer found in such an obscure passage of the Bible. No less astounding is that God answered him! The prayer of Jabez is found in 1 Chronicles 4:10 (NIV):

> "Jabez cried out to the God of Israel, 'Oh, that you would bless me and enlarge my territory! Let your hand be with me, and keep me from harm so that I will be free from pain.' And God granted his request."

Basically, Jabez found his dwelling too small and pleaded with the Landlord to add extra rooms to make the house bigger. The Landlord came through.

I still have a plaque that my mother bought me in my bedroom with the prayer of Jabez on it. It's always a good reminder of how efficient prayer is and how much favor God is willing to pour out on those who love and seek Him.

Hezekiah: He was the king of Judah and very ill. He prayed fervently to the Lord with tears, and God granted him an extra 15 years to his life to fulfill his purpose!

God basically agreed to a rental agreement extension for the king. This account, which is found in 2 Kings 20:1-6, is nothing short of amazing. Just think about the ramifications!

What would you accomplish for the Kingdom with an extra 15 years of life?

The Disciples: When the apostle Peter was imprisoned, we are told how the disciples got together and prayed for him. The full account is found in Acts 12:1-19. In verse 5 (ESV), we read:

> "So Peter was kept in prison, but earnest prayer for him was made to God by the church."

A powerful, glorious, and miraculous deliverance then took place when an angel was sent to free peter from his chains and get him out of harm's way. What's even more remarkable is that the gathered group of believers couldn't believe their prayer had been answered when Peter showed up and knocked at the door. They thought it was his ghost! In His grace, mercy, and goodness, God will sometimes answer prayers, even if we lack faith.

Yes, God is good, gracious, loving, and will do miracles on behalf of His children when they ask in earnest prayer. The Bible is filled with such accounts.

To quote late charismatic preacher, R.W. Schambach: *"You don't have any problems, all you need is faith in God."*

Sin: The Ultimate Dealbreaker

We know that faithful prayer is man's best bet in moving God to intervene favourably in the earth realm. But there is another way through which God can choose to intervene as well. This way is not recommended, though.

We see from the Scriptures that grave and overt sin gives God the legal right to intervene powerfully in the earth realm *without partnering with man*. Man's dominion is always conditional under heavenly legal jurisdiction. It can be broken through disobedience, as the Genesis account attests.

While I don't pretend to fully understand the heavenly legal ramifications of these *rules of engagement*, here is what I do understand:

- ♛ When man sins, he finds himself in legal contract breach with heaven.

- ♛ When man sins, he finds himself indebted to the Landlord. It's as if he was defaulting on his rental payment. This is partly why sin is called a debt (forgive us our debts, as we forgive our debtors).

♛ When man sins, he relinquishes his ruling privilege and legal right of dominion of the earth. That's how the Serpent was able to usurp it from man.

These "contract breach" perimeters were put in place as soon as man was created and put in the garden.

In the Bible, we see God intervening more often due to sin in the Old Testament days. The full payment of sin, the expiation or atonement, hadn't yet been fulfilled by Jesus Christ back then. For this reason, God resorted more often to swift and terminal judgment of sin in those days. There are quite a few instances where God punished men with death in the Old Testament—the Flood and Sodom and Gomorrah come to mind.

But since Christ came and paid mankind's sin debt through His sacrifice, we have been, even to some degree, collectively "under grace" for 2000+ years.

Peter himself reminds us of this in 2 Peter 3:3-9 (NKJV):

"Scoffers will come in the last days, walking according to their own lusts, and saying, 'Where is the promise of His coming? For since the fathers fell asleep, all things continue as they were from the beginning of creation.' For this they willfully forget: that by the word of God the heavens were of old, and the earth standing out of water and in the water, by which the world that then existed perished, being flooded with water. But the heavens and the earth which are now preserved by the same word, are reserved for fire until the day of judgment and perdition of ungodly men. But, beloved, do not forget this one thing, that with the Lord one day is as a thousand years, and a thousand years as one day. The Lord is not slack concerning His promise, as some count slackness, but is longsuffering toward us, not willing that any should perish but that all should come to repentance."

In this passage, Peter reminds us of how the old world, which was flooded with water, was destroyed by the Word of God. And, likewise, our present wicked age, which should be judged, but is not; this grace too is extended by the Word of God—by decree of the King.

While sin does give God the legal right to intervene directly and even swiftly, we can be thankful that He doesn't intervene every time we do sin. We are, indeed, under grace.

> While sin does give God the legal right to intervene directly and even swiftly, we can be thankful that He doesn't intervene every time we do sin. We are, indeed, under grace.

The Landlord Always Issues a Warning

When tenants are late on their payments or conducting themselves in a way that goes against the rental agreement, the landlord has legal recourse to terminate the contract and kick them out. However, this has to be done a certain way. Usually, there will be a legal warning given to the tenant before they are officially evicted. This is called an *eviction notice.*

An eviction notice is defined as: *"A formal, written statement that a landlord or property manager uses to terminate a Lease Agreement and inform a tenant to vacate the premises. It is often the first step in the eviction process."*

Also, and interestingly, an eviction notice is usually given for the following reasons:

- Unpaid rent
- Substantial damage to the property
- Violence or threats
- Illegal activities on the premises

In the biblical account, all of these would translate as sin, which is also known as *the transgression of God's law* (1 John 3:4).

But, especially in the case of collective sin, God never just barges in to begin dishing out His justice. No. He uses His prophets first to give an *eviction notice,* of sorts. Just as it says in Amos 3:7 (NIV):

> *"Surely the Sovereign Lord does nothing without revealing his plan to his servants the prophets."*

Once the prophet gets the Word from God, he then speaks it forth. Once the Word is spoken out, that's when God has full legal right to accomplish it.

The Book of Jonah is a good example of this type of collective warning from the Landlord.

Jonah was sent to Nineveh to prophesy against their sin. He said that the Lord would destroy the city in 40 days. This was a strict eviction notice.

But...

The king and the people of the city all repented of their wrongdoing. Basically, they "paid the rent they owed," promising to be good tenants once more, and the Landlord relented from evicting them.

So, the warning serves to give leeway to the possibility of repentance, or in the case of a property rental: restitution.

Notable Landlord Interventions

There are quite a few instances in the Scripture where God intervened in the earth realm because there was a contract breach, a.k.a. sin, both collective and/or individual. Here are some of the most famous:

- Adam and Eve were kicked out of Eden. That's the first and most notable eviction in history.

- The Flood. This one was the biggest landlord intervention in all of history.

- The Tower of Babel. In this particular instance, God applied a "divide and conquer" method to disperse the rebellious tenants all over the earth.

- Sodom and Gomorrah. These two corrupt cities were destroyed by fire this time!

- The Golden Calf idolatry. The Lord commanded for 3000 to be put to death, and the rest were struck with a plague.

- The Earth swallowing people up. Two hundred and fifty people were swallowed up by the earth because they conspired against Moses and Aaron (and thus against the Lord Himself). Number 26:9-11.

- King Saul. His disobedience made him lose his kingship to David. The Lord removed him from authority (1 Samuel 15).

- David's first child with Bathsheba. David's sin against Uriah and his adultery with Bathsheba got a severe punishment. God killed his firstborn child from the illicit union. Yes, this was the Lord's doing.

In all of these instances, we are reminded that *our dominion is a conditional privilege from the Lord* and is to always be exercised under the fear of God. Overt sin can get us severe reprimands, judgements, and in some cases, even death—especially under the Old Covenant.

But what about the New Testament? Are there any landlord interventions or eviction notices in the New Testament? Absolutely!

- King Herod was eaten by worms. The arrogant and wicked king wouldn't give the Landlord His due, and he was judged on the spot in a gruesome fashion (Acts 12:21-23).

- Ananias and Sapphira. Immediate judgement fell of the

couple because they lied to the Holy Spirit. This was a severe reminder for the fledgling New Testament Church that, despite His grace and forgiveness, the Landlord should still be feared (reverently obeyed).

♛ And of course, there are plenty of judgements and landlord interventions in the Book of Revelation.

We should also note that, aside from direct landlord interventions, overt, unchecked, and unrepentant sin also gives grounds to the Enemy to accuse us in the courts of heaven. He does this to gain legal access to our lives and our children's lives through footholds and generational curses. Sin gives Satan and his cohorts legal rights to cause all kinds of ill in our lives.

> Sin gives Satan and his cohorts legal rights to cause all kinds of ill in our lives.

The account of the paralytic that Jesus healed at the pool of Bethesda in John 5 shows how this is so. After he had been healed, the Lord Jesus said to him (v.14; ESV): *"See, you are well! Sin no more, that nothing worse may happen to you"*. I believe that in this particular case, the man had contracted this illness because he gave legal rights to demons to cripple him through some kind of sin or a generational curse. Jesus warned him about getting into a worse predicament.

What About Angels?

Okay, so far, we saw how God intervenes mostly (but not limited to) when we pray or sin. That's pretty straightforward.

But what about angels?

What grants angels the right to intervene in the earth realm on our behalf? Are they under the same rules of engagement as God? What consists as their green light to interfere in our affairs?

Back in chapter one, I briefly mentioned how angels are the

Kingdom's military force. But they are also much more than that. There are a variety of angelic beings of all shapes, sizes, authority, and powers who play many different roles in His Majesty's service. They act as:

- Warriors
- Messengers
- Protectors
- Servants
- Leaders
- Secret Service
- Enforcers
- Soldiers
- Envoys
- Generals, etc.

The word angel is from the Latin *"angelus"* and from the Greek *"angelos,"* which means *"messenger."* The word literally means *"messenger, envoy, one that announces,"* in the New Testament.

The least we can say is that angels are highly organized, powerful, and versatile. The Bible says of angels:

> *"Are not all angels ministering spirits sent to serve those who will inherit salvation?" ~ Hebrews 1:14 (NIV)*

This is interesting. They are not limited to ministering (serving) those who *have inherited salvation*, but they also minister to those *who will inherit salvation*—future tense. They protect God's future Kingdom citizens as well as His present ones!

I must say that I have pondered the many angelic accounts in the Bible. I did so because I wanted to know how and when they were used of God. They are used of God for the following:

- ♛ To encourage
- ♛ To help
- ♛ To give a message
- ♛ To deliver
- ♛ To prophesy
- ♛ **To kill (yes, you read that right)**
- ♛ **To wage warfare with the Enemy, etc.**

While they are often dispatched on behalf of the saints who have prayed, angels can also come to our aid without us praying. This particularity has made me quite curious about their role. I even experienced their unsolicited aid in my own life on a few occasions (and probably on many others, unbeknownst to me). This has made me reach the following conclusion:

Angels are God's secret agents, dispatched to go secretly when neither sin nor direct prayer gives God the legal right for direct earthly intervention.

> Angels are God's secret agents, dispatched to go secretly when neither sin nor direct prayer gives God the legal right for direct earthly intervention.

In other words, angels often act as God's failsafe so that He maintains indirect access to us in times of need—no matter what. Like any Good Father, while He won't break His own Word to us about the "dominion" He gave us. He made sure He could send help… even when we don't ask for it. This makes me smile because as a father myself, if I had unlimited resources, I too would make sure my children were always kept safe and protected—even if they didn't ask for my help.

While angels do not have the ability to be everywhere at once, like God, according to Kevin Zadai, a man who died, saw heaven, and had many angelic encounters, they are, nonetheless, incredibly fast and able to go around the earth up to eight times per second. This enables them to minister on behalf of countless people and save many lives in the course of a day.

Now, that's fast! Yes, move over, Flash.

The Earth: Our Inheritance

In the beatitudes, we read:

> *"Blessed are the meek, for they will inherit the earth."* ~ Matthew 5:5 (NIV)

Never forget that, while He is King, the Landlord is also our Abba, our *Daddy*. And every Good Father leaves an inheritance to His children.

It is quite common for a wealthy father to leave the estate, his property, to his children. Remember Psalm 115:16 (NKJV), *"The heaven, even the heavens, are the LORD's; But the earth He has given to the children of men."*

It was His intention to give it to us in the beginning, and it will be perfectly fulfilled in the end. As Jesus said:

> *"It is your Father's good pleasure to give you the kingdom."* ~ Luke 12:32 (ESV)

God Will Never Be Denied

No matter what, God always ends up getting His way on the earth. He has a perfect record of 1 billion victories and 0 losses, so to speak. He always finds a man who is willing to be in covenant with Him to get His will accomplished in the earth realm. Because He has given man dominion,

> God always ends up getting His way on the earth.

God uses man, a man, any chosen man, to speak forth His will before He accomplishes it on the earth.

Remember, we read in the Bible that:

> *"The Sovereign LORD does nothing without revealing his plan to his servants the prophets."* ~ Amos 3:7 (NIV)

Once the prophet has spoken the will of God, then His will is done without any restraint or hindrance.

But, let us suppose for a moment that God wouldn't find any man to partner with, that He didn't have any man to speak forth His Word. What then? Would that be sufficient to stop God? Hardly.

First of all, we know that God can access any man's heart, will, and emotions. The Book of Proverbs 21:1 (NKJV) tells us: *"The king's heart is in the hand of the Lord, like the rivers of water; He turns it wherever He wishes."*

God Can Make You Scream

I am reminded of a time when God did just that with my wife, Elisabeth. He made her scream. This happened after our move from the province of Quebec to Prince Edward Island. He had clearly mandated us to move to Prince Edward Island, but after a little more than a year, we felt homesick and decided it was time for us to move back to our native province of Quebec (I'm giving you here the short version of the story). However, we still hadn't completed our Kingdom assignment on P.E.I., and, unbeknownst to us, God had further plans for us in the tiniest province of Canada.

As we had put all the wheels in motion to obtain a job transfer and even sold our house, God wanted to halt the process of this move. He wanted us to remain on Prince Edward Island. The problem was, our house was already sold, and I had obtained the confirmation for my job transfer back to Quebec to a town called *Lachute*.

Undaunted by our plans, the Spirit of the Lord gave Elisabeth no peace about the move. Her anxiety was such that one night, she woke up screaming! But she didn't just scream for the sake of expressing panic. No. She woke up screaming the exact words: *"I don't want to move to Lachute!!!"* (the city we had obtained the transfer to).

Believe it or not, that was all it took.

From that point on, our lives took on an unprecedented turn into a major halting of all prospects of a successful move back to Quebec.

It began when my employer, Canada Post, called us to inform us that the transfer was an "administrative error" and thus cancelled it. And then, in a whirlwind of chaotic logistics, we ended up buying another house, albeit a better house, in Prince Edward Island, where we've been living ever since.

Today, in hindsight and with the passing of years, we understand all that God wanted us to accomplish and learn through this ordeal.

Our dominion-led decision, our desire to do our own thing, had been overruled by His sovereign will. And all it took was one emotionally charged, prophetic, panicky utterance from Elisabeth. He made it happen.

Screaming Stones

You've probably heard of *the Rolling Stones*, but have you ever heard of the *Screaming Stones*? Probably not.

Just for the sake of argument, let's pretend no man wants to do His will; what then? What if nobody says to God, *"Here I am, send me."* What then? Could God still get His way? The Bible clearly says 'yes,' and how this would be done might surprise you.

In Luke 19:37-40 (NIV), we read:

> *"When he came near the place where the road goes down the Mount of Olives, the whole crowd of disciples began*

joyfully to praise God in loud voices for all the miracles they had seen: 'Blessed is the king who comes in the name of the Lord! Peace in heaven and glory in the highest!' Some of the Pharisees in the crowd said to Jesus, 'Teacher, rebuke your disciples!' <u>'I tell you,' he replied, 'if they keep quiet, the stones will cry out.'</u>

God's voice will never be denied in heaven or on earth. If necessary, the stones will cry out to get the Word out. And if His voice cannot be denied, neither can His will. Psalm 66:4 (NLT) says:

"Everything on earth will worship you; they will sing your praises, shouting your name in glorious songs."

If no man were to be found, God would still use a donkey to speak His Word and get His will done (Numbers 22:21-39). And if that doesn't work, John the Baptist reminded his hearers:

"Do not presume to say to yourselves, 'We have Abraham as our father,' for I tell you, God is able from these stones to raise up children for Abraham." ~ Matthew 3:9 (ESV)

In other words, do not become prideful of the authority and dominion God bestowed upon you. Or, as Paul said:

"if anyone thinks he is something, when he is nothing, he deceives himself." ~ Galatians 6:3 (ESV)

God is sovereign no matter what. Therefore, always remain humble and thankful for the privilege we have in serving the King.

Later, in chapter 9, I address further how man's words either partner with heaven or hell in getting things done on the earth.

PART 2
THE KINGDOM:

YOUR PLACE IN IT
AND
HOW TO OPERATE IN IT

7
FAITH: THE KINGDOM'S CURRENCY
Exploring the Intricacies of Faith

"When you do business with people you need money. When you do business with God you need faith. Faith is the currency of the Kingdom of God." ~ Reinhard Bonnke

Have you ever seen the movie, *Faith Like Potatoes*? *Faith Like Potatoes* tells the true story of Angus Buchan, a South African farmer who learns, through farming, what *true faith* really is.

Angus comes to South Africa in the middle of racial turmoil and economic disruption to begin a new life for himself and his family. He purchases an old farm. The labour associated with restoring it nearly drives him nuts. Fortunately, though, God had better plans for him than that of a mental asylum. Angus, through his local church and pastor, comes to faith in Jesus Christ. He becomes born-again and a Kingdom citizen.

Angus is then challenged to share his newfound faith by telling others about what God has done in his life. In the difficulties that follow, God answers Angus' many prayers in miraculous ways. For instance, He sends rain to put out a fire, and He even uses Angus to raise a woman from the dead!

But the farmer's greatest test of faith comes when a devastating drought threatens the land. Though Angus leads the community in a prayer of healing, the drought persists.

One day, Angus believes the Lord is challenging him to risk being perceived as a fool for Him. He decides to plant water-thirsty potatoes amid this severe drought. The investment is so large that Angus puts his farm on the line for what he believes the Lord is calling him to do.

After Angus plants the field of potatoes, the rain still doesn't come. The entire community is curious to see what will happen. Even Angus is concerned.

Angus' motto, *"Just Trust God,"* is then put to the ultimate test. The equation is simple: If the crop fails, Angus loses everything. If it comes in, he will be able to pay off the farm and ensure his family's survival and the small orphanage they have opened.

Though he believes, Angus has no idea what will happen. He has grown corn in the past, which is above ground and visible, but potatoes grow out of sight. Potatoes really require faith.

As harvest time approaches, Angus' words of hope and trust are on the line. He tells a friend as they look over the dry fields, *"The condition for a miracle is difficulty. For a great miracle, it's impossibility."*

> "The condition for a miracle is difficulty. For a great miracle, it's impossibility."

This predicament he faces is the same one that all of us face when we *become fools for God.* Will his faith be rewarded, or will he become a failure because he crossed the fine line between faith and foolishness?

As the morning of the harvest comes, everyone waits with uncertainty. No one knows if Angus Buchan will be shown to be a man of faith or simply a darn fool. Angus walks across the dry field with his African friend and co-worker, Gibli. The plants are withered and dry, and the men have no idea what lies beneath their feet.

In this powerful scene, Angus begins by thanking his friend, saying: *"Gibli, my friend, before we get started, I want to tell you how much I appreciate you, what you've done for me and my family. I don't think we would have been here if it wasn't for you."* Gibli just silently stares at his friend, not too sure what to think or say. Angus continues, *"I know you love this land as much as I do. I really appreciate you."*

Angus then takes his hat off and says, *"Come, Let's pray."*

Angus begins to pray, *"God, thank you for this harvest. Thank you for giving us this land."* He looks around and adds, *"We don't know what's in this ground, but we pray that you'll bless it."*

After the prayer, Gibli takes a pitchfork and sticks it into the ground to see what's there. To his amazement, huge potatoes come up with the dirt. When Angus sees them, he begins to shout praises to God, and Gibli joins him, shouting in the Zulu tongue, *"Potatoes from God!"* Angus stops in the middle of his celebration as he sees the workers and his family and friends coming to help with the harvest. His wife, Jill, tells Angus, she had faith for the potatoes, as they embrace.

After the harvest, Angus is sitting with a group of young men from the orphanage. He asks one of the boys to take a potato. Angus says, *"Feel this. Smell it!"* Then he adds, *"Your faith in God must be like that. It must be real! You can feel it. You can smell it!"* Turning to the entire group, he adds, *"Your faith has got to be like a potato!"*

The lesson was that true faith is real, vibrant, and alive. You can feel it! You can touch it, see it, and smell it.

When we hear of stories like this or see movies such as *Faith Like Potatoes*, we get inspired. We get encouraged. It's wonderful to see such testimonies of God's faithfulness and provision! It makes us appreciate more that, to God, nothing is too hard

> If you go out in faith and are willing to look crazy for God, He will reward you with a crazy harvest.

or impossible. It teaches us that if you go out in faith and are willing to look crazy for God, He will reward you with a crazy harvest.

However, for those of us who struggle with faith or who don't fully understand how faith works, these stories don't always show us how to get to that level.

Such stories tell us about the wonderful *results of faith*, but not necessarily its process. Maybe now you're just scratching your head and rationalizing it with thoughts like:

- ♛ Well, I guess I just don't have that kind of faith; or
- ♛ Well, some have the spiritual gift of faith; or
- ♛ Well, that's what charismatics teach, and I'm a _____ (fill in the blank); or
- ♛ Well, my pastor teaches that great miracles like those of the apostles were done away with. These things have ceased, etc.

When our faith doesn't yield desired results, we explain it away. We rationalize it. We basically end up twisting the Word through theological gymnastics to prove that Jesus didn't really mean what He said in Mark 11:24 (NIV):

"Therefore I tell you, whatever you ask for in prayer, believe that you have received it, and it will be yours."

And yet, we know that God is good, right? We know that God is no liar. We know that God's Word is true. And we know that:

'Jesus Christ is the same yesterday, today, and forever.' ~ Hebrews 13:8 (NKJV)

So, if that's true, let every man be a liar then. In other words...

If you don't have miracles and prayers answered in your life, the fault must not lie with God; it must lie with you. As harsh as this statement seems, you need to come to terms with that and from there seek answers, solutions, and become teachable.

I really like what Gary Keesee, author, pastor, and entrepreneur, said in many of his teachings:

> "As God began to reveal and teach me His laws, I began to realize that every story in the Bible held keys that I needed to know in regard to how the Kingdom operated. I began to read every story in the Bible differently. I started approaching everything I read with questions: Why did that happen? Why didn't that happen? What principles are revealed in this story?
>
> How did that happen?
>
> I began to call myself a "spiritual scientist," and I was thrilled each time the Holy Spirit revealed a Kingdom law to me. I was even more thrilled to see that the laws I discovered could operate in my own life just like they did in the Bible."

I believe Kingdom citizens should always have this same blessed curiosity. We should never settle when we don't understand. Like spiritual scientists, we should always seek to find answers, especially when our questions concern seeking the Kingdom of God and how it operates.

So, how exactly does one have 'Faith Like Potatoes'? A faith that laughs in the face of seemingly impossible odds, a faith that is able to look like a fool for God, or a faith that is fully assured of things unseen?

Faith is the lifestyle of the believer. We are to live by faith:

> "Without faith it is impossible to please God, because anyone who comes to him must believe that he exists and that he rewards those who earnestly seek him." ~ Hebrews 11:6 (NIV)

And

> "The just (righteous) shall live by faith." (Habakkuk 2:4; Romans 1:17; Galatians 3:11; Hebrews 10:38)

So, not only should we live by faith and not by sight, but our faith enables us to please God.

Therefore, one could say that your faith is a basic requirement to bring you into the Kingdom and make you a citizen. After all, as the Scripture says:

> *"By grace you have been saved, through faith—and this is not from yourselves, it is the gift of God— not by works, so that no one can boast." ~ Ephesians 2:8-9 (NIV)*

So, in other words, your new citizenship in the Kingdom was acquired not by seeing but by believing—through faith. And, ever since then, your whole new Kingdom life has been exercised by faith.

It is by faith that you were saved and sealed. But that's not all...

- ♛ You believe the Bible is true... *by faith.*
- ♛ You believe God hears your prayers... *by faith.*
- ♛ You know that you will go to heaven when you die... *by faith.*
- ♛ You trust God on a daily basis... *by faith.*

You began your new life, your born-again life, *by faith.* And life in the Kingdom of God is lived... *by faith*—every minute of every day.

The well-known preacher, Charles Spurgeon, was once asked: *What is more important—praying or reading the Bible?* He replied: *"What is more important: breathing in or breathing out?"*

Faith will bring you to do both regularly, and doing both regularly will bring up your faith. *It's synergistic!*

Faith is the oxygen you breathe in the Kingdom of God—you live by it.

> Faith is the oxygen you breathe in the Kingdom of God—you live by it.

The Bible also reminds us that:

> *'God has dealt to each one a measure of faith.' ~ Romans 12:3 (NKJV)*

I've been given a measure of faith, and so have you. But, that 'measure of faith,' what exactly is it?

Well, it is comparable to your body. While we are all given a capable body, not all of us develop it the same way. Everyone who has two arms and two legs was given 650 muscles in their body. That's the number of muscles you and I both possess. But… not all of us use or develop these muscles the same way. Some develop them very highly through intensive training and discipline—like the Olympic athlete or bodybuilder. Others don't train or develop their muscles *at all.*

Did you know the guy who sits on his couch drinking beer all day has the same number of muscles as the Olympic athlete? The difference then lies in the use, training, and disciplining of those muscles.

Likewise, you were given the same measure of faith as the apostle Paul or Angus Buchan of the movie, *Faith Like Potatoes.* However, not all of us have exercised or trained our faith like they have. Some of us have 'Pot-Bellied faith' and others have 'Six-pack abs faith.'

Hopefully, you can learn how to have Olympic-level faith.

To that end, there are three main things you need to know about faith:

1. **What faith is:** *"faith is the substance of things hoped for, the evidence of things not seen."* ~ Hebrews 11:1

2. **How to get faith or be in Faith:** *"So then faith comes by hearing, and hearing by the word of God."* ~ Romans 10:17

3. **How to make your faith work for you:** *"Therefore I tell you, whatever you ask for in prayer, believe that you have received it, and it will be yours."* ~ Mark 11:24

As Kingdom citizens, we cannot live, operate, or be approved by the King without Faith. That is partly why as soon as you were saved and became a citizen of the Kingdom, He has provided you with a measure of faith to operate in His Kingdom.

> As Kingdom citizens, we cannot live, operate, or be approved by the King without Faith.

Faith, *your faith*, is your main kingdom key.

But, as with any key, it will not work:

- ♛ If you keep it in your pocket (for ex: if you don't use it)
- ♛ If you misuse it (for ex: insert it the wrong way or turn it the wrong way)
- ♛ If you don't understand how it works (for ex: the mechanics of it)
- ♛ If you don't know what it's for (for ex: the purpose for it)

Furthermore, the Bible tells us that with it, with this key, "All things are possible." Because *"all things are possible to him who believes."* ~ Mark 9:23

The main reason people do not understand or experience Kingdom living is that they do not understand what faith is, how faith works, and how it is made stronger.

So, let's consider the dynamics of faith—how you can work out your faith and make it work for you.

What Faith Is

The Amplified Bible puts Hebrews 11:1 like this:

> *"Faith is the assurance [the confirmation, the title deed] of the things we hope for, being the proof of things we do not see and the conviction of their reality [faith knowing as fact what is not revealed to your senses]."*

So, faith is an assurance, a deep conviction, a knowing.

Let me ask you a question…

196

How do you know you're saved, redeemed, and going to heaven when you die? Nobody gave you any visual or physical proof of your salvation, and yet you're so sure of it, aren't you?

And how about the colour blue, how can you be so sure of what blue is? If I were to show the colour red and tell you that it is blue, you would tell me to go fly a kite, wouldn't you? That's because you just know the truth. You have a deep knowing and conviction about the colour blue. That's what faith is. It is a deep knowing, an undeniable conviction.

The Difference Between Hope and Faith

Many believers confuse hope with faith. We need to clarify this. Faith stems from hope but is not hope. Hope is only the starting point of faith.

The definition of hope is the following: *A feeling of expectation and desire for a certain thing to happen.*

Any prayer request begins with a *desire* for something—a mental image of something good or a solution.

And the definition of faith is the following: *A complete trust or confidence in someone or something.*

One is expectant desire; the other is joyful, confident reception.

Hope is the embryo of faith, but many suffer miscarriages while waiting for the baby to be born. Hope prays for rain; faith digs ditches to receive water (see 2 Kings 3:16-18).

So many Christians say, *"I've prayed again and again. I've fasted. I've pleaded. I've petitioned. I cried out to God, etc., but*

> Hope is the embryo of faith, but many suffer miscarriages while waiting for the baby to be born.

nothing happened. I didn't get my prayers answered. And yet, I really believed it would happen."

This is a common problem. And that problem is often summed up by this: You were hoping, but you didn't have faith like a mustard seed. You were in hope, not in faith. For most, this is a tough pill to swallow.

I tell you, if hope were the requirement for us to have our prayers answered, all of us would have them answered.

The language of hope is the following:

- ♛ I hope God will answer me.
- ♛ I can't wait to see this prayer answered.
- ♛ It's going to be so exciting when…
- ♛ I'm hoping to see this come to pass soon.
- ♛ We have to keep hoping and praying, etc.

Actually, such language can be deceiving. While it does bear *the appearance of faith*, it is rather the language of hope.

Remember this: *hope always speaks in the future tense; faith always speaks in the present tense.* Hope believes that God can; faith knows that God has.

Faith receives right away. It is hope made manifest.

Remember Mark 11:24? *"Therefore I tell you, whatever you ask for in prayer, believe that you have received it, and it will be yours."*

Jesus said, *'Believe that you have received it,'* He didn't say *'Believe that you will receive it.'*

How to Get Faith or Be in Faith

So now, you might be asking, *"Okay, but how do I work out my faith so that when I pray, I believe in the present tense that I have it?"*

Good question.

Romans 10:17 says:

"Faith comes by hearing, and hearing by the word of God."

So, faith comes by hearing... *the Word of God.*

God says of His own Word in Isaiah 55:11 (NKJV):

"So shall My word be that goes forth from My mouth; it shall not return to Me void, but it shall accomplish what I please, and it shall prosper in the thing for which I sent it."

God said of His Word, *"it shall prosper in the thing for which I sent it."*

Now, a question...

In the New Testament, where did God send His word?

When Jesus explained the parable of the sower to His disciples in Luke chapter 8:11-15 (NIV), He said this:

"This is the meaning of the parable: <u>The seed is the word of God.</u> Those along the path are <u>the ones who hear,</u> and then the devil comes and takes away the word from their hearts, so that they may not believe and be saved. Those on the rocky ground are the ones who receive the word with joy <u>when they hear it,</u> but they have no root. They believe for a while, but in the time of testing they fall away. The seed that fell among thorns stands for <u>those who hear,</u> but as they go on their way they are choked by life's worries, riches and pleasures, and they do not mature. <u>But the seed on good soil stands for those with a noble and good heart, who hear the word, retain it, and by persevering produce a crop."</u>

Okay, so now, we know that faith comes by hearing (I can never emphasize the word HEARING enough here) the Word of God.

And, thanks to the parable of the sower, we know that this *audible word* is sown in the hearts of men. And then it produces a crop.

Therefore, the mechanics are simple: hearing the Word goes

through your ears, in your mind, and then down to your heart, and produces a crop.

Now, let me ask you another question…

When you speak, do you hear yourself talk? Yes, of course you do. We all do.

Now, I'll ask you another question, just bear with me for a moment…

When your read your Bible, do you hear the words? No, not really.

Why?

Because there is a marked difference between what we *read* and what we *speak*… right?

Now, before I continue… let's look at another Bible passage. It's in Joshua 1:8 (ESV):

> *"This Book of the Law <u>shall not depart from your mouth</u>, but you shall meditate on it day and night, so that you may be careful to do according to all that is written in it. For then you will make your way prosperous, and then you will have good success."*

So, God said this book of the Law shall not depart from your eyes…oh, wait, NO! *FROM YOUR MOUTH! … then you will make your way prosperous, and then you will have good success.*

There's another thing…

In most conservative denominations, we are greatly encouraged to *read the Bible.* There's nothing wrong with that. In fact, I hope you do tons of Bible reading.

However, reading is done through your eyes. And we are told the Word should not depart from our mouths—not our eyes. Therefore, the greatest faith results in our lives are achieved when we read the Word of God *out loud.*

One way to make God's Word audible back in the day was through public reading. Public reading makes the Word of God audible, and makes His word accomplish that which for it is sent out. That's why we see Ezra standing before the people of Israel, reading the law of Moses aloud in Nehemiah 8:1-3 (ESV), where it says:

> "And all the people gathered as one man into the square before the Water Gate. And they told Ezra the scribe to bring the Book of the Law of Moses that the Lord had commanded Israel. So Ezra the priest brought the Law before the assembly, both men and women and all who could understand what they heard, on the first day of the seventh month. And he read from it facing the square before the Water Gate from early morning until midday, in the presence of the men and the women and those who could understand. And the ears of all the people were attentive to the Book of the Law."

And in 1 Timothy 4:13 (NIV), Paul says to Timothy:

> "Until I come, devote yourself to the public reading of Scripture, to preaching and to teaching."

When we read aloud the Words of God, whether publicly or privately, we make His words our own, and when we make the Words of God our own, miraculous things happen.

What exactly happens when, in our personal devotional time, we speak the Words of God, pray the Words of God, and confess the Words of God?

Here is how this works...

When the Words of God roll off your own tongue—you hear them. And faith, as we saw, comes from hearing *and hearing from the Word of God.*

When we read aloud the words of God often and meditate on them, we build up our own faith.

Repeating the promises of God about an issue in your life, whether it has to do with healing or finances, or any other matter, helps you to build up your faith in what your heavenly Father says on that very matter.

For example, if I have financial trouble, and many times a day, I repeat the promise of my Father's Word, which says: *"My God shall supply all my need according to His riches in Christ Jesus."* This will gradually make my spirit come into agreement with the Word of God.

Until with all my being, I believe and agree with the Words and promises from the Word of God, my faith will not be strong enough to move mountains. And the only way to be in full agreement with the Word of God is to apply Joshua 1:8 to myself in the first person:

This Book of the Law shall not depart from my mouth, but I shall meditate on it day and night, so that I may be careful to do according to all that is written in it. For then I will make my way prosperous, and then I will have good success.

So, hearing the Word of God repetitively, methodically, and intentionally, is the best way to build up your faith.

Do you have a Bible-reading plan that includes reciting out loud God's Words and promises to you? If not, I urge you to begin this week.

There are also great Scripture compilations available that include Bible promises by topics. These are great to pray the Scriptures for specific needs in your life. They are often classified with topics such as health, family, finances, faith, etc.

In order to have powerful faith results, you must be plugged into the Word—day and night!

> "Your faith will never be greater than your knowledge of the Word."
> ~ Kenneth E. Hagin

Faith teacher, Kenneth E. Hagin, once said: *"Your faith will never be greater than your knowledge of the Word."*

How to Make Your Faith Work for You

Before I explain *how to make faith work for you*, we need to establish something crucial.

We know that God's Kingdom operates by law. God is a God of order, and He has established His creation to operate through diverse laws. We have to interact with all kinds of laws in this life. Some call them laws of nature or laws of physics. We have the law of gravity, the law of sowing and reaping, the law of reproduction, the law of cause and effect, etc.

Well, maybe you didn't know this, but *faith is also a LAW*.

In Romans 3:27-28 (NKJV), we read this insightful nugget:

> *"Where is boasting then? It is excluded. By what law? Of works? No, <u>but by the law of faith.</u> Therefore we conclude that a man is justified by faith apart from the deeds of the law."*

So, aside from the obvious context here, where Paul reminds us that we are not saved by works, he tells us that the law of faith supersedes all others.

The LAW of faith.

God, in His Word, has defined faith as a law.

But what exactly defines a law?

A law is defined as follows:

"A statement of fact, deduced from observation, to the effect that a particular natural or scientific phenomenon always occurs if certain conditions are present. For example: "the second law of thermodynamics, the law of gravity" It is also a generalization based on a fact or event perceived to be recurrent." ~ Wikipedia

With this in mind, notice the terminology of Romans 3:27, where Paul says: *the law of faith*. The superior law of faith overruled and superseded the law of sin and death (i.e., the soul that sinneth, it shall die).

So, what then can be observed about the *law of faith*? Here are a few things:

- ♛ Faith works the same way every time, all the time, everywhere! It is a law.
- ♛ It's not just a matter of asking God, and then if He wants to, He'll give you what you ask.
- ♛ God is consistent, and His laws are consistent (remember electricity, gravity?)
- ♛ Ignorance of how faith works will keep you from having what God has for you.

The main thing to remember about a law is its *consistency*. This means that when properly applied and understood, your faith will work *EVERY TIME!*

This is why Jesus said:

> *"If you abide in me and my words abide in you, ask whatever you wish, and it shall be done for you." John 15:7 (NIV)*

> *"Therefore I tell you, whatever you ask for in prayer, believe that you have received it, and it will be yours." Mark 11:24 (NIV)*

> *"So Jesus answered and said to them, "Assuredly, I say to you, if you have faith and do not doubt, you will not only do what was done to the fig tree, but also if you say to this mountain, 'Be removed and be cast into the sea,' it will be done. And whatever things you ask in prayer, believing, you will receive." Matthew 21:21-22 (NIV)*

Elsewhere, we also read:

> *Now this is the confidence that we have in Him, that if we ask anything according to His will, He hears us. And if we know that He hears us, whatever we ask, we know that we have the petitions that we have asked of Him." 1 John 5:14-15 (NIV)*

Notice in John 15:7 verse, Jesus begins by saying, "*If you abide in me and my words abide in you.*" Just like I wrote previously, this means that we are to saturate ourselves with the Words of God for this law of faith to be made manifest in our lives. The Words of God must become one with our spirit.

According to His Will

When we become saturated with the Words of God, we come to a place in our faith and prayer life where we will inevitably pray according to His will.

This, by no means, indicates that you will only pray prudent prayers. That's what I used to believe. I used to believe that praying "*according to His will*" meant uttering prayers that were timid, general, or only found in the Bible. I thought praying timidly made me humble, but in reality, I just didn't understand the privilege and power of the prayer of faith. And yet, so many men (and women) of God have shown us quite the contrary. They've asked for things that some religious folks would qualify as preposterous—and they've obtained them! The Bible tells us in Hebrews 4:16 that we can "*come boldly unto the throne of grace, that we may obtain mercy, and find grace to help in time of need.*"

When we understand the Father's deep love for us, our position with Him, and have faith in His Word, we will ask for things that we would never otherwise ask for. Also, a clear understanding of God's ways enables men to pray boldly and intelligently, directing towards the throne room prayers that are both powerful and efficient.

Steps to Moving Mountains

Now, let's look at five practical steps to make sure that this law of faith works in your life… Every. Single. Time.

1. Know Your Authority

The believer's knowledge of the authority given to Him by His King is the first and most important steppingstone to efficient, strong, and authoritative Kingdom faith. You will never move mountains unless you are convinced that you have the authority to do so.

> You will never move mountains unless you are convinced that you have the authority to do so.

authority to do so. We'll examine in more details the ramifications of the believer's authority in the next chapter.

For now, however, what you need to understand is that Jesus Christ, the King of kings and Lord of lords, has *"given you authority to tread on serpents and scorpions, and over all the power of the enemy, and nothing shall hurt you."* ~ Luke 10:19 (ESV)

And, just before He gave His disciples the Great Commission, we read: "

> *And when they saw him they worshiped him, but some doubted. And Jesus came and said to them, 'All authority in heaven and on earth has been given to me.'"* ~ *Matthew 28:17-18 (ESV)*

It is so reassuring that Jesus, to remedy His disciple's doubt, told them about His majestic and unlimited authority!

So it is, dear friend, that if you doubt, you must remind yourself of the authority of the one whom you belong to. Like Him, we do not come in our own authority, but by the authority of the One who sent us, and His authority is boundless! I address this further in chapter 8.

2. Clear the Air

Before you exercise your faith through prayer, you must do so with a clear conscience. If there is any unforgiveness or root of bitterness in your heart, these will short-circuit the efficiency of your faith. The Bible says:

Matthew 5:23-24 (NKJV): "Therefore if you bring your gift to the altar, and there remember that your brother has something against you, leave your gift there before the altar, and go your way. First be reconciled to your brother, and then come and offer your gift."

In the Lord's prayer, it says: *"forgive us our debts, as we also forgive our debtors."*

And then Jesus adds in Matthew 6:14-15 (NIV):

"For if you forgive other people when they sin against you, your heavenly Father will also forgive you. But if you do not forgive others their sins, your Father will not forgive your sins."

If you hold on to unforgiveness, it causes bitter roots to extend deeper into your heart. This will seriously damage your prayer life, faith, and blessings. The law of faith cannot operate within the confines of unforgiveness.

Hebrews 12:14-15 (NKJV) says:

"Strive for peace with everyone, and for the holiness without which no one will see the Lord. See to it that no one fails to obtain the grace of God; that no 'root of bitterness' springs up and causes trouble, and by it many become defiled."

And, for those of you who are married, *let not the sun go down on your anger.* Always forgive. A healthy marriage is the union of two forgivers. This is especially applicable to you, husbands, as the head of your household. The apostle Peter reminds you:

Likewise, husbands, live with your wives in an understanding way, showing honor to the woman as the weaker vessel, since they are heirs with you of the grace of life, <u>so that your prayers may not be hindered."</u> 1 Peter 3:7 (ESV)

I remember pastor and author, Chuck Swindoll, saying that if you make it a rule in your marriage to never go to bed angry against your spouse, you will notice that forgiveness seems to come more easily as the discussion and the night drags along. It's a lot easier to let go of our point of contention at 2 a.m. than it was at 8 p.m., when the argument began. I know this to be true from experience.

3. Show Up Filled Up

The Bible gives us this interesting account about the Lord. In Luke 11:1 (ESV), it says:

> *"Now Jesus was praying in a certain place, and when he finished, one of his disciples said to him, 'Lord, teach us to pray, as John taught his disciples.'"*

They had been with Him for some time. They observed His habits. They saw how He spent hours a day in solitude and prayer. They also saw what these hours a day translated as. They saw the results of Jesus' prayer life. They witnessed how hours of prayer equalled:

- 👑 **Commanding nature (that took Him one sentence)**
- 👑 **Raising the dead (that took Him one sentence)**
- 👑 **Casting out demons (that took Him one sentence)**
- 👑 **Healing the sick (that took Him one sentence)**

So, despite the fact they were 'uneducated,' they were still able to put two and two together. They knew what to ask Jesus. They wanted what He had. They did not ask Him to show them how to walk on water, or raise the dead, or calm a storm.

No.

They knew where the power came from. They understood the source. They knew it came from His time alone praying.

So, being smart, they asked Him to show them HOW to pray. So, they basically asked Him the secret on how to show up filled up.

It's no different with us. In order to maximize the power and efficiency of our measure of faith, we have to show up filled up too.

As Kingdom ambassadors, the power of our faith is proportionate to the quality of our devotional time with the King.

4. Eliminate Doubt

Bible teacher and man of faith, Charles Capps, put it like this: *"Faith is the ability to conceive God's Word."*

I mentioned earlier that hope is the embryo

> "Faith is the ability to conceive God's Word." ~ Charles Capps

of faith, but many suffer miscarriages while waiting for the baby to be born.

In other words, many of us fall out of faith between the *'Amen'* of our prayer to God and the *'There it is'* of His answer.

How many times have you prayed and believed for a thing, and the moment you prayed, you began doubting when it had been a little too long for the thing to manifest?

I know I've been there. In fact, too many times to remember. Too often, we are like Peter, walking on water to go to Jesus, but when things get a bit hard or too long, then we lose faith, start sinking, and shout, *"Save me, Lord!"*

The Bible tells us in James 1:6-8 (NIV):

"When you ask, you must believe and not doubt, because the one who doubts is like a wave of the sea, blown and tossed by the wind. That person should not expect to receive anything from the Lord. Such a person is double-minded and unstable in all they do."

James tells us the one who doubts *'should not expect to receive anything from the Lord.'*

Now, does doubt completely short-circuit faith? Is it the opposite of faith?

I used to think so, but I don't believe this anymore.

Sometimes, we think that having faith means a complete absence of doubt. We believe either we have faith or we have doubt. We always see faith as the absence of doubt and doubt as the absence of faith, but that is not so.

It is possible to have both faith *and* doubt.

Many of us have faith mixed with doubt. In fact, most of us do. And that is why we seldom see miraculous results in our life. Jesus said in Matthew 21:21 (ESV):

> *"Truly, I say to you, <u>if you have faith and do not doubt</u>, you will not only do what has been done to the fig tree, but even if you say to this mountain, 'Be taken up and thrown into the sea,' it will happen."*

The way this is phrased is fascinating. The word 'AND' changes much of the meaning. Jesus says, 'If you have faith <u>and</u> do not doubt.' Meaning both conditions must be met for the mountain to move.

Faith, without doubt, moves mountains. Faith with doubt might move anthills, maybe even molehills, but forget the mountains.

This is why you get prayers answered... *sometimes*. This is why you see miracles manifest... *sometimes*. It happens only *sometimes* because of faith mixed with doubt.

Remember in *Star Wars: The Empire Strikes Back*, when Yoda gets Luke's ship out of the swamp using the force? Luke then turns to Yoda and says in shock, *"I don't believe it!"* And Yoda simply replies, *"That... is why you fail."*

It's interesting to note that Luke had previously budged the ship. He had faith mixed with doubt. He was able to move an anthill, but not a mountain.

5. Speak Up

In Matthew 21:18-22 (NIV), we read:

> *"Early in the morning, as Jesus was on his way back to the city, he was hungry. Seeing a fig tree by the road, he went up to it but found nothing on it except leaves. <u>Then he said to it, "May you never bear fruit again!" Immediately the tree withered.</u>*
>
> *When the disciples saw this, they were amazed. "How did the fig tree wither so quickly?" they asked.*
>
> *Jesus replied, "Truly I tell you, if you have faith and do not doubt, <u>not only can you do what was done to the fig tree, but also you can say to this mountain,</u> 'Go, throw yourself into the sea,' and it will be done. If you believe, you will receive whatever you ask for in prayer."*

The passage says Jesus *said to the fig tree*. He spoke to it. *Out loud.* The passage also says in verse 21, *"you will <u>SAY</u> to this mountain."* Jesus *"shouted"* to Lazarus to come out. He spoke it. Jesus ordered demons out. This too was spoken.

Faith in action is always *spoken* with authority. It is spoken out loud.

The confessions of your mouth are the measure of your faith.

When Peter and John healed a lame man in Acts chapter 3, they said to him, *"Rise up and walk."*

> The confessions of your mouth are the measure of your faith.

Proverbs 18:20-21 (NKJV) says this about your speaking out, your verbal confessions:

> *"A man's stomach shall be satisfied from the <u>fruit of his mouth</u>; from the <u>produce of his lips</u> he shall be filled. <u>Death and life are in the power of the tongue</u>, and those who love it will eat its fruit."*

I will go into more detail about *the power of your tongue* in chapter 9.

8
YOUR BESTOWED KINGDOM AUTHORITY

Knowing Whose You Are, Who He Is,
and What You Have

"Kingdom authority is the God-given mandate of Christians
to exercise control over the world in the name of Jesus and
under His oversight." ~ Adrian Rogers

When I first wrote this chapter, it was intertwined with the previous one about faith. But, after re-reading and revising the content of the book, I decided to make it into a separate chapter. The reason is simple: I realized as I was explaining faith that the biggest faith fails are not just because believers don't have enough faith but because they do not understand their authority. In most cases, when our faith fails us, it is due to a misuse, underuse, or an altogether misunderstanding of our Kingdom authority.

Delegated Authority

When Jesus came to earth, He clearly possessed the authority of Heaven. During His ministry, this authority was palpable. Even His hearers *"were astonished at His teaching, for He taught them as one having authority, and not as the scribes." ~* Matthew 7:28-29 (NKJV)

And the disciples were also amazed when, after Jesus quieted the storm, they said:

"What kind of man is this? Even the winds and the waves
obey him!" ~ Matthew 8:27 (NIV)

213

But, after He died and rose again, something shifted even further. Jesus reclaimed, through His obedience and the fulfillment of His mission, *His full authority!*

In Matthew 28:18 (NIV), we read: *"All authority in heaven and on earth has been given to me."*

And what did He do with this *full authority?* He gave it to us!

In the very next sentence, Jesus said, *"Therefore GO, and make disciples..."* In essence, Jesus is saying, *"Since I was given ALL authority, I order you now to go..."*

But He didn't send us empty-handed. In Luke 10:19 (NKJV), which is before He reclaimed His full authority, He said to the disciples (and to us): *"Behold, I give you the authority to trample on serpents and scorpions, and over all the power of the enemy, and nothing shall by any means hurt you."*

Authority is *delegated power.* It is always something that we receive from someone else higher than us. Jesus confirmed this when He said:

> *"I have not spoken on my own authority, but the Father who sent me has himself given me a commandment—what to say and what to speak." ~ John 12:49 (ESV)*

A policeman has authority to direct traffic because it was given to him by the municipality or state he serves. A judge has the authority to exact justice because it was given to him by his city, state, or country. Even Pilate received from above the authority to get Jesus crucified. Jesus told the Roman governor, *"You would have no authority over me at all unless it had been given you from above."*

In a similar fashion, but to a much greater extent than we even realize, believers possess the authority bestowed by Jesus Christ Himself to exact the will of the Kingdom!

Authors of Destiny

Let's consider the word *authority*. From the 15th century on, the word has meant: *the right to rule or command, the power to enforce obedience, the power or right to command or act.*

So, *authority* is none other than *the power to rule or command.* This definition is where we also get the word *authorize* from. When we get authorized to do something, it comes from a higher power than us.

Another word we derive from *authority* is the word *author.* An author is a creator through words—a wordsmith. It is someone who uses words to achieve results. I like the image this conveys. An author, or wordsmith, is someone who writes stories or books and *weaves words into meaning and power.*

When believers use their *authority*, they use it through their *words*. This will be tackled further in the next chapter. But for now, suffice it to say that since God gets all things done through the authority of His Word, it only makes sense that His children, who are made in His image, would operate in the same way.

Like God's, our authority is displayed and used through our words. Because we were made in His image, we operate in a similar fashion as Him. Since He created the whole universe by His Word, doesn't it make sense then that we should influence our world through our words as well?

In the foreword to his bestselling book, *The Believer's Authority*, Kenneth E. Hagin wrote:

> *"As a result of my studies, I concluded that we as a Church have authority on the earth that we've never yet realized– authority that we're not using. A few of us have barely gotten to the edge of that authority, but before Jesus comes again, there's going to be a whole company of believers who will*

rise up with the authority that is theirs, and they will do the work that God intended they should do."

Individual believers and the Church as a whole cannot bring heaven to bear on the earth without a distinct awareness and use of their God-given authority. All of creation does indeed *await the full manifestation of the sons of God* (Romans 8:19)! We need not wait for our future translation into glory for it. It starts with you. It starts with me. It starts here and now!

> Individual believers and the Church as a whole cannot bring heaven to bear on the earth without a distinct awareness and use of their God-given authority.

One Fine Example

The best account we have of Kingdom faith and authority in the gospels comes from an unlikely source. It comes from a Roman centurion. This account is from Luke 7:1-10 (NIV):

> *"When Jesus had finished saying all this to the people who were listening, he entered Capernaum. There a centurion's servant, whom his master valued highly, was sick and about to die. The centurion heard of Jesus and sent some elders of the Jews to him, asking him to come and heal his servant. When they came to Jesus, they pleaded earnestly with him, "This man deserves to have you do this, because he loves our nation and has built our synagogue." So Jesus went with them. He was not far from the house when the centurion sent friends to say to him: "Lord, don't trouble yourself, for I do not deserve to have you come under my roof. That is why I did not even consider myself worthy to come to you. But say the word, and my servant will be healed. For I myself am a man under authority, with soldiers under me. I tell this one, 'Go,' and he goes; and that one, 'Come,' and he comes.*

I say to my servant, 'Do this,' and he does it." <u>*When Jesus*</u>
<u>*heard this, he was amazed at him, and turning to the crowd*</u>
<u>*following him, he said, "I tell you, I have not found such*</u>
<u>*great faith even in Israel."*</u> *Then the men who had been sent*
returned to the house and found the servant well."

In this passage, Jesus is *amazed* and says, *'I tell you, I have*
not found such great faith even in Israel.' The whole spiel from the
centurion is about his authority and understanding of how authority
works. Notice how the centurion didn't mention his faith once. And
yet, Jesus said that He was amazed at his *faith*.

The centurion said:

"I myself am a man under authority, with soldiers under
me. I tell this one, 'Go,' and he goes; and that one, 'Come,'
and he comes. I say to my servant, 'Do this,' and he does it."

What he meant was that if he, a simple centurion, could have
things done at a distance, simply by word of command; surely, Jesus,
the renowned prophet of Israel, could do likewise.

Furthermore, he called himself *"a man under authority."* This
seems a bit odd, doesn't it? Why didn't he say *a man with authority*
or *a man invested with authority*? Well, technically, there was
sound understanding in the way he put it. Often, most people do
not understand the hierarchy in the Roman army. For this reason,
it is generally believed that a centurion had an important rank
and position. But despite the way the word sounds (powerful and
authoritative), a centurion was in the lower tier of the chain of
command, having only 80 or so men under his authority.

In the Roman army's chain of command, there were many ranks
above a centurion. Above the centurion was the senior centurion,
and above the senior centurion, the sixty centurions of the Roman
legion. Above the sixty centurions were the six tribunes, and above

the six tribunes, the two consuls, and—in the imperial system—above the two consuls, the emperor himself.

And so, it was because he stood at a lower rung in this long line of delegated authority that the Roman centurion had developed this understanding of *how authority works*. He gave orders because he received orders. He had authority because he was under authority himself.

In the same way, we also need to understand that we have authority because we stand under authority. The devil flees from us only when we submit to God (James 4:7); when we put ourselves under His auhtority. So, the authority you're *under* (God) gives you authority *over* (demons, poverty, illness, etc.).

Occupy Till I Come

In the parable of the talents, the Master (a.k.a. Jesus) says to His servants to '*occupy till I come*.' This is the one explicit direction He gave to His servants just before He left them: *Occupy till I come.*

Figuratively, it is representative of what we must also do. But, what does this mean exactly—to occupy till He comes? Well, in French, the word '*occupé*' means to be busy with something. In essence, the Master told them to *get busy.*

Jesus essentially said that we are to remain occupied in working hard for His Kingdom until He returns. The English Standard Version (ESV) has translated '*occupy till I come*' as '*engage in business until I come.*' Which is to say, "*take care of my business; make it grow; look after things dutifully while I'm gone.*"

Occupy can also mean a military term. In military terms, *to occupy* means to take control of (a territory, especially a country) by military conquest or settlement. Synonyms include *capture, seize, take possession of, conquer, invade, overrun, take over, colonize.*

Isn't that interesting?!

Pastor Ken Baker said: "*The call to "take the land" ... is not a call to a new political, cultural or geographical dominance. It is Kingdom of God territory. It is the will of the Eternal God being done on earth, as it is in heaven."*

But before we can do that, we need to better understand what it means to be part of God's Kingdom.

As believers, we are part of a Kingdom—The Kingdom of God. Humanly speaking, however, few of us have an understanding or notions of what this entails. As we have seen, the reason is that nowadays, most of the countries we live in are not ruled by a king. Most of the countries we live in operate differently than a kingdom per se. We live mostly in republics and democracies. Therefore, we are not very familiar with how a Kingdom operates and how we should conduct ourselves before a King.

This ignorance of earthly Kingdom principles of operation keeps us from being fully functional and efficient as citizens of the Kingdom of God. Furthermore, and to make matters worse pertaining to our practical understanding, most of us in the West live in a democracy. In a democracy, the people decide, but not in a kingdom. This, of course, greatly affects our point of view, mindset, and even our obedience as citizens of God's Kingdom. It accentuates an already steep learning curve in our Kingdom re-education.

Who Are Kingdom Ambassadors?

All kingdoms have appointed persons who are sent to foreign lands to act as representatives of the king. These people are despatched by the king and carry with them the king's authority wherever they are sent. Those people are called ambassadors.

The Merriam-Webster dictionary defines an ambassador this way:

> *A diplomatic agent of the highest rank accredited to a foreign government or sovereign as the resident representative of*

his or her own government or sovereign or appointed for a special and often temporary diplomatic assignment.

The Bible calls us ambassadors. In 2 Corinthians 5:19-20, we read that God *"has committed to us the message of reconciliation. We are therefore Christ's ambassadors, as though God were making his appeal through us."*

As ambassadors of the Kingdom of heaven, we represent our King and His Kingdom *in a foreign land for a temporary diplomatic assignment.*

This job description aligns with the words of Peter in 2 Peter 2:11, in the New Living Translation:

"Dear friends, I warn you as 'temporary residents and foreigners' to keep away from worldly desires that wage war against your very souls."

Ambassadors are unique individuals, possessing a unique political position and respected influence everywhere they go.

In order to thrive in the Kingdom of God, you must understand what your title of ambassador comes with. You must understand the power, authority, and distinction that comes with this revered title. It is part of your Kingdom identity.

So, what are the characteristics of an ambassador? Excellent question! Dr. Myles Munroe listed 12 such characteristics of an ambassador. He wrote:

1. He is appointed by the king, not voted into position.
2. He is appointed to represent the state or kingdom.
3. He is committed only to the kingdom's interest.
4. He embodies the nation, state, or kingdom.
5. He is totally covered by the state.
6. He is the responsibility of the state.

7. He is totally protected by his government.

8. He never becomes a citizen of the state or kingdom to which he is assigned.

9. He can only be recalled by the king or president.

10. He has access to all his nation's wealth for his assignment.

11. He never speaks his personal position on any issue, only his nation's official position.

12. His goal is to influence the territory for his kingdom's government.

Note how number 4 says the ambassador *'embodies the nation, state, or Kingdom he represents.'* Remember what Jesus said concerning the Kingdom of God in Luke 17:21?

He said: *"The Kingdom of God is within you."*

Dear ambassador, *the Kingdom is within you!* As an ambassador who carries great authority, this means the following:

- ♛ Whoever attacks you, attacks the kingdom.
- ♛ Wherever you are... there is the presence of God and His Kingdom living in you through the Holy Ghost.
- ♛ Wherever you set your foot, that place becomes holy ground.
- ♛ When you speak, you represent the King of Glory and His Word.
- ♛ Your authority is the authority of the King Himself.
- ♛ Whatever you own, wear, or ride in—these become royal.

Yes, friend, even your T-shirt is royal attire. Your car is a royal chariot. And sure enough, a (believing) man's home is his castle. Why? Because the Kingdom in you through the Spirit sanctifies it and makes it so.

In my broadcast and teachings, I have often used the term *'kingdomizing'* to express this reality. As believers, we *kingdomize* what we come in contact with, be it things, places, or people. This is done supernaturally through the power of the King Himself who resides within us.

Of course, as ambassadors, because of this immense privilege, we also carry immense responsibility. I cover this at length in the book.

Ambassadors Influence Culture

Wherever they are despatched to by their respective country or kingdom, ambassadors are known to bring their country's culture along with them and influence the culture of their host country. Another definition of an ambassador is *a person who acts as a representative or promoter of a specified activity.*

To illustrate this principle, we find a great example of ambassadorial influence in the world of sports.

Back in August 9, 1988, the world of sports received the shocking news that its (arguably) greatest star, Wayne Gretzky, was traded by the Edmonton Oilers to the Los Angeles Kings.

"The Great One" was now bringing his record-shattering star power from the cold of Edmonton (Canada) to the palm trees of Los Angeles. He was moving from a small Canadian market to a buzzing and glamorous U.S. city and megalopolis.

Many hockey experts hailed Wayne Gretzky as *"the greatest ambassador for Hockey the United States had even seen."*

In hindsight, this was almost an understatement. Gretzky transformed the sport, not only in the U.S., but worldwide!

At the time, the loss was great for the Oilers, but in retrospect, it did wonders for the National Hockey League, hockey, and its popularity in the United States.

I remember before the trade, how hockey was just above tractor pulling contests in popularity in the United States (this is no joke). In other words, the NHL (National Hockey League) was far below the other major sports league in popularity: the NBA (National Basketball Association), NFL (National Football League), and MLB (Major League Baseball). Gretzky changed all that.

Gretzky's presence in Hollywood also brought him many endorsements, sponsorship deals, and TV appearances—which were seen everywhere across the country.

Since he became a "hockey ambassador" in the U.S. 30+ years ago, the sport has skyrocketed in popularity. Gretzky's record-breaking talent, natural good looks, meekness, and influence, attracted legions of young fans who now wanted to be enrolled in hockey (instead of other sports) by their parents. They wanted to emulate their newfound hero and become "The Next One."

This greatly contributed to not only the growth of the sport itself but to the talent pool expanding across the country. As a result, promising young prospects began emerging in the minor leagues across the U.S. The NHL then began drafting many young Americans on draft day, instead of just Canadians, Swedes, or others.

In turn, this enabled the United States to become a hockey superpower on the world stage right alongside Canada, Russia, and Sweden!

The popularity of Hockey was growing so much that it also provided the NHL with the opportunity to expand its teams to other American cities, including two in the state of California: The San Jose Sharks and The Anaheim Ducks.

So, what is my point with this illustration? Simply this:

If a single hockey player was able, by sharing what he was carrying, to influence the world as an ambassador for his sport, what untapped potential do ambassadors of the King of the universe carry with them? Remember:

> *"The Spirit of God, who raised Jesus from the dead, lives in you"* ~ Romans 8:11 (NLT)

> We carry the Spirit of the Living God wherever we go! This means that we carry within us limitless potential to influence and transform surrounding culture.

We carry the Spirit of the Living God wherever we go! This means that we carry within us limitless potential to influence and transform surrounding culture.

Your Sphere of Influence

You carry the glory of the Kingdom and the authority of the King within you! Where you walk becomes hallowed ground because of who you carry within. And make no mistake, this power and glory that accompanies you, the Holy Spirit's presence, can be felt strongly in the spirit realm. This is what Paul meant when he said:

> *"Thanks be to God, who in Christ always leads us in triumphal procession, and through us spreads the fragrance of the knowledge of him everywhere. <u>For we are the aroma of Christ to God among those who are being saved and among those who are perishing, to one a fragrance from death to death, to the other a fragrance from life to life.</u>"* ~ 2 Corinthians 2:14-16 (ESV)

This explains why, as a believer and Kingdom citizen, you get different reactions from people wherever you go. Some like you right away. They befriend you and are not repelled when you express your faith in speech with them. To them, you present the sweet fragrance of Jesus Christ and eternal life. These people are, most likely, called to salvation.

Yet, others manifest unprovoked hostility, even demonic hostility towards you before you even open your mouth. They might not even know why they hate you, but the spirits within them know why... and they fear you, rightfully so. Your Kingdom presence and authority is to them a fragrance of *death*. This reaction, by the way, doesn't mean they can never be saved—it just means it will require more grace, *"for where sin abounds, grace abounds more"* (Romans 5:20).

Now, three things will determine the size of your sphere of influence; they are:

1. Your faithfulness. The Lord said that to those who are faithful in little; He would assign more to rule over.

2. Your awareness. How aware you are of your bestowed Kingdom authority will determine the size of your sphere of influence.

3. Your Faith. The level of your faith will determine how willing and efficient you are at exercising your Kingdom authority.

How closely you walk in relationship with the King determines how vast your authority is felt in the spirit realm. For some, it's ten feet; for some, 30 or 100 feet, and for others, it's whole cities!

> How closely you walk in relationship with the King determines how vast your authority is felt in the spirit realm. For some, it's ten feet; for some, 30 or 100 feet, and for others, it's whole cities!

Some Kingdom men and women are so filled with the power and authority of the Holy Ghost and walk so closely to Jesus that demons flee the towns and cities wherever they show up.

Fill Your Position

One day, I was driving and thinking at the same time. By the way, this is for experienced drivers only. Just kidding. But I digress...

As I was driving, I thought of something I once heard leadership teacher, John C. Maxwell, say. He said:

> *"The position doesn't make the leader, the leader makes the position."*

And then my mind shifted to our *position* as Kingdom citizens.

I thought about how, through faith, God has given us the highest positions that could ever be conferred upon human beings.

Let's just go through a shortened list of how God has positioned us through Christ.

The Bible says:

We are a new creation: *"Therefore, if anyone is in Christ, he is a new creation. The old has passed away; behold, the new has come."* ~ 2 Corinthians 5:17 (ESV)

We are a holy people: *"But you are a chosen race, a royal priesthood, a holy nation, a people for his own possession, that you may proclaim the excellencies of him who called you out of darkness into his marvelous light."* ~ 1 Peter 2:9 (ESV)

We are His children: *"But to all who did receive him, who believed in his name, he gave the right to become children of God."* ~ John 1:12 (ESV)

We are His inheritors: *"And if children, then heirs—heirs of God and fellow heirs with Christ, provided we suffer with him in order that we may also be glorified with him."* ~ Romans 8:17 (ESV)

We are His workmanship: *"For we are his workmanship, created in Christ Jesus for good works, which God prepared beforehand, that we should walk in them."* ~ Ephesians 2:10 (ESV)

We are His ambassadors: *"We are therefore Christ's ambassadors, as though God were making his appeal through us."* ~ 2 Corinthians 5:20 (ESV)

I could go on and on because there are many more passages that speak of our unmerited yet exalted position, but I think these will suffice.

The point is this: As believers, we were given positions of tremendous authority and leadership.

> As believers, we were given positions of tremendous authority and leadership.

So, I ask you, what are you going to do about it? How can you make this position a reality?

Remember that *the position doesn't make the leader, but the leader makes the position.*

In corporate settings, there is an expression we use when a new position becomes available. We say that we need to *fill the new position.* And when someone gets hired, we say *the position has been filled*—implying that something empty has been filled.

Also, when we put on clothes, we fill them. In Romans 13:14, Paul admonishes us to *"put on the Lord Jesus Christ."*

As believers, we are given this tremendous position automatically through our new birth. But now, we are required to *fill the position.* We need to fill its every nook and cranny by becoming more and more what the position entails. We need to *grow into it,* to fill it up with all of God's righteousness and holiness. This is done by putting on the Lord Jesus Christ.

What this means is:

- ♛ Since I am a child of God, I need to grow as a child of God.
- ♛ Since I am a new creation, I need to grow as a new creation.
- ♛ Since I am holy, I need to grow in holiness.
- ♛ Since I am an heir, I need to think as someone who has no lack.
- ♛ Since I am an ambassador, I need to walk as an ambassador.

As believers, we were granted a powerful leadership position and authority upon the earth. The mandate of our lives then becomes to grow more and more into the likeness of Christ and to thus justify that position that cannot be taken from us.

In the corporate world, it's the opposite. In the corporate world, people get promotions based on their performance. Christianity operates in reverse: we get the position without merit, and then we are called to fill it by doing the works God prepared in advance and accordance with the position.

Authority *and* Power

The story is told of a Department of Water Resources representative who stops at a Texas ranch and talks with an old rancher. He tells the rancher, *"I need to inspect your ranch for your water allocation."*

The old rancher says, *"Okay, but don't go in that field over there."*

The Water representative says, *"Mister, I have the authority of the Federal Government with me. See this card? This card means I am allowed to go WHEREVER I WISH on any agricultural land. No questions asked or answered. Have I made myself clear? Do you understand?"*

The old rancher nods politely and goes about his chores.

Later, the old rancher hears loud screams and sees the Water Rep running for his life. And close behind is the rancher's bull. The bull is gaining with every step.

The Rep is clearly terrified, so the old rancher immediately throws down his tools, runs to the fence and yells at the top of his lungs, *"Your card! Show him your card!"*

Results like these can be expected for those who claim authority but have no power to back it up. It's one thing to have authority, but authority, as this story shows, can easily be thwarted by power.

Fortunately, as believers, we were given authority from Heaven *and great power to back it up*. The power we have is authoritative and is found in the name of Jesus and through the Holy Spirit. This is the power that so amazed the 72 disciples when they returned from their preaching mission. We read how:

> *"The seventy-two returned with joy, saying, 'Lord, even the demons are subject to us in your name!'"* ~ *Luke 10:17 (ESV)*

The Lord then gave them the admonition to not overly rejoice in the power but rather in their position and privilege. He said:

> *"I have given you authority to trample on snakes and scorpions and to overcome all the power of the enemy; nothing will harm you. However, do not rejoice that the spirits submit to you, but rejoice that your names are written in heaven." ~ Luke 10:19-20 (ESV)*

I often teach my children that the Name of Jesus is to be treated with tremendous reverence. I teach them not to use it in vain, of course. But I also teach them *why* the Name of Jesus is the Name above all names.

As believers, we often make the mistake of treating the name of Jesus like some sort of magic formula that will seal the deal if added at the end of a prayer. But the Name of our Lord carries so much more than that.

The account of the failed exorcism by the itinerant Jews and the sons of Sceva in Acts 19 remind us of this. I will have more to say about this as you read on.

The Least in the Kingdom

The Pharisees, who were the religious leaders in Jesus' day, constantly challenged His authority everywhere He went. We read of this particular account in the Gospel of Mark:

> *"Then they came again to Jerusalem. And as He was walking in the temple, the chief priests, the scribes, and the elders came to Him. And they said to Him, 'By what authority are You doing these things? And who gave You this authority to do these things?'*
>
> *But Jesus answered and said to them, 'I also will ask you one question; then answer Me, and I will tell you by what*

authority I do these things: The baptism of John—was it from heaven or from men? Answer Me.'

And they reasoned among themselves, saying, 'If we say, 'From heaven,' He will say, 'Why then did you not believe him?' But if we say, 'From men'—they feared the people, for all counted John to have been a prophet indeed. So they answered and said to Jesus, 'We do not know.'

And Jesus answered and said to them, "Neither will I tell you by what authority I do these things." ~ Mark 11:27-33 (NKJV)

Obviously, both Jesus and John had received their authority from Heaven. And yet, the religious leaders at the time didn't want to recognize it. This would have meant they needed to yield to Jesus.

I must warn you, as you grow in your Kingdom awareness and walk in more authority, you too will encounter opposition—especially from religious leaders. You might be perceived as a threat to some. Do not let this surprise you. This is to be expected since *"a servant is not greater than his Master"* (John 13:16).

But, as you will encounter people who ask you, *"By what authority are you doing these things?"* do not be shaken or deterred from continuing in your assignment from the Father. As you meet with their doubt, resistance, and mockery, do not let it wound you, and always answer with grace. Remember the words of the Master who said:

"Behold, I send you out as sheep in the midst of wolves. Therefore be wise as serpents and harmless as doves." ~ Matthew 10:16 (NKJV)

And remember how Jesus, speaking of John, also said:

"I tell you, among those born of women there is no one greater than John; yet the one who is least in the kingdom of God is greater than he." ~ Luke 7:28 (NIV)

What does this mean? Simply this: even the least in the Kingdom, or under the New Covenant, is greater than John the Baptist.

'The least in the Kingdom' has access to *a better covenant* which includes:

- ♛ **More authority**
- ♛ **More blessings**
- ♛ **More power**
- ♛ **More favor**
- ♛ **More gifts than John the Baptist, who was deemed "the greatest born of women"**

This is the authority the Father invested in you through the Son. Walk in it humbly but walk in it surely.

What's in a Name?

Although the quote is often cited and quite poetic, Juliette, in Shakespeare's masterpiece, *Romeo and Juliette,* spoke naively when she said to Romeo: *"What's in a name? that which we call a rose. By any other name would smell as sweet."* ~ William Shakespeare

While a rose would probably smell as sweet if it had been named differently, the Bible shows us beyond the shadow of a doubt just how important names are in the Kingdom of God.

Names, like words, have power.

The Scriptures are replete with examples and instances when things were either named or renamed—and it was never done lightly. Names in the Word of God were always given with thought and purpose.

- ♛ Places were named or renamed.
- ♛ People were named or renamed.
- ♛ Dates and times were named.

- ♛ The stars were named by God.
- ♛ Books were named.
- ♛ Animals were named, etc.

In Genesis, we are told that one of the first tasks of Adam, as one with dominion, was to name the animals. Genesis 2:19-20 (NKJV) says:

"Out of the ground the Lord God formed every beast of the field and every bird of the air, and brought them to Adam to see what he would call them. And whatever Adam called each living creature, that was its name. So Adam gave names to all cattle, to the birds of the air, and to every beast of the field."

I mentioned in chapter 2 that whatever we name, we have authority over. This is verifiable. Indeed, we name our children, our businesses, our pets, and we have authority over all of these.

Another interesting thing to note is that in the realm of the demonic, ask most deliverance ministers, and they will confirm this: *knowing and calling out the name of the entity you are casting out can make for a smoother process.* While it doesn't give the believer more authority (Kingdom authority through the name of Jesus does that), it does seem to "address" the problem better—pun intended. Calling them out by name gives more of a grip on those slimy evil entities.

This makes sense. For example, if you were walking down the street and heard your name called out, wouldn't you turn around? Of course, you would. While this doesn't imply that the person calling out your name has authority over you, it nonetheless brings an appropriate response on your part. It makes you pay attention. It also facilitates communication.

Jesus: The Name Above All Names

Now, let's talk about the Name of Jesus, through which we have and exercise our authority.

There is a strange book included in the two-volume *Old Testament Pseudepigrapha* compilation I own (published by Hendrickson). The Pseudepigrapha are falsely attributed works or texts, whose claimed author is not the true author. Many of them, nonetheless, offer some value to the reader, whether historical or otherwise.

Now, this particular book, *The Testament of Solomon* (which is falsely attributed, according to scholars), tells the story of how King Solomon, through the use of a ring given to him by the Archangel Michael, was given the power to enslave demons to help with the building of the Jerusalem temple.

In the book, before assigning their tasks, King Solomon asks every demon a series of intriguing questions. Also, physical descriptions are given of every single demon that presents itself before Solomon, which is interesting. The questions he asks them are:

- ♕ **The demon's name.**
- ♕ **What harm/symptoms the demon causes in people (i.e., headaches, sleeplessness, miscarriages, etc.)**
- ♕ **And finally, the name of the Angel who thwarts them.**

These questions are significant, but especially the last one.

Back in Old Testament days, exorcists were not yet given the authority of the name of Jesus to cast out demons. They needed to know the names of the angels that could assist them in getting the demons out. Each demon had an arch-nemesis, so to speak, that could drive him away. Therefore, exorcists used the names of angels to gain the upper hand in casting out demons. Besides that, they (exorcists) used a more ritualistic deliverance method as well, somewhat akin to those performed in the Catholic Church.

This is where it got very interesting, and I'm sure you'll agree. In the Scripture, we are told that:

"God has highly exalted him (Jesus) and bestowed on him the name that is above every name, so that at the name of Jesus every knee should bow, in heaven and on earth and under the earth, and every tongue confess that Jesus Christ is Lord, to the glory of God the Father." ~ Philippians 2:10-11 (ESV)

Under the New Covenant, the name of Jesus became the greatest name with the greatest authority and with the most power.

Before Christ came, other names were used to deliver people from demons—the various names of angels. This was such a widespread practice that the author of Hebrews spends all of chapter 1 explaining *why the name of Jesus is superior to the names of angels.*

We read in the epistle to the Hebrews, chapter 1:1-4 (NIV):

"In the past God spoke to our ancestors through the prophets at many times and in various ways, but in these last days he has spoken to us by his Son, whom he appointed heir of all things, and through whom also he made the universe. The Son is the radiance of God's glory and the exact representation of his being, sustaining all things by his powerful word. After he had provided purification for sins, he sat down at the right hand of the Majesty in heaven. So he became as much superior to the angels as the name he has inherited is superior to theirs."

It is interesting to note that the transition between using the name of angels and the Name of Jesus towards exorcisms was obvious in the recorded events of Acts 19:13-17, where the itinerant Jews and the sons of Sceva (a Jewish chief priest) found out the hard way how NOT use the Name above all names—the Name of Jesus. They used the Name of Jesus without prior regeneration or faith in Him. In other words, they had no bestowed authority. As a result, they were attacked violently by the possessed man and left that house battered, bruised, naked, and bloodied.

Now, you understand better why the author of the Book of Hebrews felt it was necessary to address the matter of angels. It was to set the record straight for the Hebrews. It was to bear testimony to the ultimate Kingdom power of the Name Above All Names, that of *Yahushua HaMashiach*, Jesus Christ, the Lord of lords and King of kings!

> *"In that day you will ask nothing of me. Truly, truly, I say to you, whatever you ask of the Father in my name, he will give it to you. Until now you have asked nothing in my name. Ask, and you will receive, that your joy may be full."*
> ~ *John 16:23-24 (ESV)*

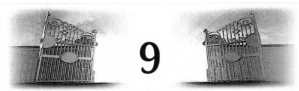

9

WHAT YOU SAY IS WHAT YOU GET

Uncovering the Power of the Tongue

"The magic of words is that they have power to do more than convey meaning; not only do they have the power to make things clear, they make things happen." ~ Frederick Buechner

In chapter two, I mentioned how in order to understand the Bible, the Book of Genesis is the key. Indeed, if we don't understand the beginning of a thing, how can we tell its end or understand its purpose?

We are told that in the beginning:

> *"God said, let us make man in our image, after our likeness. [...] So God created man in his own image, in the image of God created he him; male and female created he them." ~ Genesis 1:26, 27 (KJV)*

Man was created in the image of God. And we know that while sin has disfigured or marred this image, we retained it, nonetheless.

So, make no mistake, to this day, we are still made in the image of God.

I'm sure, dear reader, that you already know this important truth. Therefore, and for this reason, many of God's attributes can still be found in man. We were given many of His mighty attributes, such as language, creativity, love, emotions, thought, freedom, etc. More could be added here, but it would be overly tedious for me to begin expounding on the attributes of God in man at this point in the book.

Nevertheless, I would like to focus on one particular attribute here: *the power of creative speech.*

Intelligent speech, first spoken and then written, is the greatest differentiator between man and animal. Conversely, we could say that intelligent speech is man's most God-like attribute. Not only is it God-given, but it is, yes, *God-like.*

And God Said...

One of the King's greatest and most interesting attributes is His power to speak things into existence—*His creative speech.*

We are told in the Genesis creation account (Genesis chapter 1) that *"God said"* and *"God called"* everything into being. In fact, in chapter one alone, this is recorded a whopping 16 times (10 x "said") + (6 x "called")! This is why Hebrews 11:3 (ESV) says: *"By faith we understand that the universe was created by the word of God."*

And Psalm 33:8-9 (ESV) says:

> *"Let all the earth fear the Lord; let all the inhabitants of the world stand in awe of Him. For He spoke, and it was done; He commanded, and it stood fast."*

But, is it a fair assertion to say that God, when He made man in His image, also gave Him the power of *creative speech*? Isn't this a little far-fetched? Besides, isn't this a New Age teaching or belief? Well, I often say that the New Age hasn't invented anything, and nothing is new under the sun. Furthermore, we want to see what the Bible says, don't we? And the Bible does indeed say that our speech and our tongue have tremendous power. In fact, it is safe to say that we do get what we say in large part during the course of our lives.

This, for some, is a fallacy. For others, a scary prospect. But for you, dear reader, I hope it is good news and the prospect of a better future as you learn to master your speech.

In the Master's Own Words

In the Book of James, the apostle goes to great lengths in explaining how our tongues are instruments of great power, blessing, or even calamity. In fact, the larger part of James chapter 3 (v. 1-12) is consecrated to the power of the tongue and the dangers of its misuse.

Another interesting fact is that while James is known as one of the chief apostles, he was also the (half) brother of Jesus. This means he grew up alongside Jesus in the same household. The Bible doesn't mention how much Jesus, as an elder brother, taught James prior to his apostleship. However, we can suppose that James was privy to many valuable lessons from his elder brother growing up.

But one thing is for sure, Jesus also knew and understood the power of the tongue when He said:

> *"I have not spoken on my own authority, but the Father who sent me has himself given me a commandment—what to say and what to speak. And I know that his commandment is eternal life. What I say, therefore, I say as the Father has told me." ~ John 12:49-50 (ESV)*

Jesus only spoke the words He heard from God. Think about that! And, if we consider that Jesus was also sinless, it brings us to reconsider the importance of how we speak.

The words we say and those we don't say determine much of how we live before God. Our words either defile us or make us holy. Our words can make us clean or unclean (Matthew 15:11, 18).

The prophet Isaiah, when he found himself brought before the Lord of creation, was distraught and fearful about one thing. He said:

> *"Woe is me! For I am lost; for I am a man of unclean lips, and I dwell in the midst of a people of unclean lips; for my eyes have seen the King, the Lord of hosts!" ~ Isaiah 6:5 (ESV)*

Isaiah, like our Lord, understood the power of the tongue and our accountability in its use.

Yes, we will be held accountable for how we wield our tongue—this mighty weapon of blessing or destruction. Jesus said:

> *"I tell you, on the day of judgment people will give account for every careless word they speak, for by your words you will be justified, and by your words you will be condemned."*
> *~ Matthew 12:36-37 (ESV)*

The Fruit of Your Words

The story is told of the Roman emperor Nero's mother. When Claudius became Emperor of Rome, Agrippina was restored to her rank and fortune. At once, she again took up the management of her child, the future Nero. As a child, he was beautiful, and in this, his mother took a special pride. From his youth, it seems that her main and only desire was to have her boy raised to the rank of Emperor. Astrologers and soothsayers warned her that his elevation to the throne would mean her murder. To all their dark prophecies of the future, she had but one reply: *"Occidant dum imperat,"* which means, *"Let him slay me, if only he reigns."* As history tells us, the cruel Nero put his very own mother to death.

Sadly, Agrippina's words became the death of her. She ate the sour fruit of her own words.

Another wicked man, Aleister Crowley, was a world-renowned dark occultist who lived from 1875 to 1947. The British press once dubbed him *"The Wickedest Man in the World."*

Crowley was born to a wealthy family in Royal Leamington Spa, Warwickshire. Early in his youth, he rejected his parents' strict Christian Plymouth Brethren faith to pursue an interest in Western esotericism.

Aside from his dabbling in all wicked practices and debauchery, he became the inventor of the religion of *The Thelema*, which was summed up by only one commandment: *"Do what thou wilt shall be the whole of the law."* This was obviously a knock towards Christianity's more thorough Ten Commandments.

Most people wonder how Crowley could develop into such a perverse human being in the first place. I believe I have, at least, a partial answer to this question.

You see, Crowley was rambunctious as a boy. In reaction to high energy and turbulence, his mother, Emily Bertha Crowley (née Bishop), often called him *"the Great Beast, the unholy monster of the Apocalypse,"* when he was growing up. Well, guess what? She spoke this upon her son, and it came to pass. That's what he became, *a beast.* Later, he even used that moniker to describe himself.

So, in her ignorance, Emily Bertha Crowley ate the fruit of her words—and they tasted very bitter.

The Book of Proverbs is full of admonitions about the use of our words. In it, Solomon, also known as the wisest of men, repeats in many places how not to speak words that are out of place, untimely, foolish, or ill-chosen.

Solomon reminds us in Proverbs 18:21 (NKJV) that:

> *"Death and life are in the power of the tongue, and those who love it will eat its fruits."*

In all honesty, for the longest time, I didn't understand these passages in the Book of Proverbs that emphasized the importance of words. Or rather, I didn't understand what was implied here and the extent of its application. I thought Solomon made too big a case out of our words. I believed he meant that if we didn't curse, swear, or use the Lord's name in vain, that was it for the Christian. I figured that if we didn't use lewd language and made efforts to season our speech with grace and kindness, that was more than enough. I failed to understand the greater power of our words—their creative power. This is what Solomon alluded to in many places in the Book of Proverbs.

> The words we speak act as seeds.

We should know that the words we speak act as seeds. There was definitely a time in my life when I didn't understand this fact. As a result, I sowed many weeds in the garden of my life which later became weeds.

When Elisabeth and I purchased our first house, we were three years into our marriage. We had already suffered many trials as a young couple. We had money troubles, extended family troubles, etc.

But this particular season was very trying for us. It brought us to the breaking point, and I had very little clue as to why this was. I didn't understand why we had so many hardships.

At the time, although we had both been believers for some time, we had a rather pessimistic outlook on life. I, for one, had been through much in my life, and this had bred a spirit of bitterness within me. I didn't understand much of the spiritual realities of the Kingdom. And I certainly didn't think much of the impact of our words. I thought such teachings were all derived from New Age hocus-pocus. All this to say that my words reflected the state of my soul—they were bitter. The glass was always half-empty, and I called it so. I was negative. I was a complainer. I thought the grass was always greener in my neighbour's yard. And guess what? For years, I ate of the fruit of my words.

Here is what happened to us in the span of about one to two years as new house owners…

👑 Two months after we moved into the house, thieves broke in while we were at work and stole our jewelry, precious keepsakes, and other goods. We felt violated.

- ♛ Later that year, a big tree broke and fell in our backyard after a bad storm.

- ♛ Also that year, a fire broke out in our backyard in our trash bins. It turns out I didn't know ashes could be dangerous. Okay, maybe that wasn't the fruit of my tongue. Perhaps it was just me being dumb. So, scratch that and keep reading...

- ♛ Later, while we were away on vacation in Florida, the sump pump back at our house broke, and our basement got flooded. We had thousands of dollars in damage and lost many family pictures and goods of all kinds.

- ♛ Later still, wasps made a nest into the inner wall of our house, which necessitated the services of an exterminator.

- ♛ We also got into a big car accident. Our Ford Escort Wagon got hit sideways by an 18-wheeler truck. If it hadn't been for angelic intervention, we would've died.

- ♛ And, last but not least, Elisabeth got pregnant around that time. Our first child, a daughter, died a few minutes after birth. I told you this sad story back in chapter five.

All of this happened in a very short span of time of about two years, maybe a bit more. It was excruciating on an individual level, and it took such a toll that it almost destroyed our marriage. I was beginning to feel cursed.

Of course, this was due mostly to the Enemy attacking us in no uncertain way. I figured that quickly enough. But what I didn't understand was how the devil had obtained a legal right to do so, mostly through the careless use of my own words. With my own tongue, I had cursed myself repeatedly.

Every day, my negative and careless words gave the Enemy a legal right to come against my wife and me.

For example, if I received an unexpected check, I would say something like: *"Well, this extra money is nice, but with the way our life goes, it probably won't last long."*

Well, guess what? It didn't last long. My car would break down the same week, or some other thing would happen that required some of that money—or all of it.

If my seniority at work enabled me to get some good summer vacation weeks, I would say something stupid like: *"Well, sure, we got some nice weeks off in July, but with our luck, we won't have enough money to enjoy ourselves during our time off."* Well, guess what? July came, and sure enough, we were broke. We were stuck on a staycation instead of enjoying a fun vacation.

Our lives went on like this for years.

One blessed evening, I listened to a podcast where the host was interviewing Pat Holiday, a deliverance minister from Florida. She spoke about the use of the tongue. She said:

> *"Most of the time, people are their own worst enemy. They give the devil a legal right to steal, kill, and destroy in their life through the words they speak. Many people I deal with in my ministry have cursed themselves."*

This was the first time I heard someone in ministry explain how the tongue operates and how it can bless or curse us. This revelation brought me on a path of renewed understanding. It also brought me on a healing journey and gave me the wisdom to choose my words more carefully. Did it happen overnight? No. It took years for me to just begin to curve my negative verbal habits. In fact, I'm still far from where I want to be. The fruit of my tongue is still not satisfactory to me. But, by the grace of God, I'm now lightyears ahead of where I used to be.

The Power of Words

"Words are the most powerful thing in the universe…words are containers. They contain faith, or fear, and they produce after their kind." ~ Charles Capps

My life experiences taught me the hard way about the power of words. It used to be that when I read in the Bible about words, what to speak, when to keep silent, carefully choosing our words, et al., I thought this meant that words could cut deep, or hurt feelings, or make us seem foolish, or lead us to blaspheme. There is no denying that ill-chosen words can do all these things. However, I thought words had power in a limited sense only—mostly how they affect thoughts or feelings. I couldn't fathom that words might have power in a supernatural, positive, and creative sense as well. I didn't believe our words could affect our lives or our circumstances. In that respect, I was not different from most evangelicals.

I concur with Reinhard Bonnke, the German evangelist who said: *"Christianity is either supernatural or nothing at all."*

"Christianity is either supernatural or nothing at all." ~ Reinhard Bonnke

This statement aligns with Kingdom reality. It's supernatural!

While most believers will never deny the power of *God's Word* itself, what they perceive as its power, or the reason for its power, may greatly differ. The most conservative believers will tell you that only God's Word has power when spoken directly by Him, while the most charismatic among us will say that we wield in our tongues the God-given power to create as we speak. So, which is it? Or is the truth somewhere in-between?

Abracadabra? *Say What?!*

I find it distressing and sad that most people involved in witchcraft have a better handle and understanding of the power of words than the average Christian. In my book, *The Law of Attraction: Is It for Christians?* I spoke about this fact. I wrote:

"Those who practice magick and the occult understand the power of the tongue and apply it more than believers, albeit in their own twisted way. Ever think about where we got the term 'magick spells' from? The word 'spell' comes from the word 'spelling' i.e. how we write or say words. Our utterances have power, more than we can ever know."

Even the popular word they coined, *'abracadabra'*, expresses their grasp of the power of words. While no one is sure about the exact origin of the strange word, many have said that it is from the Aramaic *'avra kadavra'*, meaning *'it will be created in my words'* or *'I create as I speak'*.

Contrary to what most churchians believe, the power of the tongue isn't, as the church lady would probably coin it, *"a satanic doctrine reserved for witches and warlocks"* (although the devil would have us stick to those guns). It is an actual and effectual biblical truth that occultists have cleverly hijacked.

Remember, witches cannot operate outside of the laws God has set of His own authority. God's Word settles all matters. He has chosen to create man with the ability to speak words with the intent to achieve results. Therefore, witches simply found selfish, ignorant, and misdirected ways to use this law, and others, to achieve results. When they cast spells, they do it from soulish, fleshly, or demonic motives.

This now brings the question: *Can believers have wrong motives when speaking words, declarations, and decrees, and thus inadvertently engage in witchcraft?* The short answer is *yes*. Unfortunately, it happens, but mostly out of ignorance, as was the case for me in my earlier years. Anything that is not of the Spirit is of the flesh.

Also, there is, unfortunately, such a thing known as "charismatic witchcraft," which is simply done when a believer intentionally speaks ill-advised, selfish, fleshly, or evil words outside of the will of God. After all, we were charged to pray according to the will of God, and Jesus said we would be held accountable for all idle words spoken. But this whole topic would take us on a whole other tangent.

Ironically, the word *"occult"* means hidden. Furthermore, the etymology of the word *esoteric* means: secret; intended to be communicated only to the initiated; profound, 1650s, from Latinized form of Greek *esoterikos "belonging to an inner circle."*

Satan has indeed *hidden* many things from those whom he wants to deceive. All in all, by keeping Christians in the dark about the power of their tongue, Satan has pulled off a threefold coup:

1. He prevented much of the Church's authority from being used intentionally and powerfully.

2. He brought many believers to curse themselves by turning negative thoughts into negative words.

3. He empowered his own by giving them this hidden knowledge to use for his kingdom and against the Kingdom of God.

The fact remains though, we do indeed create much of our reality by the words we use.

The Bible confirms this. In Proverbs 13:3 (NKJV), we read:

> *"He who guards his mouth preserves his life, but he who opens wide his lips shall have destruction."*

And in Proverbs 12:14(a) (NKJV), it says:

> *"A man will be satisfied with good by the fruit of his mouth…"*

So, whether we speak ill or blessing, the word of God tells us that we do reap what we sow, including with our tongue. Words are seeds we sow, and make no mistake about it, they too are subject to the universal Kingdom law of *sowing and reaping*.

There is a slew of reasons and ramifications that explains how this is so. And to be honest, this complex and fascinating subject could be made into a book, even a series of books!

Nevertheless, we could sum it up with these vital points:

- We are made in His image. This simple truth's depth is often misunderstood. When He speaks, worlds are created, and mountains crumble. To a lesser degree, He has endowed faith-filled human beings to accomplish similar feats. This is why Jesus said: *"Truly I tell you, <u>if anyone says</u> to this mountain, 'Go, throw yourself into the sea,' and does not doubt in their heart <u>but believes that what they say will happen</u>, it will be done for them."* ~ Mark 11:23 (NIV) (emphasis mine).

- When we speak the Word of God, we agree with Heaven and thus loose the Word of God to *accomplish what He desires and achieve the purpose for which He sent it* (Isaiah 55:11).

- When we speak biblical words of purpose, faith, and power, we build up our faith and align ourselves with the Word of God concerning our destiny and assignment, setting ourselves up, through faith, for success, provided we back it up with purposeful action (Joshua 1:8).

- When we speak negative, foolish, or careless words, we may inadvertently curse ourselves, others, or worse: give the devil a legal right to attack our lives and cause harm to ourselves or even our loved ones. Negative words cause chinks in our armor that can sometimes bring years of trials upon us and even our loved ones. This is why Solomon said:

"When there are many words, wrongdoing is unavoidable, but one who restrains his lips is wise." ~ Proverbs 10:19 (NASB)

I would now like to give you two powerful examples of the power of words spoken over our lives.

Speak Life... Always!

Life and death are indeed in the power of the tongue. One woman found out just how true this is back in 2001. The amazing story of both her and her husband is told in the May 2020 issue of *Victory Magazine*.

Jim and Christa Tomlin are both committed Kingdom believers. One night back in 2001, Jim suffered a violent demonic attack that was meant to kill him. It all began when he surprised his teenage son, Zane, in the den, watching MTV. They were playing Marilyn Manson songs backwards (notice a pattern here: songs = words, backward demonic words released into the atmosphere). He immediately rebuked his son and shut off the TV because MTV was not allowed in their home. Jim then walked out.

A few moments later is when the attack happened.

Jim felt an incredible pain in his chest. In his own words, he described it *"As though someone reached inside and grabbed me between my heart and stomach. The pain was incredible. Worse than anything I'd ever experienced."*

He said he could feel a demonic force pulling him downward. His spirit was brought in utter darkness, and he saw two demons dragging him deeper and deeper in utter darkness. That's when he collapsed.

The loud thud and groan from Jim awakened his wife, Christa, who had gone to bed earlier that night.

She got out of bed and found her husband face down on the kitchen floor with his right cheek up, and his arms splayed out. He was convulsing, and his eyes were rolled back in his head. He let out one breath, and that was it. He didn't let out another. Jim wasn't moving; he wasn't breathing.

Zane, their son, also witnessed the scene, and he was in shock at the sight of his father laying still on the floor.

All kinds of voices crept into Christa's mind at that point, and fear began to grip her about her life without Jim. But Christa was not your average Christian—she was a Spirit-filled Kingdom woman who had been filling her heart and mind with the Words of God for weeks before this tragic event. For days on end, she would listen to uplifting Kingdom teachings and content. Therefore, she knew the fearful voices in her head were not of God, and she understood *the power of words*. She knew that whatever words she spoke at this time had to be chosen carefully.

So, after a moment of still silence and keeping her cool and her faith, she stood over her dead husband and with bold authority, declared: *"In the Name of Jesus be made whole!"*

Nothing happened.

Undaunted, she grabbed Jim's shoulders and turned him on his back. Again, she said: *"In the Name of Jesus be made whole!"*

She didn't utter another word. She knew better.

She and Zane both stood still and waited.

Meanwhile, Jim, who was probably out of his own body and still in demonic darkness, heard Jesus speak not once, but twice! Jim turned around and saw the Lord! Then, Jesus grabbed him and pulled him back into his body!

He was back. Bruised but alive.

Jim eventually made a full and miraculous recovery following this ordeal.

So, through his wife's faith-filled words, Jim was brought back to life. Christa spoke life, and sure enough, *life happened!*

The account in the magazine brings many more details to this incredible testimony, but the gist of it is here. Words, spoken in faith, have tremendous power!

But what about negative words? Do they possess the same power? This next story serves more as a serious cautionary tale...

The Fateful Words of a Sports Hero

On January 26, 2020, the world of sports was shaken with the terrible news that basketball star, Kobe Bryant, died in a terrible helicopter accident along with his 13-year-old daughter—Gianna, basketball coach—John Altobelli, five other passengers, and the pilot.

Bryant was *"Regarded as one of the greatest players of all time, who helped the Lakers win five NBA championships, and was an 18-time All-Star, a 15-time member of the All-NBA Team, a 12-time member of the All-Defensive Team, the 2008 NBA Most Valuable Player (MVP), and a two-time NBA Finals MVP. Bryant also led the NBA in scoring twice, and ranks fourth on the league's all-time regular season scoring and all-time postseason scoring lists."* (Wikipedia)

It was a tragic accident, and although I am not a basketball fan (I'm more of a hockey fan), I remember it well, and I too, felt the weight of the sad news.

A few days later, one of Kobe's best friends and NBA star in his own right, Tracy McGrady, gave a short interview on ESPN's show, *The Jump*. As he confided to the show's host, Rachel Nichols, he was in tears and visibly still very shaken.

What he said that day, however, eventually went viral and shocked people everywhere.

The interview didn't go viral because it concerned one of the greatest legends of the NBA. No. It went viral because of the weight it carried, humanly speaking.

Tracy McGrady, talking about a younger Kobe Bryant, said the following:

"This sounds crazy, but Kobe spoke this," McGrady said.

"He spoke this. He used to say all the time, 'I want to die young.'"

"Really?" interjected Rachel Nichols, visibly shocked, bringing a trembling hand to her own mouth.

McGrady continued: *"He used to say: 'I want to die young. I want to be immortalized. I want to have my career be better than Michael Jordan, and I want to die young.' And I just thought he was so crazy for saying that."*

In a different interview, former teammate John Salley, when told of McGrady's interview, was asked if he had heard Kobe say this.

He answered, *"No, what I heard, and how he would say it to me, is, he said: 'I do everything young. I do it all young.'"*

Kobe Bryant said these things mostly as a young man entering the NBA. It was no doubt attributable to his youthful zeal and bravado. Surely, as a 41-year-old father of four precious daughters, he had no true desire to die. And yet, the words he spoke, probably more than once, had a tremendous impact on his destiny. This sad demise indeed serves as a powerful cautionary tale when it comes to *the use of your tongue.*

I believe that by speaking these words, Kobe Bryant unwittingly brought it upon himself, just as I had in my early married life, and most probably gave a legal right to the Enemy to launch a merciless and sudden attack on his life.

The Bible tells us that the thief comes indeed to steal, *kill,* and destroy (John 10:10). And we must never give him ammunition through the use of our words.

There's Power in Agreement

In the stories told so far in this chapter, there is an underlying and powerful Kingdom principle at work. In all cases, the persons involved were either in agreement with heaven or with hell—and that, knowingly or not.

For Christa Tomlin, she was in agreement with Heaven, with the Holy Spirit, and based on His witness and hers, she spoke life. The result was miraculous. As for Kobe, unfortunately, through the power of his words, he (unwittingly) came in agreement with the wrong voice, and it spelled disaster.

In the Lord's prayer, we are taught to come in agreement with heaven when we pray: *"Thy will be done on earth as it is in heaven."* The Bible tells us about this agreement/witnessing principle in many instances.

> *"A single witness shall not suffice against a person for any crime or for any wrong in connection with any offense that he has committed. Only on the evidence of two witnesses or of three witnesses shall a charge be established."* Deuteronomy 19:15 (ESV)

> *"I call heaven and earth as witnesses today against you, that I have set before you life and death, blessing and cursing; therefore choose life, that both you and your descendants may live."* Deuteronomy 30:19 (NKJV)

> *"But if they will not listen, take one or two others along, so that 'every matter may be established by the testimony of two or three witnesses.'"* Matthew 18:16 (NIV)

> *"Again, truly I tell you that if two of you on earth agree about anything they ask for, it will be done for them by my Father in heaven. For where two or three gather in my name, there am I with them."* Matthew 18:19-20 (NIV)

> *"This will be my third visit to you. 'Every matter must be*

established by the testimony of two or three witnesses." 2
Corinthians 13:1 (NIV)

*"And the Spirit is the one who testifies, because the Spirit is the
truth. For there are three that testify: the Spirit and the water
and the blood; and these three agree." 1 John 5:6-8 (ESV)*

So, two or three witnesses, when in agreement, can be a powerful
thing. This works through people but also is found in principles of
creation and spiritual reality.

Here are some instances where two witnesses are pictured as
principles in the Bible:

- God created the heavens and the earth (Genesis 1:1)
- God created light and darkness (Genesis 1:3-4)
- God created night and day (Genesis 1:5)
- God created land and sea (Genesis 1:9-10)
- God created the sun and the moon (Genesis 1:16)
- God created male and female (Genesis 1:27)
- God created heaven and hell

I could go on and on, but you now see that this principle of
witnesses in agreement is prevalent throughout Scripture. It is found
throughout creation as a *principle*.

Finally, we are told that at the time of the End, God will send
His two witnesses (Revelation 11). While we do not know for sure
if it will be Enoch and Elijah, or Moses and Elijah, or perhaps some
others; these two (Moses and Elijah) were nonetheless witnesses at
the Mount of Transfiguration along with the three apostles (Peter,
James, and John) in Matthew 17:1–8, Mark 9:2–8, and Luke 9:28–36.

But why was it Moses and Elijah on the mountain speaking
with Jesus? Why these two in particular? Because, as the most
suitable representatives of the Law (Moses) and the Prophets

(Elijah), they testified that Jesus did, indeed, come to accomplish the law and the prophets (Matthew 5:17). They were acting as those two witnesses then.

And speaking of Peter, James, and John; in many instances, Jesus brought them along with Him wherever He went to serve as His witnesses.

This just goes to show that there is a definite power in having people or the Holy Spirit witnessing and in agreement with you to accomplish your Kingdom destiny.

This then begs the question... *Who are you coming in agreement with generally?* Do you often agree with Heaven or with Hell?

When in Doubt, *Keep It Shut*

As important as speaking the right words is, until we get to a point where our words are seasoned with Kingdom grace, wisdom, meaning, and power, there is one thing that we can do more easily. And that would be keeping our mouth shut. Yes, you read that right. As a general rule, when in doubt, *keep it shut*.

In all honesty, this has been (and still is) very challenging for me. When I was younger and found myself in social settings, I used to get nervous. And when I got nervous, my reflex was to speak and jest more. As you can imagine, this got me in all kinds of *"foot in mouth"* situations that I regretted—some to this day.

So, take it from me, if you're going to master this deceitful little organ known as the tongue, the best way to get started is to speak... *less*. In fact, there are no ill side-effects to speaking less, except perhaps, risking to appear boring. But as we have seen, there can be horrid consequences when we say too much.

A friend of mine once posted a fascinating compilation of Scriptures on Social Media. The compilation was titled: *When to Keep Your Mouth Shut*. Here it is:

1. Don't open your mouth…

2. In the heat of anger. (Proverbs 14:17)

3. When you don't have all the facts. (Proverbs 18:13)

4. When you haven't verified the story. (Deuteronomy 17:6)

5. If your words will offend a weaker brother. (1 Corinthians 8:11)

6. If your words will be a poor reflection of the Lord or your friends and family. (1 Peter 2:21-23)

7. When you are tempted to joke about sin. (Proverbs 14:9)

8. When you would be ashamed of your words later. (Proverbs 8:8)

9. When you're tempted to make light of holy things. (Ecclesiastes 5:2)

10. If your words would convey a wrong impression. (Proverbs 17:27)

11. If the issue is none of your business. (Proverbs 14:10)

12. When you are tempted to tell an outright lie. (Proverbs 4:24)

13. If your words will damage someone's reputation. (Proverbs 16:27)

14. If your words will destroy a friendship. (Proverbs 25:28)

15. When you are feeling critical. (James 3:9)

16. If you can't speak without yelling. (Proverbs 25:28)

17. When it is time to listen. (Proverbs 13:1)

18. If you may have to eat your words later. (Proverbs 18:21)

19. If you have already said it more than once (then it becomes nagging). (Proverbs 19:13)

20. When you are tempted to flatter a wicked person. (Proverbs 24:24)

21. When you are supposed to be working instead. (Proverbs 14:23)

All of these admonitions sum up Proverbs 21:23 (NLT) nicely:

> *"Watch your tongue and keep your mouth shut, and you will stay out of trouble."*

Kingdom Declarations and Decrees

I opened this chapter with the words of Jesus saying:

> *"I have not spoken on my own authority, but the Father who sent me has himself given me a commandment—what to say and what to speak. And I know that his commandment is eternal life. What I say, therefore, I say as the Father has told me." ~ John 12:49-50 (ESV)*

So, Jesus only spoke the words the Father told Him—the Words of God, which bear the authority (are authored by) of God. Well, if this is good for Jesus, shouldn't it be good for us as well?

Speaking out loud the Words of God or uttering declarations based on the Word of God is called decreeing and declaring. A decree and a declaration

> Jesus only spoke the words the Father told Him—the Words of God, which bear the authority (are authored by) of God.

are alike and have similar results, but they are not the same.

The definition of a declaration is *a written or oral indication of a fact, opinion, or belief.*

And the definition of a decree is *an edict or law.*

From a Kingdom perspective, this is quite interesting. A *decree* is usually spoken directly by a monarch, an emperor, or a king. It is the official word of a ruler, which is then binding to the Kingdom he rules and becomes law for its citizens. This is why the Word of God is so powerful. Whatever a king decrees becomes law in the kingdom He rules. Therefore, since God is King, His Word is law.

In daily practice, we should use our tongues to both declare and decree God's promises over our lives and the lives of our loved ones through intercession.

When a Kingdom citizen decrees a thing, he basically reiterates out loud the promises and Words of the King over his life.

For example, if I say out loud this scripture every day: *"My God shall supply all my need according to his riches in glory by Christ Jesus"* (Philippians 4:19), I am indeed decreeing the Word of God. Because it is the Word of God, albeit adapted in the first person, it is a *decree*. Using our tongue to decree God's Word is immensely powerful! We then become partners with our King in releasing His Word. And God said of His Word:

> *"So shall my word be that goeth forth out of my mouth: it shall not return unto me void, but it shall accomplish that which I please, and it shall prosper in the thing whereto I sent it." ~ Isaiah 55:11 (KJV)*

Whereas *a declaration* is an adaptation of truth that I say out loud. For example, if I were to say out loud: *"Because God loves me, He sends angels to protect me and brings me in the path of prosperity,"* I am declaring a *Kingdom truth*, even though it is not necessarily a Kingdom Law (the exact Words of the King, a.k.a., a decree).

Whether you decide to *decree* things over your life or *declare* things over your life, the results will bless and empower you to fulfill your Kingdom assignment. You will, through your lips, open up the favor of the Father on your path.

I know some of my readers will say, *"This is the Name-it-and-claim-it heresy! It's a Charismatic thing."* To that, I answer: No. *It is a God thing.* It is a Kingdom thing. It is a faith thing. Make no mistake about it; it shall be done unto you according to your faith and your words.

> Make no mistake about it; it shall be done unto you according to your faith and your words.

As much as we like to assign labels to make ourselves feel better, this is not the way of the Kingdom.

As citizens of the Kingdom of God, we should always use the language that aligns with that of our homeland.

There are two official languages in Canada: English and French. If I did not speak either, I would struggle here. It would hinder my chance of employment, success, and relationships. So, speaking these languages benefits me greatly as a Canadian citizen. The same can be said of us as Kingdom citizens. The official languages in the Kingdom are *Prayer, Fasting, Supplication, Intercession, Decrees, and Declarations*. When we use these "Official Kingdom Languages," we are in alignment with the King, with Heaven, and with His will for us on the earth. We thus benefit from what the Kingdom has to offer.

Hey, if this was good enough for Jesus, it's good enough for all of us.

And now, decree this:

> *"You will also declare a thing, and it will be established for you; so light will shine on your ways." ~ Job 22:28 (NKJV)*

Calling Things That Are Not

We are reminded in Romans 4:17 (NKJV) that God *"gives life to the dead and calls those things which do not exist as though they did."*

And, faithful to His Father in heaven, Jesus did just that while on earth. He called things that did not exist as though they did. He also named things or people. And we saw the significance and authority behind naming things or people. Jesus judiciously used His own tongue and understood the power of words said in faith.

So, here are a few examples of Jesus *calling things that are not as though they are* during His ministry:

- ♛ Amidst the storm, He rebuked the wind and said to the waves, "Be still" (Matthew 8:23–27, Mark 4:35–41, and Luke 8:22–25). So it was.

259

- ♛ He changed Simon's name to Peter, a.k.a., the rock (Matthew 16:16-18; John 1:42). He was.

- ♛ He rebuked the fever from Peter's mother-in-law (Luke 4:38-39).

- ♛ He told the paralytics (two of them) to "rise up and walk" (Matthew 9:1-8; Mark 2:1-12; John 5:1-17). They did.

- ♛ He said that Jairus' daughter was asleep instead of agreeing with those who said she was dead (Mark 5:21-43). Indeed, she was asleep.

- ♛ He said Lazarus' sickness was not unto death, but to serve for the glory of God and His Son (John 11:4). It did.

- ♛ He cursed the fig tree which didn't yield any fruit (Mark 11:12-21). And cursed it was.

- ♛ He calls us by name (John 10:3). And we follow Him.

Now, I know what some of you might be thinking. You might reason, *"But that is good for God, and for Jesus, not for me."* Really? Are you sure?

Don't forget that you are made in His image. He creates as He speaks. And as this chapter proved, just like our Father in heaven, our words can and do (to a lesser extent than God, of course) bring forth what we say—whether consciously or not. Furthermore, the Lord said we would do greater things than He (John 14:12). And just think about the Great Commission's added benefits given to us in Mark 16:17-18 (ESV), which states:

> *"And these signs will accompany those who believe: in my name they will cast out demons; they will speak in new tongues; they will pick up serpents with their hands; and if they drink any deadly poison, it will not hurt them; they will lay their hands on the sick, and they will recover."*

Be a Thermostat, Not a Thermometer

Renowned faith teacher, Charles Capps, once gave a powerful analogy of how to use our faith and words by aligning them with Kingdom reality instead of earthly reality. He wrote the following:

> *"I have come to the conclusion that there are two kinds of Christians. There are Christians who act like thermometers. They rehearse the problem over and over, but never do anything to change it. Then there are some who function as thermostats and change things for the better. The thermostat on the wall of your home is wired to the heart of that unit which is designed to control the temperature in your house. That thermostat has a built-in thermometer to reveal the present condition (temperature) and a dial to make the desired change. When you change the dial setting, it makes a demand on the heating and cooling unit. The thermometer only tells you how it is at the present time. But by setting the thermostat to what you desire, you can change present facts."*

So, in the Kingdom, there is no sickness, poverty, or death. Jesus always spoke the things of the Kingdom into existence in the earth realm. By always speaking His Father's words and not of His own authority, He brought God's authority into all matters.

> *"Ask yourself: 'How is it in heaven? Is there sickness, disease, poverty?' No. Then you have authority to bind it here on earth." ~ Charles Capps*

And to do this, you need to know how to use your tongue for the Kingdom.

When You Get Tongue-Tied

In Romans 8:26-27 (ESV), the apostle Paul tells us:

> *"Likewise the Spirit helps us in our weakness. For we do not*

know what to pray for as we ought, but the Spirit himself intercedes for us with groanings too deep for words. And he who searches hearts knows what is the mind of the Spirit, because the Spirit intercedes for the saints according to the will of God."

It is common for even the strongest believers to not know what or how to pray. Depending on circumstances, it can happen to the best of us. Fortunately, we know from this scripture that the Spirit intercedes in our favor when this occurs.

When we just don't know what to speak, the Spirit comes through for us *"with groanings too deep for words."*

The Spirit also comes through for us through *glossolalia*, better known as *speaking in tongues*. Those who were baptized in the Holy Ghost enjoy the privilege of this gift. They testify as to how many times the Spirit of God has interceded on their behalf in an unknown language during prayer times. Speaking in tongues brings the believer into the most intimate fellowship with the Lord. It makes the believer's spirit call through and to the Spirit of God, or, as the Scripture says, *"Deep calls unto deep"* (Psalm 42:7).

The Spirit of God knows perfectly how to speak the language of God in a way that far surpasses any words we can come up with on our own. Whether He does it through speaking in tongues, or through deep groanings, or desperate sighs of the heart, He makes sure that our prayers pierce the thick darkness and reach the throne room of the King of Glory.

> The Spirit of God knows perfectly how to speak the language of God in a way that far surpasses any words we can come up with on our own.

10

TRUSTING IN KINGDOM WEALTH AND PROVISION

Rethinking Your Way to Abundance

"When I think on God's Kingdom, I am compelled to be silent because of its immensity, because God's Kingdom is none other than God Himself with all His riches." ~ Meister Eckhart (14th century mystic)

Have you ever heard the story of the rich man who was near death? He was very grieved because he had worked so hard for his money, and he wanted to be able to take it with him to heaven. So, he began to pray that he might be able to take some of his wealth with him.

An angel heard his plea and appeared to him. *"Sorry, but you can't take your wealth with you,"* he said.

The man implored the angel to speak to God on his behalf to see if He might bend the rules. The man continued to pray that his wealth could follow him to heaven. The angel reappeared and informed the man that God has decided to allow him to take one suitcase with him. Overjoyed, the man gathers his largest suitcase and fills it his wealthiest possession: *pure gold bars*. He then set his suitcase beside his bed at the ready.

Sure enough, soon afterward, the man dies and shows up at the Gates of Heaven, where St. Peter greets him. The apostle, seeing the suitcase, says, *"Hold on, you can't bring that in here!"*

The man then explains to St. Peter that he was granted special permission from God and asks him to verify his story with the Lord. Sure enough, St. Peter checks and comes back saying, *"You're right. You are allowed one suitcase, but I'm supposed to check its contents before letting it through."*

St. Peter then opens the suitcase to inspect the worldly items that the man found too precious to leave behind and exclaims, *"Unbelievable! You were granted a unique privilege and could have brought untold riches, and you chose to bring... pavement?!"*

I always liked this story because it truly portrays the unlimited wealth of the Kingdom. Indeed, the streets of the heavenly city are paved with gold (Revelation 21:21). This clearly indicates how wealthy the King is. His wealth is limitless. In fact, despite what the devil would have us believe, God still owns it all! Consider these verses:

- 👑 **Exodus 19:5:** *"All the earth is Mine."*
- 👑 **Deuteronomy 10:14:** *"Behold, to the LORD your God belong heaven and the highest heavens, the earth and all that is in it."*
- 👑 **Job 41:11:** *"Whatever is under the whole heaven is Mine."*
- 👑 **Psalm 24:1:** *"The earth is the LORD's , and everything in it, the world, and all who live in it."*

A Kingdom of Paradoxes

While our Father and King own it all, the way we access this wealth and provision is not something that comes easy to most people. I like what educator Kent M. Keith said about the paradoxical and unexpected ways of the Kingdom:

"Jesus used paradoxes to help us see the kingdom of God. His paradoxical statements turned the secular world upside down. As we have already noted, He said that 'whoever wants to become great among you must be your servant, and whoever wants to be first must be your slave.' He said

*that 'the last shall be first, and the first shall be last.' He said:
'I tell you the truth, unless you change and become like little
children, you will never enter the kingdom of heaven.' He
said that 'Whoever finds his life will lose it, and whoever
loses his life for My sake will find it.'"*

The least we can say is that the Kingdom of God is, unlike most of
our latest tech, counter-intuitive. Indeed, the Kingdom is a system of…

1. **Exaltation through Humility (James 4:10)**
2. **Strength through Weakness (2 Corinthians 12:10)**
3. **Freedom through Servitude (Romans 6:18)**
4. **Gaining through Losing (Philippians 3:7-8)**
5. **Living through Dying (John 12:24)**
6. **Finding through Losing (Matthew 10:39)**
7. **Receiving through Giving (Acts 20:35)**
8. **Leading through serving (Luke 18:27)**

For the new believer and the seasoned one alike, this requires
some getting used to—especially in the areas of money, work,
provision, and giving. This is because: "

> *"The children of this world are more shrewd in dealing with
> the world around them than are the children of the light." ~
> Luke 16:8 (NLT)*

In other words, the unregenerate children of this world, *of which
we once were*, elbow their way through life. It's no wonder since we
are told from youth that "it's a dog-eat-dog" world and that it's all
about "survival of the fittest." As a result, we strive, push, and shove
to make a place for ourselves in a very loud and competitive world.

Famous evangelist, Billy Graham, once said:

> *"If a person gets his attitude toward money straight, it will
> help straighten out almost every other area in his life."*

> "If a person gets his attitude toward money straight, it will help straighten out almost every other area in his life." ~ Billy Graham

And yet, this is very challenging. Why is that?

Because in the world system ruled by Satan, people are always in survival mode. For those who operate in the system of this world, the curse (of Genesis 3) hasn't been lifted, so shrewdness is common—even necessary in some cases. In other words, for those who aren't born again, the way to sustenance and provision is still through painful toil and sweat alone, as the King decreed it in Genesis 3:17-19:

> *"Then to Adam He said, 'Because you have heeded the voice of your wife, and have eaten from the tree of which I commanded you, saying, 'You shall not eat of it': 'Cursed is the ground for your sake; in toil you shall eat of it all the days of your life. Both thorns and thistles it shall bring forth for you, and you shall eat the herb of the field. In the sweat of your face you shall eat bread till you return to the ground, for out of it you were taken; for dust you are, and to dust you shall return.'"*

The curse of Adam made obtaining our daily bread very difficult. The ground didn't yield its fruit effortlessly anymore. This meant that Adam now needed to set his alarm clock every morning, reluctantly get up, and go do a job that he found hard, unrewarding, and painful.

When Christ came to re-establish all things and brought access to the Kingdom of God; however, we were given another way, a different way, a new way—an alternate reality of sorts. Suddenly, in the Kingdom, we were brought to the realization that we do not need to elbow our way to survival anymore. We are told to:

> *"Seek first the kingdom of God and his righteousness, and all these things will be added to you." Matthew 6:33 (ESV)*

Nevertheless, for most believers, myself included, living out this new Kingdom reality is easier said than done. Unfortunately, for most, they still cling to the old way of doing things because they find it requires too much faith to live according to the new way.

Although they despise painful toil and sweat and the devil's eat-or-be-eaten ways, they cannot wrap their minds, and much less their faith, around the words of Christ. Besides, they're now used to the world system. It's what they know. They've grown accustomed to it. Ironically, and sadly, for many believers, it's a case of *the devil we know is better than the Christ we don't know.*

Restoration from Trauma

Embracing Kingdom living is a gradual, sometimes painful, and sometimes lengthy *process,* not unlike trauma recovery.

Living under the ways of the devil for so long before we come to Christ has its effect on our identity, psyche, and outlook. Only the love, care, and provision of God can undo these negative effects. In many ways, the present world system traumatizes us. It keeps us in fear—fear of failure, fear of lack, and fear of man. But praise be to God, the King, because His *"perfect love casts out fear"* (1 John 4:18).

> In many ways, the present world system traumatizes us. It keeps us in fear—fear of failure, fear of lack, and fear of man. But praise be to God, the King, because His "perfect love casts out fear"

Trauma is defined as *"the lasting emotional response that often results from living through a distressing event or ongoing stress."*

I would surmise that living under the power of the Prince of this world before conversion would qualify as ongoing stress-inducing trauma, wouldn't you?

This is why it takes time for a Kingdom citizen to begin living out and benefiting from the ways of the Kingdom where strength is through weakness, exaltation is through humility, and riches come through giving. This isn't what we're told, and for most of us, it isn't what we've experienced either.

Rejoice! You Work for the King Now

This world can be an abusive place. Everybody suffers under painful toil and sweat in this cursed earth system.

If you've ever worked under an abusive boss or amidst a corrupt company culture, you know just how bad it can get. It takes its toll physically, mentally, and emotionally. It can lead to exhaustion, bitterness, and burn-out. These are the ways of the world system operated by the devil. These ways are not made to benefit you; they are made to benefit him and his kingdom of darkness.

But once you're a Kingdom citizen, you've literally obtained a job transfer. Our updated CV (Curriculum Vitae) can now read as *"rescued us from the kingdom of darkness and transferred into the Kingdom of his dear Son"* ~ Colossians 1:13 (NLT)

This means that you're now working for a new boss. His ways are as day and night compared with the devil's ways. (See picture).

God	Satan
Stills you	Rushes you
Reassures you	Frightens you
Leads you	Pushes you
Enlightens you	Confuses you
Forgives you	Condemns you
Calms you	Stresses you
Encourages you	Discourages you
Comforts you	Worries you

I once saw a *Burger King* ad the company had put out for the purpose of mass hiring. The ad read: *"Work for a king (not a clown). We're hiring!"* While this clever advertisement made me laugh, it also made me think about our own employment predicament as believers. Although born-again believers belong to the King, many are deceived and unwittingly still work for the devil.

Misgivings About Giving

Under the King's jurisdiction, there is a better way, a Kingdom way to obtain provision.

> *"If anyone is in Christ, he is a new creation; old things have passed away; behold, all things have become new."* ~ *2 Corinthians 5:17 (NKJV)*

The use of the term *"all things"* is not superlative here. It is true. And this includes the way to obtain our daily bread, make an income, and obtain provision for our individual Kingdom assignment.

You and I, as believers, are under a *new government.*

And like many things in the Kingdom, the way to obtain provision seems counter-intuitive.

Jesus shared this recipe when He said:

> *"Give, and it shall be given unto you; good measure, pressed down, and shaken together, and running over, shall men give into your bosom. For with the same measure that ye mete withal it shall be measured to you again."* ~ *Luke 6:38 (KJV)*

This is to say that as Kingdom citizens, our minds need to shift from *"how do I get more?"* to *"how do I give more?"*

Author N.T. Wright put it this way:

> *"The kingdom that Jesus preached and lived was all about a glorious, uproarious, absurd generosity."*

Unfortunately, many believers today have little understanding of what giving means and does in the Kingdom of God.

For example, how thrilled would you be if God gave you a conviction to give $500 to someone in your church today?

Or how about $5,000 to a ministry?

Or, what if God asked you to empty your bank account for a cause tomorrow? Would you do it?

If we're honest, most of us would probably show some resistance to such levels of giving.

Why? Because most of us have *misgivings about giving.*

> "The kingdom that Jesus preached and lived was all about a glorious, uproarious, absurd generosity."
> ~ N.T. Wright

As per our experience in this world system, we see giving as a sacrifice and not as a privilege. This is due to what I would call our *pre-Kingdom trauma.*

Jesus knew this when He said in Luke 12:32-34 (NIV):

> *"Do not be afraid, little flock, for your Father has been pleased to give you the kingdom. Sell your possessions and give to the poor. Provide purses for yourselves that will not wear out, a treasure in heaven that will never fail, where no thief comes near and no moth destroys. For where your treasure is, there your heart will be also."*

For the children of this world, in the earth curse system, giving is a sacrifice, and can be scary. But for the children of God, it's a privilege.

And here is why...

With Great Power...

One of the most iconic and inspirational phrases in all of pop culture is that of Peter Parker's (Spider-Man) Uncle Ben, who said, through the pen of Stan Lee, that *"With great power comes great responsibility."*

The Bible tells us (in the KJV text) in John 1:12:

> *"But as many as received him, to them gave he power to become the sons of God, even to them that believe on his name."*

The *power to become sons of God* is the greatest power ever given to men.

> The power to become sons of God is the greatest power ever given to men.

And, as we have seen so far in this book, with that *great power* comes many great responsibilities, one of which is that we are to be *generous souls*.

As Kingdom sons, citizens, and ambassadors of Christ, we have a great responsibility in keeping the flow of money alive in the Kingdom of God.

This is done by us not hanging on to it but by letting ourselves become conduits for it. This is a source of great blessing.

We should emulate Corrie Ten Boom, who said: "

> *"I have learned to hold all things loosely, so God will not have to pry them out of my hands."*

Kingdom Ca$hflow

A pastor once shared the story of how the Lord pressed him to give $500 to the guy next to him on an airplane. This amount was all he had left. While he obeyed the voice of the Lord, he only did so with great reticence. Well, the next day, he got home and found he had a check of $5000 waiting in his mailbox. Someone had sown the amount into his ministry.

Even though it seemed counter-intuitive, he didn't resist the prompting of the Holy Spirit and was rewarded for his faithfulness.

In fact, when the Spirit of the Lord tells us to give, He has our best interest at heart as well as the recipient. This story also shows us that money constantly flows in the Kingdom, like a river.

So, he gave $500, but another gave him $5000. And we can surmise that this other person who gave him $5000 got what was coming to him as well.

This principle of the flow of wealth is a *Kingdom law*. The Kingdom of God has the ultimate cash flow.

Wealth, in the Kingdom of God, operates by laws. Those who understand and apply these laws become wealthy. Those who do not understand and do not apply these laws remain poor. I explain these matters in much greater detail in my book: *5 Reasons God Wants You to Prosper* (available on Amazon).

God expects wealth to flow freely and without resistance in His Kingdom. This is why the Bible condemns the hoarding of money.

Ecclesiastes 5:13 (NIV) says:

> *"I have seen a grievous evil under the sun: wealth hoarded to the harm of its owners."*

And, in the New Testament, Jesus greatly condemned the hoarding of money, especially in the parable of the rich fool found in Luke 12:13-21 (NIV):

> *"Someone in the crowd said to him, 'Teacher, tell my brother to divide the inheritance with me.' Jesus replied, 'Man, who appointed me a judge or an arbiter between you?' Then he said to them, 'Watch out! Be on your guard against all kinds of greed; life does not consist in an abundance of possessions.' And he told them this parable: 'The ground of a certain rich man yielded an abundant harvest. He thought to himself, 'What shall I do? I have no place to store my crops.' 'Then he said, 'This is what I'll do. I will tear down my barns and build bigger ones, and there I will store my surplus grain.*

And I'll say to myself, 'You have plenty of grain laid up for many years. Take life easy; eat, drink and be merry.' But God said to him, 'You fool! This very night your life will be demanded from you. Then who will get what you have prepared for yourself?' 'This is how it will be with whoever stores up things for themselves but is not rich toward God.'"

Notice how he is called *a fool*, by God no less!

The early Church in the Book of Acts understood Kingdom wealth when they put everything in common. There was no hoarding in the early Church because they understood that hoarding is for fools.

In God's Kingdom economy, money is meant to be in constant movement, changing hands regularly to fulfill its mission from place to place—blessing many along the way.

> In God's Kingdom economy, money is meant to be in constant movement, changing hands regularly to fulfill its mission from place to place— blessing many along the way.

The Blessing of Giving

In Acts 20:35 (NIV), we read an interesting verse. In it, Paul says:

"In everything I did, I showed you that by this kind of hard work we must help the weak, remembering the words the Lord Jesus himself said: 'It is more blessed to give than to receive.'"

These words of Jesus are found nowhere else in the New Testament. Strange, isn't it? They might have been given as a Rhema Word to Paul, or perhaps he heard it from the other disciples as they recounted to him things Jesus said.

But the point is, *it is more blessed to give than to receive.*

In all honesty, I used to think it was more blessed to receive. I compared the thrill I got out of both activities. I compared how I felt when I gave with how I felt when I received. As a youth, it seemed to me that receiving was way more fun, therefore, more blessed.

To be honest, when I was younger, I just didn't see it. I mean, giving feels good, sure. *But I really loved receiving!*

I didn't understand God's kingdom laws about wealth back then. I didn't understand the blessedness associated with giving.

The blessedness of giving with purpose is not just because it makes you feel nice inside, *but because it puts you in a position of expectancy through God's Kingdom LAW of return.*

The *law of return* is best expressed by the Lord when He says in Luke 6:38 (NIV):

> *"Give, and it will be given to you. A good measure, pressed down, shaken together and running over, will be poured into your lap. For with the measure you use, it will be measured to you."*

And Paul said in 2 Corinthians 9:6 (NKJV):

> *"But this I say: He who sows sparingly will also reap sparingly, and he who sows bountifully will also reap bountifully."*

Once Upon a Supper of Pastors

A pastor who was teaching on the blessings of giving was expounding about these things and explained that when he got together with other pastors who understood how blessed it was to give, they actually got into fights.

But their quarrels were not on theological issues. Not at all.

He was saying how, since they are all gathered as kingdom citizens, they all fought over who would pick up the tab at the end of the meal.

Why?

Because they each wanted the blessing that comes from paying a meal to other men of God.

They understood the blessing of giving, of sowing into other Kingdom men's lives. They understood how it is, indeed, more blessed to give than to receive.

Giving to a King

Now, giving has its own rewards, but *where you give* will also determine the extent of that reward. When you sow into the Kingdom, you are in effect, giving to a King—the King of kings and Lord of lords.

Here is a principle you might not know:

> *A King, in order to preserve His glory, will never allow himself to be outgiven or outdone by anyone.*

When you give to a King, you can always expect to get back more than you gave. This principle is very much present and applicable in the Kingdom of God.

> A King, in order to preserve His glory, will never allow himself to be outgiven or outdone by anyone.

God, as King, will never allow Himself to be outgiven by anyone. This would diminish His glory, and He said it Himself:

> *"I am the Lord; that is my name; my glory I give to no other, nor my praise to carved idols." ~ Isaiah 42:8 (ESV)*

So, if as a child of God, you sow generously into His Kingdom, you're shopping for a blessing. You're not just going to get back from Him as a citizen of His Kingdom, but also as a child of the King. It's a double portion of blessing.

If it were even possible to outgive a King, you'd make Him look bad. Now, if an earthly king wouldn't have it, *how much more the King of glory?!*

Think about that.

A Wise Queen

One person who understood the principle of giving to a king better than anyone in the Bible is *the Queen of Sheba.*

Here is what we read about her in 2 Chronicles 9:1-4 (NIV):

"When the queen of Sheba heard of Solomon's fame, she came to Jerusalem to test him with hard questions. Arriving with a very great caravan—with camels carrying spices, large quantities of gold, and precious stones—she came to Solomon and talked with him about all she had on her mind. Solomon answered all her questions; nothing was too hard for him to explain to her. When the queen of Sheba saw the wisdom of Solomon, as well as the palace he had built, the food on his table, the seating of his officials, the attending servants in their robes, the cupbearers in their robes and the burnt offerings he made at the temple of the Lord, she was overwhelmed."

And then, in verses 9-12 (NIV), we read:

"Then she gave the king 120 talents of gold, large quantities of spices, and precious stones. There had never been such spices as those the queen of Sheba gave to King Solomon. (The servants of Hiram and the servants of Solomon brought gold from Ophir; they also brought algumwood and precious stones. The king used the algumwood to make steps for the temple of the Lord and for the royal palace, and to make harps and lyres for the musicians. Nothing like them had ever been seen in Judah.) King Solomon gave the queen of Sheba all she desired and asked for; he gave her more than

she had brought to him. Then she left and returned with her
retinue to her own country."

The Queen of Sheba understood deeply and experientially the
principle of giving to a king (she was of royal blood herself). She
brought as much as she could to Solomon.

That was wise.

As a result, the Bible tells us:

*"King Solomon gave the queen of Sheba all she desired and
asked for; he gave her more than she had brought to him."*

My advice: Be like the Queen of Sheba when it comes to giving
to the Lord. Give, sow generously into His Kingdom. This way, you
will have an abundance
on earth, and more
importantly, a treasure in
heaven.

> "If you want to prosper,
> prosper God." ~ Sherry K. White

"If you want to prosper, prosper God." ~ Sherry K. White

A Prophet's Reward

Jesus said the following in Matthew 10:40-42 (NIV):

*"Anyone who welcomes you welcomes me, and anyone who
welcomes me welcomes the one who sent me. Whoever welcomes
a prophet as a prophet will receive a prophet's reward, and whoever
welcomes a righteous person as a righteous person will receive a
righteous person's reward. And if anyone gives even a cup of cold water
to one of these little ones who is my disciple, truly I tell you, that person
will certainly not lose their reward."*

What reward was He referring to? What is a prophet's reward?

Well, to answer this question, let us consider an event in the life
of the prophet Elijah.

We find this story in 1 Kings 17:7-24 (NIV):

"Some time later the brook dried up because there had been no rain in the land. Then the word of the Lord came to him: 'Go at once to Zarephath in the region of Sidon and stay there. I have directed a widow there to supply you with food.' So he went to Zarephath. When he came to the town gate, a widow was there gathering sticks. He called to her and asked, 'Would you bring me a little water in a jar so I may have a drink?' As she was going to get it, he called, 'And bring me, please, a piece of bread.'

'As surely as the Lord your God lives,' she replied, 'I don't have any bread—only a handful of flour in a jar and a little olive oil in a jug. I am gathering a few sticks to take home and make a meal for myself and my son, that we may eat it—and die.'

Elijah said to her, 'Don't be afraid. Go home and do as you have said. But first make a small loaf of bread for me from what you have and bring it to me, and then make something for yourself and your son. For this is what the Lord, the God of Israel, says: 'The jar of flour will not be used up and the jug of oil will not run dry until the day the Lord sends rain on the land.'

She went away and did as Elijah had told her. So there was food every day for Elijah and for the woman and her family. For the jar of flour was not used up and the jug of oil did not run dry, in keeping with the word of the Lord spoken by Elijah.

Some time later the son of the woman who owned the house became ill. He grew worse and worse, and finally stopped breathing. She said to Elijah, 'What do you have against me, man of God? Did you come to remind me of my sin and kill my son?'

'Give me your son,' Elijah replied. He took him from her

arms, carried him to the upper room where he was staying, and laid him on his bed. Then he cried out to the Lord, 'Lord my God, have you brought tragedy even on this widow I am staying with, by causing her son to die?' Then he stretched himself out on the boy three times and cried out to the Lord, 'Lord my God, let this boy's life return to him!'

The Lord heard Elijah's cry, and the boy's life returned to him, and he lived. Elijah picked up the child and carried him down from the room into the house. He gave him to his mother and said, 'Look, your son is alive!' Then the woman said to Elijah, 'Now I know that you are a man of God and that the word of the Lord from your mouth is the truth.'"

In this story, we see how the woman got *a prophet's reward*. She welcomed Elijah by faith *as a prophet*, and she got a prophet's reward: food amidst famine and her son raised from the dead. These two things would not have been possible without her welcoming the prophet in faith. In fact, it's a good bet that she would have lost both her life and her son's if she hadn't.

The widow is a perfect example of a woman who applied the anointed words of king Jehosaphat who exhorted his people by saying:

> "Believe in the Lord your God, and you shall be established; <u>believe His prophets, and you shall prosper.</u>" ~ 2 Chronicles 20:20 (NKJV)

Good Ground, *Every Time!*

Whatever you sow into the Kingdom is multiplied back unto you.

"Give and it shall be given back to you," Jesus said.

Jesus understood Kingdom giving, Kingdom economy, and Kingdom return better than anyone. That's why He asked to see what they already had before He fed the 5000.

"Five loaves and two fish" was the answer from His disciples who had obtained this meagre provision from a lad in the crowd. In the natural, it's not much when you're trying to feed 5000+ people. But Jesus didn't work in the natural.

The Bible tells us He then blessed the loaves and fish. In other words, He offered what they had to the King—His Heavenly Father. As a result, it came back multiplied many, many times.

He sowed the food, which was all they had, into the Kingdom, and the miraculous result is recorded in the Bible for our benefit and Kingdom instruction. The Kingdom of God is always good ground.

So, now, after all we've considered, do you understand?

Do you understand what Jesus meant in Luke 12:32-34 (NIV)?

> *"Do not be afraid, little flock, for your Father has been pleased to give you the kingdom. Sell your possessions and give to the poor. Provide purses for yourselves that will not wear out, a treasure in heaven that will never fail, where no thief comes near and no moth destroys. For where your treasure is, there your heart will be also."*

How to Give Generously

In the previous passage, Jesus firstly tells us *not to be afraid* BECAUSE the Father is pleased to give us the Kingdom.

And then, He proceeds to exhort us to give liberally, without any constraints.

First, we must get rid of our fear. Giving is an act of faith. Often, what holds us back from giving is our fear—irrational fear. Any fear associated with sowing into God's Kingdom is irrational. Imagine for a moment if a farmer refused to plant his fields for fear of losing his seed. That wouldn't make any sense, would it?

Many fears hold believers back from being generous, but the main ones are:

- ♛ **Fear of lack**
- ♛ **Trauma from previous lack**
- ♛ **Fear of being 'had' by wolves in sheep's clothing**

We must always yield to the Holy Spirit as to who to give to or *where to give*. This isn't always obvious, but if you ask God: *Where should I give?* He will direct you to where He wants money to flow to.

Unquestionably, there are false prophets and greedy preachers in the world. But, if you are firmly anchored in the Word of God, you will see right through them. Or, you will feel a warning in your spirit concerning them, an intuition. You will know them by their fruit.

The point is this: When we are assured of the Kingdom's (and the Father's) all-sufficiency to provide more than enough for our needs, we do away with the fear of giving.

The Bible says that perfect love does away with fear. So, basically, when we are assured of our Father's perfect love for us, we will be assured that He will provide for all our needs. In turn, this will give us the assurance to give liberally and cheerfully.

When we have this assurance, we give generously regardless of:

- ♛ **Our past scarcity**
- ♛ **Our bad experiences with wolves in sheep's clothing**
- ♛ **Our trauma endured at the hands of the cursed earth system**

A Hard Question...

Jesus' mission was all about bringing and teaching the Kingdom of God to His disciples in the hope that they would carry the same torch and spread its fire across the world and across centuries.

In some respects, and meaning no disrespect, although the Church still exists today and partly thrives, they failed—and so have we, the Church.

As we saw in an earlier chapter, the gospel of salvation taught today is *not* the same as the gospel of the Kingdom Jesus entrusted to His disciples. The gospel of the Kingdom began waning in its preaching as early as the second century, i.e., after the death of the apostles and first disciples.

Nonetheless, Jesus really wanted His disciples to understand how the Kingdom of God operates. He wanted them to do the works He did. It is for this reason that He tested them before the 5000 who were hungry.

> *"Jesus lifted up His eyes, and seeing a great multitude coming toward Him, He said to Philip, 'Where shall we buy bread, that these may eat?' But this He said to test him, for He Himself knew what He would do." ~ John 6:5-6 (NKJV)*

In the Gospel of Matthew, it is said that they were all put to the test:

> *"When it was evening, His disciples came to Him, saying, 'This is a deserted place, and the hour is already late. Send the multitudes away, that they may go into the villages and buy themselves food.' But Jesus said to them, 'They do not need to go away. You give them something to eat.'" ~ Matthew 14:15-16 (NKJV)*

The disciples retorted something that we, as ex-traumatized earth-curse toilers, probably all would have said. They said:

> *"Shall we go and buy two hundred denarii worth of bread and give them something to eat?" ~ Mark 6:37 (NKJV)*

One denarius was a day's wage for an unskilled labourer (Matthew 20:2), so two hundred denarii would represent about seven months' wages. Now, interestingly, from the text, it seems that they might have had it in their treasury possession. But, notwithstanding, they gave a reply that had everything to do with the old way of doing things. They gave a *"painful toil and sweat"* answer on a Kingdom test. They failed.

Would I have done any better? Probably not.

Now, some time later, Jesus was disappointed to see that they still didn't understand the economy of God's Kingdom.

We read this account in Mark 8:14-21 (NIV):

> *"The disciples had forgotten to bring bread, except for one loaf they had with them in the boat. 'Be careful,' Jesus warned them. 'Watch out for the yeast of the Pharisees and that of Herod.' They discussed this with one another and said, 'It is because we have no bread.'*
>
> *Aware of their discussion, Jesus asked them: 'Why are you talking about having no bread? Do you still not see or understand? Are your hearts hardened? Do you have eyes but fail to see, and ears but fail to hear? And don't you remember? When I broke the five loaves for the five thousand, how many basketfuls of pieces did you pick up?'*

'Twelve,' they replied.

'And when I broke the seven loaves for the four thousand, how many basketfuls of pieces did you pick up?' They answered, 'Seven.'

He said to them, 'Do you still not understand?'"

Do you still not understand? This is a hard and piercing question from the King. It's not just for the disciples back in the day. It is just as much for us—for today. It is a question for you and me when we fret, worry, or stress.

So, *do you still not understand?*

- ♛ Who you are?
- ♛ Who you are serving?
- ♛ Whose you are?
- ♛ What Kingdom you belong to?
- ♛ Who your Father is?
- ♛ What you were given?
- ♛ What is at your disposal?

EMBRACING YOUR KINGDOM IDENTITY
Developing a Kingdom Mindset

> *"Insight is the God given ability for you to know your identity, your Kingdom I.D.; your spiritual DNA; your uniqueness in the earth and in the body of Christ. There is no one like you. You are predestined for greatness." ~ Chuck Pierce*

Believe it or not, the greatest plight of most believers doesn't have anything to do with the trials of this life, with persecutions, or with the relentless attacks of the Enemy. No. The greatest difficulty to overcome for those who seek the Kingdom has to do with discovering and embracing their true Kingdom identity.

We're all prodigals who have gone astray. We've all been traumatized to some degree by this fallen world system and the "Prince of the Power of the Air" who operates his deceptions through it.

> The greatest difficulty to overcome for those who seek the Kingdom has to do with discovering and embracing their true Kingdom identity.

In many ways, the biggest lie, the biggest deception we face, is the one about ourselves.

Whether in church or out of the church, we are told lies about ourselves from birth. Unwittingly, our parents perpetuate in us the lies they themselves believed and were told by their parents and teachers, and so forth. These lies cover the whole spectrum of existential philosophy, ranging from '*you evolved from primordial slime,*' to '*you are nothing,*' to '*you are an intelligent ape,*' to '*you are God.*'

At the beginning of this book, I told you that by reading it, you were undertaking your very own *Kingdom Quest*. I also promised that through this quest, if you sought the truth with all your heart, it would bless you greatly. I was writing these words of encouragement from experience.

In my own life, I think nothing has blessed me more than finally believing and embracing what God says about me—His truth. Conversely, I can also say that being in ignorance of my true Kingdom Identity, even as a believer, has been quite detrimental to my spiritual, mental, and emotional well-being. It also stunted my growth for many years.

Restorative identity is one of the main benefits of Kingdom understanding. Without it, it really doesn't matter what you know about the world, the Bible, or any other stuff. If your identity isn't restored supernaturally, you're still lost, broken, and missing out on God's best for you. The Kingdom of God is *within* you. This is where it begins, on the inside, through your restored identity in Christ.

If your identity is blurred by lies, you are still a prodigal... even if you're saved.

For this reason, I feel it is important in this chapter on *restoring your identity and developing a Kingdom mindset* to revisit the parable of the prodigal son, which teaches us so many foundational Kingdom truths.

Have You Thrown Away Your Birthright?

Most of us are familiar with the parable of the prodigal son. It's the story of, well, us... when we came to our senses and came back to the Father in repentance, right?

But, when we take the time to read this story, study it, and consider how most Christians lead their lives, we notice something very peculiar—even troubling.

First, take the time to read the parable afresh taken from Luke 15:11-32 (NIV):

"Jesus continued: 'There was a man who had two sons. The younger one said to his father, 'Father, give me my share of the estate.' So he divided his property between them.

Not long after that, the younger son got together all he had, set off for a distant country and there squandered his wealth in wild living. After he had spent everything, there was a severe famine in that whole country, and he began to be in need. So he went and hired himself out to a citizen of that country, who sent him to his fields to feed pigs. He longed to fill his stomach with the pods that the pigs were eating, but no one gave him anything.

When he came to his senses, he said, 'How many of my father's hired servants have food to spare, and here I am starving to death! I will set out and go back to my father and say to him: Father, I have sinned against heaven and against you. I am no longer worthy to be called your son; make me like one of your hired servants.' So he got up and went to his father.

But while he was still a long way off, his father saw him and was filled with compassion for him; he ran to his son, threw his arms around him and kissed him.

The son said to him, 'Father, I have sinned against heaven and against you. I am no longer worthy to be called your son.'

But the father said to his servants, 'Quick! Bring the best robe and put it on him. Put a ring on his finger and sandals on his feet. Bring the fattened calf and kill it. Let's have a feast and celebrate. For this son of mine was dead and is alive again; he was lost and is found.' So they began to celebrate.

Meanwhile, the older son was in the field. When he came

near the house, he heard music and dancing. So he called one of the servants and asked him what was going on. 'Your brother has come,' he replied, 'and your father has killed the fattened calf because he has him back safe and sound.'

The older brother became angry and refused to go in. So his father went out and pleaded with him. But he answered his father, 'Look! All these years I've been slaving for you and never disobeyed your orders. Yet you never gave me even a young goat so I could celebrate with my friends. But when this son of yours who has squandered your property with prostitutes comes home, you kill the fattened calf for him!'

'My son,' the father said, 'you are always with me, and everything I have is yours. But we had to celebrate and be glad, because this brother of yours was dead and is alive again; he was lost and is found.'"

There are many lessons we can learn from this timeless parable of our Lord.

If you're like me, most of the lessons you were taught in church about this particular passage of Scripture were about the younger son who, after being famished and dirt poor, comes to his senses, repents, and decides to make his way back to his loving father.

We are often told it is a story of repentance and forgiveness, and it is.

But there is *sooo* much more to this story than meets the eye. It is more than what you've been told.

So, let's dig deeper...

The Rebellion

The story first begins with the younger son asking for his 'share of the estate.' In other versions, the son calls it 'the portion of goods that falls to me.' He asks for his inheritance ahead of time.

The younger son thus sets the stage for 'his declaration of independence.'

As you know, we are sinful from birth—born in sin. Theologians and Bible teachers often compare sin with *being or acting independently from God and His will.'* This is quite accurate.

While believers have Ten Commandments to abide by, Satanists adhere to one rule only, which we saw earlier in the book summed up by Aleister Crowley. This one rule, or one law, known as *the Thelema*, states: "*Do what thou wilt shall be the whole of the Law.*"

In other words, when we do what we want instead of what God wants, we are living like pagans, like the world, in rebellion. We are, by default, living independently from God and so, in rebellion or sin.

This is why the Bible says in 1 Samuel 15:23 (KJV): "*Rebellion is as the sin of witchcraft, and stubbornness is as iniquity and idolatry. Because thou hast rejected the word of the LORD.*"

The unbeliever who refuses to come to Christ is in open rebellion against the Father because He seeks to live life His way and do His own thing.

In many ways, when God granted human beings free will, He gave them a 'share of the estate.'

And, like the younger son in the story, with this *share of the estate*, or free will, many have engaged in what the story calls 'wild living'—better known as *partying* today.

So, the story begins with the young son rebelling against the Father, which is reminiscent of how we all used to be—doing our own thing.

Separation from the Father

In the story, the young son's first impulse is to put distance between himself and the Father. It says that he first *'set off for a distant country.'* So, the boy first went as far as he could from the Father and then engaged himself in crazy living, partying, and all kinds of debauchery.

If you yourself, or if you've ever witnessed a friend or relative who became backslidden, the first thing they do is put some distance between themselves and holy influences in their life.

When people become rebellious or backslidden, they want to live life on their own terms, and they want to make sure they silence any voice in their surroundings that might be hinting at their own sin or tugging at their conscience. They want to silence anything reminiscent of God, The Father, in their lives.

Proverbs 18:1 (ESV) says *"Whoever isolates himself seeks his own desire; he breaks out against all sound judgment."*

Therefore, they distance themselves from Church, godly friends and family; they stop reading the Scriptures, etc.

This is what the young son did. He put some distance between himself and his father, and then lived like a demon.

Realization and Repentance

Then, in the story, comes the young man's realization and repentance.

Realization and repentance rarely come to us when we have a full bank account and a life of plenty. No. More often than not, our repentance comes when we start seeking. And we most often start seeking when we are missing something—when we are in lack.

In the case of this young son, he missed his three-square meals a day and the comforts of home. When you start looking at what pigs are eating, and it looks good to you, you know you're in trouble.

The Bible says the pigs were eating *pods*. This refers to the pods of the carob tree, which closely resembles a small horn. These were commonly used for fattening swine. These sad dried-up pieces of 'swine food' were also seen as an article of food by poor people in the day. Pods definitely do not qualify as a delicacy, especially when trampled and drooled on by pigs.

The story also tells us that although he was a hungry and working man, *'no one would give him anything.'*

So, we could assume that in his present employment as a swine feeder, he was forbidden to eat the pigs' food.

That's when the story tells us *'he finally came to his senses.'*

When we live deep in sin and rebellion against the Father, we live in an almost inebriated state. It's like we are drunk or high. But, when the effect dissipates, we *'come to our senses.'* And the effect dissipates quite fast when we wallow in pig dung. That's a huge wake-up call.

Now, for those who live in the western world, we may find it difficult to identify with a guy who is feeding pigs. In our modern life, this could be compared to when we lose our job, or our marriage, or wake up in the bed of a stranger, or when we have to crash at a friend's house for a while because we're homeless or in some other kind of trouble.

So, the son decided to repent and go back to his father's house... as a servant.

He fabricated a speech that he repeated and memorized over and over in his mind:

> *"Father, I have sinned against heaven and against you. I am no longer worthy to be called your son; make me like one of your hired servants."*

And I absolutely love verse 20, which says:

> *"So he got up and went to his father."*

Here, it implies a stern decision made. It doesn't say that he got up, went to see his boss, and resigned. It doesn't tell us he got up and went to wash himself first. No. He simply got up and began the journey back to his father right away. There is high resolve there. There is something special about getting back up when we fall, and we all fall down. But, like the son, we have to *get up and go to our father.* We don't even need to wash up first, even if we wallowed in pig dung.

This verse is the turning point in the story.

- ♛ He was down, but not out.
- ♛ He could still get up, and he did.
- ♛ Les Brown once said that "When we fall, if we can look up, we can get up."
- ♛ His decision was made: he got up.
- ♛ When we're in a ditch, climbing out begins with us getting up.
- ♛ Getting back up is the starting point from where we are to where we want to be or should be.

So, *he got up* and went to his Father.

Forgiveness and Restoration

The most beautiful part of this story is the Father's forgiveness and restoration of his son.

The story tells us that *'When he was still a long way off the Father saw him and was filled with compassion.'*

Did you know that God, our Father, has compassion on us even before we pray to Him to ask forgiveness? He too sees us when we are still a long way off.

And when we are repentant, resolute, and we get up to go to Him, before we even make that first step, He is already running towards us!

If there are 1000 steps that separate us from God and we make one small step towards our Father in heaven, He will cover the remaining 999 steps as He runs towards us. He covers us with His grace and embraces us, just like in the story.

And then comes the restoration.

Identity Restored

This is the part of the story that seems to evade so many Bible teachers.

We love to talk about the repentance of the prodigal son and the forgiveness of the Father, but we seem to miss the part about the son's *restoration*.

> We love to talk about the repentance of the prodigal son and the forgiveness of the Father, but we seem to miss the part about the son's restoration.

And the restoration is the most crucial part of understanding the whole story.

The story shows us how the Father has a sense of *urgency* in restoring his son.

He says, *"Quick! Bring the best robe and put it on him. Put a ring on his finger and sandals on his feet. Bring the fattened calf and kill it. Let's have a feast and celebrate. For this son of mine was dead and is alive again; he was lost and is found."*

Let's look at these symbolic gestures and objects one by one.

1. The Robe. The Father quickly requested a robe to be put on His son.

Back in Bible times, the common attire was a tunic. Common people wore a tunic.

A robe, back in Bible times, was a looser and longer kind of tunic. It was a garment that was worn by nobility and important people. Scripture indicates its use by kings (I Samuel 24:4), prophets (I Samuel 28:14), and nobles (Job 1:20).

Joseph was set apart from his brothers when Jacob honored him with the *coat of many colors* (Genesis 37:3).

So, the robe is chic, perhaps even *royal attire*. It was no small thing to be clothed in one. In today's terms, this would be the equivalent of wearing a Giorgio Armani suit.

2. The Ring. Back in Bible times, common people did not wear rings. Rings were a symbol of affluence, prominence, and authority.

Kings would often wear rings to symbolize their status and power. These were decorated with distinct carvings or shapes that became official signatures when the king pressed his ring into wax that sealed a document or letter.

The term *signet ring* indicates a particular object or logo engraved on the ring. It was used by nobles and kings for making a royal sign or for sealing official documents with wax.

When Joseph went from the prison to the palace, the Pharaoh publicly affirmed his new role in Genesis 41:41-42 (NIV):

> *"Then Pharaoh said to Joseph, 'I now put you in charge of Egypt; Then Pharaoh took off his <u>signet ring</u> and put it on Joseph's finger. He had Joseph dressed in robes of fine linen and put a gold chain around his neck."*

This is the designated Joseph's position and status in the kingdom of Egypt. Someone wearing the king's ring could exercise the king's authority.

So, in like manner, the son, being given a ring by His father, indicates that He is given his Father's authority in the household. He is being greatly honored with power and authority.

3. The Sandals. The sandals, like the other two items, signified the son was not a servant. Usually, the servants did not wear any sandals.

The following lyric in the *Song of Solomon (7:1)* confirms sandals were worn by the high-born.

> *"How beautiful are your feet in sandals, O noble daughter!"*
> *(ESV)*

Furthermore, a common custom back in Bible times was to wash the feet of people who came to your house. Back then, people travelled great distances, often on foot, to go from one place to another. Their feet were often sore, dry, and dirty. A common courtesy for people having guests back then was to assign servants to wash their feet. This explains Jesus' rebuke of Simon the Pharisee's failure to wash His feet when Simon condemned the woman with the alabaster jar of fragrant oil (Luke 7:44-47). It also highlights even further the powerful significance of Jesus washing the disciples' feet at the last supper (John 13:1-17).

So, if you were to put sandals on their feet after washing them, this would have been the icing on the cake as far as honor goes.

4. The Fatted Calf. To celebrate his son's return and his restoration, the father ordered that they kill the fatted calf for a feast.

Back in biblical times, people would often set aside one livestock that was fed a special diet to fatten it up. This made it more flavorful when prepared as a meal. Slaughtering this fatted animal for a feast was done only on rare or special occasions.

So, when the prodigal son returns, the father *"kills the fatted calf"* to show that the ordained celebration is out of the ordinary.

All in all, what the father bestowed upon his son indicates that this man was very wealthy. He was not a commoner. He had servants, property, rings, cattle, robes, etc.

Even more so, our Father's wealth is so grandiose that it is out of this world!

The Pride of Excessive Humility

One of the greatest lessons in the prodigal son's story is the lesson about what He is given.

As believers, Kingdom citizens, and sons, we too were given the same honors as the younger son in the story.

The robe, the ring, the sandals, the feast… these are summed up well by the apostle Peter when he says in 1 Peter 2:9 (NIV):

"But you are a chosen people, a royal priesthood, a holy nation, God's special possession, that you may declare the praises of him who called you out of darkness into his wonderful light."

And Revelation 1:6 (NIV) says He:

> *"Has made us kings and priests to His God and Father, to Him be glory and dominion forever and ever. Amen."*

Even after all this honor, we often show signs, not of pride, but of *excessive humility*.

What is *excessive humility*? Is that even a thing? Yes, it is.

Excessive humility, in the story, would be translated as the refusal to wear the robe, the ring, or the sandals, and the refusal to attend the ceremony and eat the fatted calf.

"Who would do such a foolish thing," you ask? And yet, as crazy as this sounds, this is exactly what many Christians do today.

This strange behaviour is induced by *religious thinking* and is lived out by many Christians regularly.

The story of the prodigal son is also a story in which we are shown a stark contrast between the *Kingdom of God* and *religion*.

Imagine for a moment if the son, coming from afar, had stuck to his guns.

Imagine if he had told the Father, *"No, you don't understand… I am not worthy of all this honor. I sinned against heaven and against*

296

you. I will not wear your precious attire. I came back to be as one of your servants and that's all there is to it!"

For sure, the father would still have been glad his son came home. And yet, he would have been sadly robbed of the joy of honoring and restoring his son.

In such a scenario, the son would not have served the father in his full capacity. It would have grieved the father deeply to see his son walking in dishonor among his servants and not enjoying *everything He had to give.*

Furthermore, by associating himself with the servants, the son would *relinquish his given authority.* He would not be able to run the affairs of his father in full authority and adequately.

The son is supposed to lead, to be the head and not the tail. And yet, in such a scenario, he would voluntarily choose to be the tail.

You might find this amusing, or maybe even ridiculous, but many believers do the exact same thing!

Religious thinking induces *excessive humility, which is pride in disguise.*

> Religious thinking induces excessive humility, which is pride in disguise.

To further illustrate, proper humility says, *"Although I do not deserve these gifts, I will accept them, run with them, and use my God-given authority for the glory of my Father and His kingdom."*

Excessive humility says: *"I do not deserve these gifts. I am just a sinner saved by grace, and I am not fit to rule. I am a lowly servant of God and therefore, I cannot be elevated this way."*

Is it clear now?

Excessive humility disfigures the believer's true and rightful identity. It comes from the constant barrage of lies that we are submitted to through religion. It robs God from defining us and embraces man's definition of us.

In my book, *The Law of Attraction: Is It for Christians?* I wrote about how religion can massacre our identity through constant repetition of *who we used to be*. I wrote:

You've probably heard the following on most Sundays at Church:

- ♛ **You're a sinner (saved by grace).**
- ♛ **Your heart is corrupt (Jeremiah 17:9).**
- ♛ **You are undeserving of God's grace.**
- ♛ **You are inherently evil.**
- ♛ **You are fallen.**
- ♛ **You are fallen in Adam and a slave to sin, etc.**

Unfortunately, while these biblical facts are essential and should be stated in order to understand our need of Christ *before salvation*, they can severely damage your mindset if repeated constantly *after salvation*—which in many churches and denominations is the case.

I will now state something that might shock you: *Excessive humility is just another form of rebellion.*

You read that right. Excessive humility, despite its façade, is actually a form of pride.

It was excessive humility on the part of Moses that pushed God to snap at Moses when, after having patiently shown him how He would be with him, Moses still didn't feel he was equipped for the job.

We read this account in Exodus 4:10-14 (GNT):

> *"But Moses said, 'No, Lord, don't send me. I have never been a good speaker, and I haven't become one since you began to speak to me. I am a poor speaker, slow and hesitant.' The Lord said to him, 'Who gives man his mouth? Who makes him deaf or dumb? Who gives him sight or makes him blind? It is I, the Lord. Now, go! I will help you to speak, and I will tell you what to say.' But Moses answered, 'No, Lord, please send someone else.' <u>At this the Lord became angry with Moses...</u>"*

Moses was trying to shirk responsibility by repeatedly playing the card of *'I am not good enough, capable enough, worthy enough, etc.'*

There is no denying that in the Bible, we are exhorted to serve and to be humble. I have mentioned multiple times on my broadcasts or podcasts how important it is to be good servant-leaders. I've also emphasized the importance of humility on multiple occasions. So, I am far from saying here that there is something wrong with humility—on the contrary!

I like how C.S. Lewis defined proper humility when he said:

> *"Humility is not thinking less of yourself; it's thinking of yourself less."*

As Kingdom sons, we must never forget this vital truth:

Citizens in the Kingdom of God are exhorted to serve and anointed to rule.

Citizens in the Kingdom of God are exhorted to serve and anointed to rule.

Religion vs. Kingdom

Let's talk about the differences between the two sons. Up until this point in the parable, we know zilch about the older brother.

But when he makes his appearance in the story, the narrative takes quite an interesting turn. It shows a huge contrast between the two brothers.

Here is a spoiler of sorts: I believe the older brother represents religious people.

I once saw an insightful bumper sticker that said:

> *Religion is for people afraid of going to hell, spirituality is for those who have been there.*

This, I believe, sums up the main difference between the two brothers.

The prodigal younger son is the one that has gone through hell and found his way back to the Kingdom of His Father. He is now fully aware of everything it means to be living in his father's household. As a result, he understands his riches, privileges, and authority.

This will make him an efficient servant-ruler in his father's house.

The older son is the one afraid of going to hell (or disobeying), who never understood His Father, His Kingdom, and His inheritance.

In other words, *he does all the right things for all the wrong reasons.*

He obeys not out of love but out of misplaced fear. That's why he got so upset at the father feasting and celebrating his younger brother's return.

Notice the older brother's religiously slanted statement when he says:

> *"Look! All these years I've been slaving for you and never disobeyed your orders. Yet you never gave me even a young goat so I could celebrate with my friends. But when this son of yours who has squandered your property with prostitutes comes home, you kill the fattened calf for him!'* ~ Luke 15:29-30 (NIV)

He says, *"I have been slaving for you."*

In essence, he is saying, *"I have been a good obedient slave and you never gave me anything."*

Now, if he lived today and he spoke Christianese, he would be saying something along the lines of, *"I have been going to Church, reading my Bible, using Christian lingo, evangelizing, bringing more food than all the others at our church potluck suppers, etc."*

Notice also how he says his Father never gave him a goat to celebrate with his friends. The text doesn't say that he actually *asked for a goat.* In other words, although he did all the right things, he didn't have a relationship with his father. And, as one with no relationship, he didn't ask his father for anything, but he expected so much. The Lord told us, *"Ask, and it will be given to you"* (Matthew 7:7). And the apostle James clearly tells us, *"You do not have because you do not ask God"* (James 4:2).

The father pleads with his older son and tries to explain proper Kingdom perspective to him when he says:

> *"You are always with me, and everything I have is yours. But we had to celebrate and be glad, because this brother of yours was dead and is alive again; he was lost and is found."*

This is the father's way of saying: *"My son, you are in my kingdom and I love you. As such, you have direct access at all times to all of my riches—and to me."*

Religion is a nasty word, literally. The word comes from the Latin *"religare,"* which means *"to bind."*

> Religion is a nasty word, literally. The word comes from the Latin "religare," which means "to bind."

Indeed, those who are religious are bound. Whether they believe it, know it or not, admit it or not, they are in servitude to a system of belief. Perhaps then these are the ones Christ came for. These are the ones He came to set free (Luke 4:18).

Jesus was rightly indignant and angry with the Pharisees and religious leaders of His day. He accused them of putting people in bondage through religion. He said to them:

> *"Woe to you, scribes and Pharisees, hypocrites! For you shut the kingdom of heaven in people's faces. For you neither enter yourselves nor allow those who would enter to go in."* ~ *Matthew 23:13-14 (ESV)*

And do not kid yourself; this is still going on today. Many pastors and religious leaders are keeping people bound in man-made religious systems. They teach their followers a counterfeit Kingdom of God and therefore *shut the Kingdom of Heaven in people's faces.*

Restored Identity = Restored Relationship

In the story of the prodigal son, we are shown a profound truth. We can be sons and not feel like sons. We can be sons and not act like sons. We can be sons and not access the full benefits and blessings of sons.

In the beginning of this book, I share the analogy of the grand hotel to illustrate this truth. The Kingdom of God is like this grand hotel, but many believers wind up in the lobby and think, *"This is it."* That's where they stop. As a result, they miss out on all the good stuff.

The younger son in the story was a son when he asked for his inheritance and wanted to leave. He was in the lobby, and he thought that was it. He thought the lobby (religion) sucked, and he wanted out.

He was also a son during his party days, and he was still a son when feeding those pigs. The point is, he never stopped being a son. But he was "dead," meaning he was rebellious and unrepentant—and so, he was estranged from his father.

So, what changed? He did.

Naturalist John Burroughs was right when he said:

> *"The Kingdom of heaven is not a place, but a state of mind."*

The younger son's state of mind changed. His perception of his father and of his kingdom changed. He understood that even the employees in his father's 'grand hotel' had plenty. So, he repented and went back to his father with a renewed heart. He became "alive again." The son was willing to come back as a hotel employee because he now understood what the hotel had to offer. The father then restored the son's authority and position in the family business.

As for the older son, he too was in the grand hotel, but he acted like an employee, not a son. He wasn't in the lobby. Rather, he was in the laundry room; he washed toilets, vacuumed the hallways, and spent time in the hotel's basement. He too secretly thought that this was it. And he too thought that it sucked. But unlike his younger brother, he didn't dare do anything about it. Bottom line: he too needed restoration. But there cannot be restoration without realization. He didn't realize he wasn't being a son. For all intents and purposes, he thought he was. He thought that by acting like an employee, he would have the father's blessings as a son. But he lacked a relationship with his father. He was estranged in the father's own house.

This is true of many believers today. They're in the Kingdom, in the father's household, in His Grand Hotel, but they are either stuck in the lobby or acting like employees; never enjoying the perks and benefits the hotel has to offer. They are, for the most part, dissatisfied, but wouldn't dare admit it.

Remember: The Kingdom of God is within you. That's where it all starts. It begins by realizing all that the Father is, all that He wants for you, all that He has, and all that He has *for you*.

The Keys of Knowledge

To that end, there you need to get your mind right concerning your Kingdom identity.

There are seven principles or keys that will unlock your mindset to your Kingdom identity and purpose. These are, I believe, at least part of what Jesus called *'The Key to Knowledge'* that the teachers of the law (Bible experts) in Jesus' day hid from the people. He strongly rebuked them for this, saying:

> *"Woe to you lawyers! For you have taken away the key of knowledge. You did not enter yourselves, and you hindered those who were entering." ~ Luke 11:52 (ESV)*

Undaunted, Jesus gave us back, not only the key of knowledge, but also the keys of the Kingdom when He said:

> *"I will give you the keys of the kingdom of heaven, and*

whatever you bind on earth will be bound in heaven, and
whatever you loose on earth will be loosed in heaven." ~
Matthew 16:19 (NKJV)

Likewise, these same keys today will free you from the bondage
of religion and enable you to develop a strong Kingdom mindset and
relationship with the King. I've broken down the key of knowledge
into seven *'knowings.'*

1. **Know who you are.** Identity is the first and greatest hurdle
   to a Kingdom mindset. You can know the Bible by heart
   and be a master theologian, but if you do not have a deep
   knowing of *who you are*, you cannot bear your full fruit in the
   Kingdom. Once redeemed and brought into the kingdom,
   your complete identity shifted from one of an orphan to one
   of an accepted and cherished son.

2. **Know whose you are.** Closely linked to who you are is the
   knowledge of who you belong to. You are not serving a
   distant or wrathful God. While He is just, and sits as judge
   over the nations, you are nonetheless serving a tender, loving,
   all-powerful Father. He is your Abba and the King of the
   universe for whom nothing is impossible. As redeemed sons,
   we are *"not appointed unto wrath"* (1 Thess. 5:9).

3. **Know why you're here.** Wherever you are, you are not here
   by accident. I tell this to my listeners all the time. There is a
   definite and precise reason you live in the country you live,
   in the skin you're in, and in the time you're in. Your salvation
   was only the beginning of this powerful existential discovery.
   Why you're here, the reason God despatched you, defines
   your Purpose, with a capital "P."

4. **Know where you're going.** The direction you are going
   comprises many different purposes, with a lower case "p"
   this time. This path you are on and the direction God wants

you to go will acquaint you with many seasons of life and many varied assignments from the Father. Your career, your spouse, becoming a parent, your ministry; these are all part of where you are going and a vital key to your fulfillment.

5. **Know what you have.** Everybody has different talents, abilities, and gifts from the Holy Spirit. Knowing what you carry is such an important key to knowing yourself and determining what God wants you to do. What you carry will determine what you need to give. The apostle Peter reminds us: *"God has given each of you a gift from his great variety of spiritual gifts. Use them well to serve one another." ~ 1 Peter 4:10 (NLT)*

6. **Know who you serve.** The Bible is explicit that we should serve one another in love. Nevertheless, within the body, there are many different groups of people. While you are called to love all people and preach the gospel to all, your specific gifts, calling, and purpose will have you serve *specific people*. This is what we usually refer to as ministry (service). For example, some are called to serve women. Some are called to serve children, or the elderly, or the homeless, or students. Even Jesus and Paul knew who they specifically came to serve. Jesus said: *"I was sent only to the lost sheep of Israel" (Matt. 15:24)*. And Paul said: *"I have written you quite boldly on some points to remind you of them again, because of the grace God gave me to be a minister of Christ Jesus to the Gentiles. He gave me the priestly duty of proclaiming the gospel of God, so that the Gentiles might become an offering acceptable to God, sanctified by the Holy Spirit." ~ Romans 15:15-16 (NIV)*

7. **Know your enemy.** We each have a powerful enemy who seeks to deter us from our Kingdom's purposes and assignment. Believers who ignore his devices will fall into all kinds of snares. These snares may lead them to perverse thinking and wrong beliefs. As I said before, God doesn't will

the ill in your life, but the devil does. He comes to steal, kill, and destroy (John 10:10). And the doorway to most of his attacks is usually your mind. Your mind is the trump card in spiritual warfare. This is why developing a strong Kingdom mindset is so necessary for believers. We cannot afford to be *ignorant of his devices* (2 Corinthians 2:11).

Back in Jesus' day, the *'Key of knowledge'* was held from the people by teachers of the law and Pharisees. They knew truths that could have freed the people's minds and hearts and enable them to enter a proper relationship with God. But for different reasons, they held back from teaching them to the people. If revealed to the people, some of these truths might have cost them greatly in the religious culture of the day, as it did Jesus.

We have the same problem today. Many pastors and teachers will teach only 'accepted doctrine' or keep away from truths that might offend because they fear that:

- ♕ **They will lose their job or position.**
- ♕ **They will be called heretics.**
- ♕ **They will lose money in tithes and offerings, etc.**

As a result, we have many churchgoers who have become 'churchians' and are stuck in the muck of religious goo—unable to advance themselves and unable to advance the Kingdom.

While these aforementioned seven 'knowings' are merely a starting point to move from religious bondage to a Kingdom mindset, they are nonetheless crucial.

> We have many churchgoers who have become 'churchians' and are stuck in the muck of religious goo—unable to advance themselves and unable to advance the Kingdom.

Developing a Strong Kingdom Mindset

Religion has proved quite inefficient in providing believers with ways to *"be transformed by the renewing of your mind"* (Romans 12:2). This renewing of the mind is made possible by a (Holy) Spirit *"of power, and of love, and of a sound mind"* (2 Timothy 1:7).

Unfortunately, this is seldom taught in religious institutions. We are often taught love, sure. But power and a sound mind? Not so much.

There is a story told about a couple one Sunday who was exiting church. The middle-aged woman said to her husband:

'Do you think that Nicholson girl is tinting her hair?'

'I didn't even see her,' admitted the husband.

'And that skirt the pastor's daughter was wearing,' continued the woman. *'Don't tell me you thought that was suitable attire for a young mother?'*

'I'm afraid I didn't notice that either,' said the husband.

'Huh,' said the woman. *'A lot of good it does you going to church!'*

While this probably made you laugh, unfortunately, for some people, that's pretty much all they learn in Church. For such people, church is just a social club, a weekly gathering, a dead religion. And dead religion can only induce religious thinking.

In many cases, religious thinking is toxic. It is religion that teaches us that:

- ♛ Poverty is a virtue.
- ♛ We are just sinners saved by grace (instead of saints called to rule).
- ♛ God loves us, but He doesn't really need us.
- ♛ God is good, but your cancer, the death of your child, and the loss of your job; those were all His will.
- ♛ Miracles and healings were just for the times of the apostles, etc.

Rest assured, all of these I will not address here. But all I can say is this:

Such religious indoctrination can be toxic and detrimental to a healthy mindset. Beliefs such as these certainly do not contribute to a strong Kingdom mindset.

There are three steps needed for us to reset our identity and walk in Kingdom authority.

1. The first step needed to get out of the hotel lobby is the realization of our sonship.

2. The second step is embracing the Father (as sons).

3. The third step is to walk as His Kingdom sons every day.

Once we address and redress the problems related to realizing our identity and embracing it, we need to maintain a *strong Kingdom mindset*. The Bible says to not be conformed to the pattern of this world, but to be *transformed*.

Believers are sanctified. The word 'sanctified' means set apart. We are 'set apart'. God set us apart. The Father made us sons and gave us a higher calling. He gave us a different way to think and do things. He made us into salt and light to the world. He gave each of us a particular purpose and assignment.

As 1 Peter 2:9 (ESV) says:

> *"You are a chosen race, a royal priesthood, a holy nation, a people for his own possession, that you may proclaim the excellencies of him who called you out of darkness into his marvelous light."*

So, dear brother, sister, and fellow Kingdom citizen, you march to the beat of a different drummer. Therefore, your mindset should reflect this.

As a believer, your mindset should reflect the culture of the Kingdom of God and be based on the Word of God.

So, before you can walk out your purpose and assignment with assurance, before you can be a towering lighthouse shining the light of the Kingdom for a world in darkness, before you can impact the sands of time with your presence here on earth, before you can leave a godly legacy in the hearts of others, you will need *a strong Kingdom Mindset!*

What does this look like and how is it achieved? Well, for starters, remember that you're never alone and that the Holy Spirit desires this for you—which makes for a great start!

Characteristics of a Strong Kingdom Mindset

Once your identity as a son is fully restored, and you know who you are and whose you are, then comes the responsibility of maintaining a strong Kingdom mindset.

So, in order to help you understand what this is like, here are seven key characteristics of a strong Kingdom mindset.

1. **What is it about?** A strong Kingdom mindset is about *who you really are* (sons of the Most High King) and what you are called to accomplish as a result.

2. **What is its main tenet?** A strong Kingdom mindset believes that "you can do all things... *through Christ who strengthens you.*" It believes that limits can be overcome through faith because *"nothing is impossible to God."*

3. **What strengthens it?** A strong Kingdom mindset is reinforced by reading Scriptures (the Words of God), meditating on Scriptures (the Words of God), and speaking Scriptures out loud (decreeing the Words of God).

In Matthew 4:4 (NIV), when Jesus was being tempted by the devil, He answered him through the Scriptures (every time). He notably said:

"It is written: 'Man shall not live on bread alone, but on every word that comes from the mouth of God.'

And in Matthew 12:37 (NKJV), Jesus said:

"For by your words you will be justified, and by your words you will be condemned."

Guess what? If you make God's words your own by reading, meditating, and speaking them every day, you will develop a strong Kingdom Mindset—guaranteed!

God says of His own Word in Isaiah 55:11 (NIV): "So is my word that goes out from my mouth: It will not return to me empty, but will accomplish what I desire and achieve the purpose for which I sent."

So, if you make His words your own, you will see powerful results in your life.

4. **What is it used for?** A strong Kingdom mindset is used to reach your *full potential and purpose* for God's Kingdom and glory and to bless others by pointing them to God and His Kingdom in the process.

Irenaeus, the church father, said:

"For the glory of God is the living man, and the life of man is the vision of God."

Some mistranslated this by saying:

"The glory of God is in man fully alive."

"For the glory of God is the living man, and the life of man is the vision of God." ~ Irenaeus

Well, mistranslation or not, there is much truth in this saying. Indeed, the glory of God is in man fully alive!

Jesus put it this way:

*"Let your light shine before others, so that they may see your
good works and give glory to your Father who is in heaven."*
~ *Matthew 5:16 (ESV)*

5. **Who does it serve?** A strong Kingdom mindset serves God,
   yourself, and God's Kingdom on the earth for the sake of
   others.

And, just for the record, you don't need to serve God solely
through religious positions, ministries, or institutions. Remember
the seven-mountain principle?

Case in point: Christian-owned businesses like *Chick-fil-A*
and *Buck Knives* have understood this principle. They use their
companies as platforms to point others to God and to glorify Him
in the process. Much of their profit is used to benefit works and
ministries that glorify God and expand Kingdom influence. Even if
their companies provide secular products or services, their culture is
a Kingdom culture because they have developed a Kingdom mindset.

6. **What is it based on?** A strong Kingdom mindset is based
   on your conviction about what God tells you about yourself
   (building belief in what God's Word says you are).

The Word of God is filled with Scriptures about who you are as
believers—about your inheritance, your calling, your authority, your
worth, your sonship, etc.

On our website, we recorded a downloadable Mp3 Audio file
containing 85 biblical declarations about who you are and what you
have. You can download this file for FREE by visiting https://www.
thrivingonpurpose.com/

7. **What does it lead to?** A strong Kingdom mindset leads to
   the realization that *'His power is made perfect in weakness.'*

It leads to a more balanced lifestyle where rest doesn't make you
feel guilty. It leads you to the knowledge and peaceful acceptance

that only He is limitless. It leads to the firm and confident assurance that your help:

> "Comes from the Lord, who made heaven and earth. He will not allow your foot to be moved; He who keeps you will not slumber" (Psalm 121:2-3; ESV).

It leads to a bold faith that says: "

> I can do all things through Christ who strengthen me" (Philippians 4:13).

While you will continue to seek to better yourself and your circumstances, it will be done through His grace, power, and faithfulness. This trust in Him will lead you to, like Psalm 23 says: "Green pastures and still waters." It will lead you to fulfill His assignment and your destiny, which were prepared in advance for you. And last but not least, *it will lead you to victory!*

Are *YOU* a king then?

Before our Lord was crucified, Pilate asked Him this question:

> "Are You a king then?" Jesus answered, 'You say rightly that I am a king.'" ~ John 18:37 (NKJV)

In this verse, the NKJV translators added the word 'rightly', feeling it perhaps conveyed better sense in the text. However, in the other gospels and other Bible versions, Jesus seems vaguer.

For example, in the Gospel of Mark chapter 15 v. 2, in the NKJV, Jesus answered Pilate, "It is as you say." In other versions, the same passage is translated as, "You have said so" or "You say so." He easily could have been more direct.

Nevertheless, further in the conversation, Jesus confirmed His Kingship by speaking of *His Kingdom not being of this world.* But why the overall covertness?

While Jesus knew His identity perfectly, He was still holding back from proclaiming it. He had done this for the length of His ministry. He often told people to remain silent and rebuked demons forbidding them from saying who He was. Jesus gave strict orders to three different audiences not to speak about him:

♛ To demons/unclean spirits (Mark 1:24; 1:34; 3:12)

♛ To crowds and recipients of healing (Mark 1:43; 5:43; 7:33–36; 8:22–26)

♛ To His disciples (Mark 8:30; 9:9)

When before Pilate, He still kept this important fact hush-hush. His mission had yet to be fulfilled in this dark hour.

Only after He rose again did He proclaim openly His indisputable sovereignty when He said, *"All authority in heaven and on earth has been given to me"* ~ Matthew 28:18 (ESV)

At this point, His own words came to pass:

> *"The time is coming when everything that is covered up will be revealed, and all that is secret will be made known to all. Whatever you have said in the dark will be heard in the light, and what you have whispered behind closed doors will be shouted from the housetops for all to hear!"* ~ Luke 12:2-3 (NLT)

These secrets include not only the bad ones held by those in darkness, but also the good ones, such as those we are privy to in the Kingdom.

And with that, He, in turn, bestowed us with His own mighty authority for us to go and shout the Kingdom message from the housetops.

He is King, and we are heirs with Him. We are also sons of the Most High God, the King of all creation. So, what does that make us? What does that make you?

I remember my dad once tried to explain identity to me this way; he asked me, *"Who is the son of a monkey?"* Unsure where he was going with this, I replied hesitantly, *"Well, um, a monkey?"* To which he replied, *"Exactly! Never forget your inheritance. We are sons of the King of the universe. This makes us royalty."*

The parable of the prodigal son, which we explored at length in this chapter, clearly proved this point. Remember the robe? The ring? And the sandals?

Now, the Book of Revelation makes it very clear as to what our inheritance and identity is in Christ. In chapter 1 v. 6 (KJV), we read that He *"hath made us kings and priests unto God and his Father; to him be glory and dominion for ever and ever. Amen."*

Furthermore, when we read of the triumphant Christ at the end of Revelation, we are told that:

> *"On his robe and on his thigh he has a name written, King of kings and Lord of lords"* ~ Revelation 19:16 (ESV)

I used to think this title on His garment indicated *only* Jesus' title, authority, and rulership over His enemies: the evil rulers, kings, and lords of this world. But the Lord showed me that it also includes good rulers, lords, and kings. It includes all kings and all lords! And since the Bible calls us kings, it also includes you and me!

In other words, He is the KING, with a capital "K," and *all* are subject to Him. But, praise be to God, *we too are kings*—lower case "k."

So, if you are ever asked by someone, *"Are YOU a king?"* Your answer can be a resounding, *"YES! Praise be to God! By His grace, I am."*

CONCLUSION

""If you have not chosen the Kingdom of God first, it will in the end make no difference what you have chosen instead."
~ William Law

In chapter one, I shared with you a prophetic dream that God gave me. Do you remember it? I was climbing a hill and saw a big treasure chest rising from the ground, and the Lord spoke to me, asking, *"Are you all in?"*

It was a short question, but there was such a weight of pondering associated with it!

Well, dear friend, this question was not just for me. I believe this question applies to all believers.

The Kingdom of God's abundance and blessings multiply to those who seek it and His righteousness first. It is the treasure that keeps on giving, but we must be found worthy of it.

In the Gospel of Thomas, found outside of our accepted scriptures, there is a powerful saying attributed to the Lord that demonstrates nicely the process and results of seeking after the Kingdom:

"Jesus said, 'Let one who seeks not stop seeking until that person finds; and upon finding, the person will be disturbed; and being disturbed, will be astounded; and will reign over the entirety." ~ Gospel of Thomas, part 2

By now, I'm willing to bet that some of the content of this book has, at the very least, disturbed you. That's good. It's a good start for any Kingdom quest.

The Kingdom is hard to find, sure. Its standards are lofty and not easily upheld. Its King is Holy, and despite His loving, generous, and gracious disposition, it can be an intimidating force and quite demanding. And yet, He never asks something He doesn't equip us to do.

As the saying goes, *"God does not call the equipped, He equips the called."*

That said, yes, there is a high cost associated with pursuing the Kingdom of God and His righteousness.

The Cost of Kingdom Quest

In the Bible, Jesus tells us about the cost associated with being "all in" for the Kingdom. In Luke 14:25-33 (ESV):

> *"Now great crowds accompanied him, and he turned and said to them, "If anyone comes to me and does not hate his own father and mother and wife and children and brothers and sisters, yes, and even his own life, he cannot be my disciple. Whoever does not bear his own cross and come after me cannot be my disciple. For which of you, desiring to build a tower, does not first sit down and count the cost, whether he has enough to complete it? Otherwise, when he has laid a foundation and is not able to finish, all who see it begin to mock him, saying, 'This man began to build and was not able to finish.' Or what king, going out to encounter another king in war, will not sit down first and deliberate whether he is able with ten thousand to meet him who comes against him with twenty thousand? And if not, while the other is yet a great way off, he sends a delegation and asks for terms of peace. So therefore, any one of you who does not renounce all that he has cannot be my disciple."*

I would be lying if I told you there is no cost in being *"all in"* for the Kingdom. In fact, I believe I still have ways to go before I can say I am "all in" for the Kingdom and His glory. I still have much dying to self to do. Some days, I find myself counting the cost and wondering if I've done enough, or even if I should keep going. There have been times when I have felt John Bunyan's *Giant Despair* gripping me by the throat, choking me with the *"worries of this life."* Pursuing the Kingdom first is not something we do for a day, a month, or a year—it is a lifelong commitment.

I believe the late Kathryn Kuhlman hit the nail on the head one day when she spoke to a large gathering who came for her wonderful healing gift. Many wondered how they too, could be blessed with a similar grace, power, and anointing. Not holding back, she said to them:

> "It costs everything. If you really want to know the price. If you really want to know the price, I'll tell you... It will cost you everything." ~ Kathryn Kuhlman

"It costs everything. If you really want to know the price. If you really want to know the price, I'll tell you... It will cost you everything. Kathryn Kuhlman died a long time ago. I know the day. I know the hour. I can go to the spot where Kathryn Kuhlman died. But you see, for me, it was easy because I had nothing. I had nothing."

"I had nothing," she said. In sharing this, Miss Kuhlman was implying that, for those who have much, it can be tough. We are shown this in the scriptures through the story of the Rich Young Ruler, for example. For him, he thought the cost was just too much.

Like me, like Miss Kuhlman, and like the Rich Young Ruler, you too dear reader, will have to *count the cost*. Depending on how much you have, depending on where you live, and depending on who you are, the cost might vary between high or not-so-high. But there is a cost, nonetheless, and it will be up to you to decide if you will pay it.

Here I Am, *Send Me!*

At this point, I am hoping this book has made one thing very clear, and that is: *The Kingdom of God is fully available to you.*

What a wonderful news for the believer who knows everything that the Kingdom has to offer and how to appropriate it. What a wonderful news for the one who has been embraced by the Father and who embraced the Father back! God, in His grace, has withheld nothing from us.

The Bible tells us:

> *"He who did not spare his own Son, but gave him up for us all—how will he not also, along with him, graciously give us all things?"* ~ Romans 8:32 (NIV)

All that He has is available to His children. God holds nothing back from those who ask, seek, and knock—from those who press in persistently.

But the success of your mission, and mine, here on earth, relies not only on the availability of the Kingdom for you but on your availability for the Kingdom.

John F. Kennedy was speaking of a much lesser kingdom when he pressed the American people's prerogative with his famous phrase, *"Ask not what your country can do for you—ask what you can do for your country."*

Now, we know just how much the Kingdom can do for us. But the same question remains for all believers. As Kingdom citizens, what shall we do for the Kingdom? So, the real question is: *The Kingdom of God is available to you, but are you available to the Kingdom?*

> The real question is: The Kingdom of God is available to you, but are you available to the Kingdom?

The prophet Isaiah saw the King of glory and said enthusiastically:

"Here I am. Send me!" ~ Isaiah 6:8 (NIV)

Jesus said:

"Blessed are those who have not seen and yet have believed."
~ John 20:29 (ESV)

Blessed are those of us who, having not seen a heavenly vision, can still say like Isaiah: *"Here I am. Send me!"*

The Duty of Obeying the King

In an earlier chapter, I explained how, as Kingdom ambassadors, we are tasked with representing the King's will, His rule, and His authority wherever we're sent.

We are not our own anymore because we have been bought at a price. This requires obedience. In many instances throughout history or in certain cultures, the code of honor demands that when someone saves your life, you use the remainder of your life to serve them faithfully.

This is what William Carey meant when he said:

"Surely it is worthwhile to lay ourselves out with all our might in promoting the cause and kingdom of Christ."

Western believers seem to have a lax concept of what it means to have been redeemed by the King of glory.

Obedience after salvation, while perceived as optional by many, is not to be taken lightly. There can be nothing glorious achieved or any Kingdom expansion without a committed and surrendered obedience to the King.

The story is told of Sir Leonard Wood, who once visited the king of France. The king was so pleased with him that he was invited for dinner the next day.

Sir Leonard went to the palace and the king, meeting him in one of the halls, said:

> *"Why, Sir Leonard, I did not expect to see you. How is it that you are here?"*

"Did not your majesty invite me to dine with you?" said the astonished guest.

"Yes," replied the king, *"but you did not answer my invitation."*

Then it was that Sir Leonard Wood uttered one of the choicest sentences of his life. He replied: *"A king's invitation is never to be answered, but obeyed."*

In Christian circles, we are often told that we *"accept Christ"* or *"accept His invitation."* But make no mistake, when you came to Christ, you obeyed a *Royal invitation.* You could have refused, sure. There are many who do just that every day. But

> In Christian circles, we are often told that we "accept Christ" or "accept His invitation." But make no mistake, when you came to Christ, you obeyed a Royal invitation.

what is said of those who refuse this invitation in the Gospel of Luke? In the parable of the ten servants, in Luke 19, the King (who is clearly Jesus) says at the very end (v.27):

"Bring here those enemies of mine, who did not want me to reign over them, and slay them before me." (NKJV)

This seemingly stern and unlikely saying of Jesus is a serious reminder that He, nor His invitation in the Kingdom, are not to be taken lightly. While God is gracious, He is King. Although we are not mere subjects but also sons, He should still be treated as a Monarch. Yielding to the King's will and voice is still key to be counted worthy of the Kingdom. Obedience is a fruit of the fear of God, which is highly lauded in the Kingdom.

From Glory to Glory... *to Glory?!*

"The frontiers of the kingdom of God were never advanced by men and women of caution." ~ J. Oswald Sanders

One of my goals in the writing of this book was to contribute, in some way, to the *"revealing of the sons of God"* (Romans 8:19).

While we are not yet all that we will be, we are more than we were, thanks be to God. And, in yielding to the Spirit

> "The frontiers of the kingdom of God were never advanced by men and women of caution." ~ J. Oswald Sanders

of God daily, we are changed "from glory to glory" evermore (2 Corinthians 3:18).

I am a firm believer in the power of individual awakening. Individual reform precedes corporate reform. And when someone is brought to the understanding of the Kingdom of God and their place in it, this brings about a powerful personal awakening. It ignites their birthright with a tremendous fire. It takes an individual out of the Grand Hotel lobby and into the full benefits of the Kingdom's power and influence. This type of awakening is very needed in our day and age. And, as I said at the beginning of this book, it is this type of awakening that will fulfill the preaching of the Kingdom of God to all nations before the end comes (Matthew 24:14).

When a believer gets out of religion (the lobby) and into greater Kingdom understanding, things start shifting for the better in the earth and the Kingdom. This individual begins walking in the greater assurance of their assignment. It gives them great conviction and enables them to walk in greater power on behalf of the King.

I believe there are three main stages in a believer's spiritual journey.

🜲 **The first one** is the new birth. Being born again or born from above. This is how you obtained your Kingdom citizenship. It's your heavenly passport.

👑 **The second one** is the baptism of the Holy Spirit. And I know there is much misunderstanding and controversy surrounding this doctrine. Nevertheless, there is undeniable scriptural and supernatural evidence that points to its truth, its manifestation, and its power. We all need the baptism of the Holy Spirit in order to fully operate in the Kingdom of God.

👑 **The third one** is coming to an understanding of what the Kingdom of God is, how it operates in the earth realm, and most importantly, how it operates in you, for you, and through you.

Now, the chances are that you are familiar with the first two spiritual stages as a believer.

But the third stage is not usually part of the believer's arsenal or experiences. That's because, as we saw, it is barely taught in most religious circles, churches, or denominations. Also, because it comes through a quickening of your understanding, a paradigm shift in your beliefs, rather than a spiritual experience. That said, it does bring the first two spiritual experiences (the new birth and baptism of the Holy Ghost) to their fuller expression.

I am thoroughly convinced, as I mentioned earlier, that Jesus' deep desire was for the gospel of the Kingdom to be fully understood and taught by His followers, as Acts 1:3 (NIV) clearly states:

> *"After his suffering, he presented himself to them and gave many convincing proofs that he was alive. He appeared to them over a period of forty days and spoke about the kingdom of God."*

Once you come into a deeper Kingdom understanding, it changes your whole outlook, identity, and walk with God, as this book has clearly demonstrated at this point. It also enables you to…

Fulfill Your Heavenly Book

Did you know that in heaven there are many books? In fact, there are libraries in heaven that would make any bibliophile salivate! The Bible tells us about some of the books found in God's abode in a few passages. For one, Revelation 20:12 (NIV) tells us about two types of books:

> "And I saw the dead, great and small, standing before the throne, and books were opened. Another book was opened, which is the book of life. The dead were judged according to what they had done as recorded in the books."

This passage mentions "books," plural, and *"The Book of Life,"* which is the main book in which are found the names of all those who are born from above. It is mentioned quite a few times in the Book of Revelation (Revelation 3:5; 13:8; 17:8; 20:12, 15; 21:27). This is the book Jesus told His disciples about when He said:

> "Do not rejoice in this, that the spirits are subject to you, but rejoice that your names are written in heaven." ~ Luke 10:20 (ESV)

The book of life is also mentioned in Exodus 32:32-33 and Daniel 12:1. It's also referred to in extra-biblical literature, such as the Book of Jubilees and the Dead Sea Scrolls.

As for "the books," these seem to indicate that they contain the records of everything everybody has ever done. This is where God records your every word and deed. These are the books that will be opened when we will appear before the King to account for how we lived our lives. They are also mentioned in Daniel 7:10.

Kevin Zadai is a well-known Bible teacher who was given the

privilege of an unusual experience. During a routine dental surgery, he died and was brought to heaven, where he had an amazing encounter with Jesus. Many things were revealed to him then, but one particularly stood out. According to Dr. Zadai, he saw books in heaven, many books! But these were not just any kind of books; *they were books written by God about… you, me, and everyone!*

In his own words, he wrote:

> *"When I was with Jesus in heaven, I saw that each person had a book of destiny written about them. It was a personal book that contained God's heart for us. Each person's book showed how they would affect their generation and even generations to come. I saw that each book was conditional, according to how we had allowed our heavenly Father to implement its contents into our lives by yielding to His will. I saw that the Holy Spirit was called alongside us to counsel us into the perfect will of God by moving upon us in a powerful way."* ~ Kevin Zadai, It's Rigged in Your Favor, p. 29.

This revelation is nothing short of astounding! And yet, it makes all the sense in the world, doesn't it? After all, Psalm 139:16 does say:

> *"In your book were written, every one of them, the days that were formed for me, when as yet there was none of them."* (ESV)

So, when I heard Dr. Zadai's testimony, I was both wowed and not surprised at the same time. It brought to light what I suspected all along: we are each sent here with a specific and divine purpose—*a pre-written Kingdom Assignment.* The closer we follow the King and His Kingdom's constitution (The Bible), the more we align ourselves with finding and ultimately fulfilling this high calling.

It's just as the Bible says:

> *"We are God's handiwork, created in Christ Jesus to do good works, which God prepared in advance for us to do."* ~ Ephesians 2:10 (NIV)

These good works are not just general ones like obeying the Ten Commandments and sharing the gospel. They are also specific to each of us. They have been pre-written in your book in ages past for you to fulfill at this specific time and place in history. And your heavenly book cannot be fulfilled unless you are born again and yield to His will daily. Only then will you be given the eternal validation of these invaluable words:

> *"Well done, good and faithful servant! You have been faithful with a few things; I will put you in charge of many things. Come and share your master's happiness!" ~ Matthew 25:23 (NIV)*

Called to Kingdom Significance

"The only significance of life consists in helping to establish the kingdom of God." ~ Leo Tolstoy

Everybody wants to feel significant. The dictionary defines *significant* as *"the quality of being worthy of attention; importance."* We all want to feel important. It is a human desire, and even a need, to feel like what we do matters. This desire is not happenstance. It was placed in your heart and mine on purpose by God

> "The only significance of life consists in helping to establish the kingdom of God." ~ Leo Tolstoy

Almighty! God desires you to be significant. He didn't create any of us to be insignificant.

Author Os Guiness once said that *"there can be no calling without a caller."* Indeed, God has called each of us to a lofty purpose. He is the One who calls us to a higher ideal. God doesn't just want you to be successful; He desires you to become significant—Kingdom significant!

Everybody is significant in the Kingdom of God simply because, positionally, we are sons of the Most High. Our identity gives us significance. This significance is inherent to our being. It gives us value.

Nevertheless, not all His children do what He asks. Not all are invested in fulfilling the interest of His Kingdom. This is the reason Jesus lamented:

> *"Why do you call me 'Lord, Lord,' and not do what I tell you?" ~ Luke 6:46 (ESV)*

The Great Abide

I found a great text on the web which illustrates just how important it is for believers to stay connected and obedient to the King. I looked thoroughly for the source but couldn't find it. I'm sharing it anyway because it is too good not to share:

> *"When God wanted to create the fish, He spoke to the sea, when God wanted to create the trees, He spoke to the earth but when God wanted to create Man, He spoke to Himself.*
>
> *Then GOD said, "Let US make Man in Our image, according to Our likeness.*
>
> *You see, if you take a fish out of the water, it will die. And when you take a tree out of the ground, it will also die. Similarly, when Man is disconnected from God, he dies.*
>
> *God is our natural environment. We were created to live in His presence. We must be connected to Him because only in Him there is Life. Therefore, Stay connected to God.*
>
> *Remember...*
>
> *God without man is still God, but man without God is Nothing."*

Truly, the measure of your influence and Kingdom significance will expand according to your connectedness and obedience to the King's will. For indeed, without God, we are nothing.

> Indeed, without God, we are nothing.

Christ said it to His disciples:

> *"Abide in Me, and I in you. As the branch cannot bear fruit of itself, unless it abides in the vine, neither can you, unless you abide in Me. "I am the vine, you are the branches. He who abides in Me, and I in him, bears much fruit; for without Me you can do nothing." ~ John 15:4-5 (NKJV)*

Abiding and obeying, therefore, are keys to promotion in the Kingdom of God.

Oswald Chambers, in his masterpiece, *My Utmost for His Highest*, said: *"Never be hurried out of the relationship of abiding in Him. It is the one thing that is apt to fluctuate but it ought not to."*

Sometimes, believers, in order to sound spiritual or godly, will say they are willing to die for Christ. While this may sound noble, what God is really looking for are people who are willing to live for Christ, even if what He asks can sometimes be difficult, such as dying to self.

Here is a true story to illustrate this:

> Believers, in order to sound spiritual or godly, will say they are willing to die for Christ. While this may sound noble, what God is really looking for are people who are willing to live for Christ.

It is said of King Henry of Bavaria that at one time, becoming weary of court life, he determined to enter a monastery. When he presented himself to Prior Richard, the faithful monk gave him the strict rules of the order. The king listened eagerly and enthusiastically expressed pleasure at the prospect of such complete consecration. Then the prior insisted

327

that obedience, implicit and unquestioned, was the first requisite of sainthood. The monarch promised to follow his will in every detail.

"Then go back to your throne and do your duty in the station that God assigned you," was the prior's word to him.

The king took up his sceptre again, and from then until he died, people said of him, *"King Henry has learned to govern by learning to obey."*

> *"Greatness in the kingdom of God is measured in terms of obedience."* ~ John Stott

Greatness Beckons

There is an oft-told factual story about President Abraham Lincoln and Dr. Finnes Gurley, a pastor and good acquaintance of Lincoln.

Back during his presidential days, Lincoln would often slip out of the White House on Wednesday evenings to listen to the sermons of Dr. Finnes Gurley at New York Avenue Presbyterian Church. He generally preferred to come and go unnoticed. So, when Dr. Gurley knew the president was coming, he left his study door open.

On one of those occasions, the president slipped through a side door in the church and took a seat in the minister's study, located just to the side of the sanctuary. There he propped the door open, just wide enough to hear Dr. Gurley's message.

During the walk home, an aide asked Mr. Lincoln his appraisal of the sermon. The president thoughtfully replied, *"The content was excellent; he delivered with elegance; he obviously put work into the message."*

"Then you thought it was an excellent sermon?" questioned the aide.

"No," Lincoln answered. *"It failed,"* he added.

"But you said that the content was excellent. It was delivered with eloquence, and it showed how hard he worked," the aide pressed.

"That's true," Lincoln said, *"But Dr. Gurley forgot the most important ingredient. He forgot to ask us to do something great."*

Dear friend, as you have now reached the end of this most important book, I too will feel that I will have failed if I do not urge you to do something great.

Our Lord gave us the GREAT Commission. I believe you are now armed with extensive knowledge of what made this commission so great. You understand more fully what the Gospel of the Kingdom was intended to bring, which is much more than just the salvation message.

Our King sandwiched His commission between two powerful statements:

1. Firstly, He confirmed that ALL authority had been given to Him (v.18).

2. Secondly, He assured us of His everlasting and continuous presence and assistance (v.20).

Furthermore, in-between these two grandiose and empowering statements, He ordered us to *"GO therefore and make disciples."*

Notice, the Lord didn't ask us to just make converts, but disciples. There's a huge difference between the two. Jesus isn't much into proselytizing but into *reproduction.* The message of salvation alone makes converts, but the message of the Kingdom is meant to make disciples. Kingdom citizens are fishers of men who make more fishers of men.

> The message of salvation alone makes converts, but the message of the Kingdom is meant to make disciples.

A disciple is where we get the word *discipline* from. We are to be *disciplined* learners and make others into disciplined learners.

Christian philosopher, Dallas Willard, said: "

> *A disciple is a learner, a student, an apprentice, a practitioner. Disciples of Jesus are people who do not just profess certain views as their own but apply their growing understanding of life in the Kingdom of the Heavens to every aspect of their life on earth."*

God doesn't need more people crowding church pews on Sunday morning; He needs disciplined citizens crowding streets, places of business, schools, organizations, workplaces, and all spheres of society with the culture and the message of the Kingdom.

Pastor and author, John Willis Zumwalt, said it this way: *"The Church has no reason to exist except for the advancement of His Kingdom into areas it has never been before!"*

Indeed, those seven mountains of culture won't climb themselves, and no one will land at their top by accident.

The Great Reset

As I am writing these lines, we are past one of the most challenging years in modern history: 2020.

In 2020, the world became a victim of a vicious attack on our freedoms and liberties. Using the excuse of a created virus-turned-bogeyman, the governments of the world tightened their grip of control over our rights to freely conduct business, over our way of life, over our families, over our right to assemble, and even over our right to breathe freely.

These corrupt and self-serving leaders have also brought about economic woes, the likes of which have never been seen before. Even the Great Depression seems like a walk in the park compared to what we witnessed in 2020.

During these forced lockdowns and confinements, there have been repeated talks from these Luciferian oligarchs of a 'Great Reset,' an idea advanced by Klaus Schwab, founder and executive chairman of the *World Economic Forum* in Switzerland. It is a global push to overhaul economic systems in the wake of the COVID-19 'plandemic'. It even has its own name, logo, website, annual summit meetings, and a virtual series of online "dialogues" to push the goals of the movement.

According to the organization's website, *The Great Reset* has among its goals, no less than *"a rapid post-pandemic overhaul of economic systems, business models and societies."*

For the biblically informed, we understand this to be nothing less than further steps taken into implementing the globalist agenda of the Beast system—the system of the Antichrist.

But guess what…

God also is planning *His Great Reset,* and it's going to be a *WHOPPER!*

God's Great Reset

Throughout the Scriptures, we see it. For millennia, the Kingdom of God has been at war with the kingdom of darkness. And, despite appearances from the 2020 debacle and seeming progress of the latter, we needn't worry or fret. God is still firmly anchored on His throne and unphased by anything the Enemy has been doing. The King of glory has never for once lost a battle.

In Psalm 2, we read of one of the few instances in the Bible where God actually laughs. So, you may ask, *"What makes Him laugh?"* We are told that the conspiracies of the wicked make Him laugh:

> *"Why do the nations conspire and the peoples plot in vain?*
> *The kings of the earth rise up and the rulers band together*

against the Lord and against his anointed, saying, "Let us break their chains and throw off their shackles." The One enthroned in heaven laughs; the Lord scoffs at them. He rebukes them in his anger and terrifies them in his wrath."
~ Psalm 2:1-5 (NIV)

While the wicked are conspiring against all and planning their Great Reset, the Almighty is planning His.

I believe we are on the cusp of a major End-Times shift.

For years, many doomsday prophets have been speaking of, among other things, a future pole shift that will bring unprecedented destruction to our planet. I believe the pole shift they have been expecting in the End Times might not be physical at all—it will be in the Spirit! The Great Reset of God will usher in a great revival, and I believe, a *Great Reversal*—a spiritual pole shift! This great reversal will make the first become last, the last become first, and even the poor become rich in order to fulfill Kingdom works in the last days. Many expect this to happen only during the future earthly reign of Christ, but I believe we will see it, at least in part, on this side of the millennium.

Before the final falling away and the cataclysmic events of the great tribulation, there will be one last and mighty push of the Spirit of God on the earth. God's Great Reset will bring about more repentance and more converts than at any other time in history. There will be a great trembling and a mighty revival on the earth that will be spearheaded in the United States of America, most likely through much pain, travail, and suffering. But, in the end, God's Great Reset will bring about a scriptural prophetic fulfillment of epic and unprecedented proportions.

Indeed, just like Jesus said:

"And this gospel of the kingdom will be preached in the whole world as a testimony to all nations, and then the end will come." ~ Matthew 24:14 (NIV)

In alignment with this verse, it was said by revivalist John Wesley:

"Give me one hundred men who love only God with all their heart and hate only sin with all their heart and we will shake the gates of hell and bring in the kingdom of God in one generation."

Later, in 1939, faith healer and preacher, Smith Wigglesworth, prophesied a vision to his mentee, Lester Sumrall, about the final wave of

> "Give me one hundred men who love only God with all their heart and hate only sin with all their heart and we will shake the gates of hell and bring in the kingdom of God in one generation." ~ John Wesley

God's glory with tears of joy streaming down his cheeks. He said:

"After that, after the third wave, I see the last day revival that's going to usher in the precious fruit of the earth. It will be the greatest revival this world has ever seen! It's going to be a wave of the gifts of the Spirit. The ministry gifts will be flowing on this planet earth. I see hospitals being emptied out, and they will bring the sick to churches where they allow the Holy Ghost to move."

May God make us witness such a generation and such a day!

The Coming Great Transfer of Wealth

Back in 1997, late evangelist and faith teacher, Morris Cerullo, wrote a short book titled: *The Last Great Transfer of Wealth*. In it, he explains from the Scripture how God will supernaturally transfer the wealth of the wicked to the righteous before the End of the Age comes.

Likewise, another well-known Bible teacher and prophetic voice, Peter C. Wagner, wrote one last book before going to be with the Lord in 2016. In his book titled, *The Great Transfer of Wealth*, he shared with the world his hope and insight concerning what he saw as a soon-to-be transfer of wealth. He too, spoke of a time when God will supernaturally transfer the wealth of the wicked into the hands of the righteous, not unlike what the Israelites experienced when they left Egypt under Moses and plundered the Egyptians.

In the Bible, we read that:

> *"The wealth of the sinner is stored up for the righteous."*
> *~ Proverbs 13:22b (NKJV)*

I believe this statement from Solomon bore prophetic significance. I also believe this wealth has been stored up since the days of King Solomon—perhaps even earlier. And, speaking of prophetic voices, it was said by the prophet Isaiah to God's people:

> *"Lift up your eyes and look about you: all assemble and come to you; your sons come from afar, and your daughters are carried on the hip. Then you will look and be radiant, your heart will throb and swell with joy; the wealth on the seas will be brought to you, to you the riches of the nations will come." ~ Isaiah 60:4-5 (NIV)*

Indeed, in this last push to spread the *Gospel of the Kingdom*, you and I will witness amazing moves of God that will leave us flabbergasted, crying with joy, and on our knees worshipping the King. While this is merely my opinion, I believe we will see *the wealth of the nations* come to much of the Body of Christ before the end comes.

The people of God have benefited in the past from similar wealth transfers. For example, Abraham obtained much of his wealth by transfer from the wicked (the Pharaoh in Egypt). Jacob supernaturally obtained much of his wealth from Laban (in the form of cattle). Later, Joseph was appointed as prime minister in Egypt; he controlled much of its wealth, which came from Pharaoh. Much later, when the Israelites were delivered from the hand of Pharaoh and brought out of slavery by God's mighty hand, they plundered the Egyptians of much of their wealth. Solomon obtained much of his wealth because the heathen brought it to him.

Remember, this is possible because God owns it all! In the last days, in order to spread the Gospel of the Kingdom all over the world, I believe history will repeat itself: God will supernaturally transfer wealth into the hands of men and women of the Kingdom who have proven themselves worthy—whose character is exemplary.

The Royal Wedding

This coming glorious revival and wealth transfer may seem like an odd concept to some of you, and yet, when we think about it, it makes solid biblical sense.

We are told in the Scripture that Christ is coming back soon as King to take the Church as His bride, right?

History and human culture (and my own personal experience) show us that the time a man spends the most money in the shortest amount of time is when he is about to take a wife. In the west, this may mean purchasing an expensive ring, investing in all the wedding preparations, new furniture, and in some cases, even a house. In other cultures, it may mean providing a large number of heads of cattle. But regardless of where you live, taking a bride requires the husband-to-be to spend lavishly in preparing for a comfortable life with his new bride.

Now, keep in mind that the Lord is a mighty King—the wealthiest and greatest! When He comes for her, He will not suffer His bride to wear rags before the great day. Now, whether that rags-to-riches, Cinderella-like transformation occurs before or after He comes, is where you and I may beg to differ. Personally, I believe the Church will get a taste of it *before* the wedding feast. After all, every bride needs money to purchase her bridal trousseau, right?

Get Ready, Get Ready, Get Ready!

In the summer of 2020, Elisabeth was praying with my then 8-year-old daughter, Marissa, before bedtime. As they were holding hands and Elisabeth was praying, Marissa heard the voice of the Lord. He said to her repeatedly: *"You shall prepare."*

Marissa shared this prophetic word immediately with us, and we have been preparing ever since.

Preparing how? For what? We have been preparing for His return. We have been preparing spiritually, sure, but also physically and mentally. If He is coming back soon (and I believe He is), it will not be an easy season for the saints. This is the season where we cannot afford to be likened to the foolish virgins. We need fresh oil for fresh fire. We all need to prepare and have our lamps filled up to the brim. And yes, we need to prepare in the physical as well. I always tell my listeners on our broadcast that seeing the evil days and wisely stocking up on emergency provisions doesn't make you any less spirit-filled.

As the Kingdom of God and the kingdom of darkness prepare for their final showdown, things are going to get rowdy, even for the saints. As such, there is nothing dumb or silly in having extra food stored, self-defense weapons, and physical silver and gold. That said, physical prepping shouldn't take precedence over your spiritual and mental preparation. Furthermore, it should not be done out of fear of what is to come but rather out of faith, understanding, and wisdom. Proverbs 27:12 (NLT) says: "

> Seeing the evil days and wisely stocking up on emergency provisions doesn't make you any less spirit-filled.

A prudent person foresees danger and takes precautions.
The simpleton goes blindly on and suffers the consequences."

Remember in the days ahead, just as always:

> *Whether you turn to the right or to the left, your ears will*
> *hear a voice behind you, saying, "This is the way; walk in it."*
> *~ Isaiah 30:21 (NIV)*

Following the King into Glory

Someone once observed:

> *"Jesus does not make claims as a dictator removed from the*
> *battlefield but rather goes before us leading the charge as*
> *King of the Kingdom of God."*

Yes, Jesus is the consummate ruler with a steel will and a compassionate heart. He is the ultimate leader of the ultimate Kingdom. This, the Bible confirms as it comes to its victorious crescendo in the Book of Revelation.

> *"Then I saw heaven opened, and a white horse was standing*
> *there. Its rider was named Faithful and True, for he judges*
> *fairly and wages a righteous war. His eyes were like flames*
> *of fire, and on his head were many crowns. A name was*
> *written on him that no one understood except himself. He*
> *wore a robe dipped in blood, and his title was the Word of*
> *God. The armies of heaven, dressed in the finest of pure*
> *white linen, followed him on white horses. From his mouth*
> *came a sharp sword to strike down the nations. He will rule*
> *them with an iron rod. He will release the fierce wrath of*
> *God, the Almighty, like juice flowing from a winepress. On*
> *his robe at his thigh was written this title: King of all kings*
> *and Lord of all lords." ~ Revelation 19:11-16 (NLT)*

German philosopher, Karl Wilhelm Friedrich Schlegel, rightly observed when he said:

> *"Novels tend to end as the Paternoster begins: with the*
> *kingdom of God on earth."*

So will our present age end with the Kingdom being fully brought in glory.

While I have strived throughout this book to emphasize the presence of the *Kingdom now* for obvious and lengthily detailed reasons, we cannot ignore its future manifestation in *full glory*. This comprises our future and blessed hope (Titus 2:13)! Someday, hopefully soon, we will indeed see the Kingdom become manifest in all its glory right here on the earth. Christ, our King, will confirm His majesty through an indisputable, impeccable, and perfect rule right here on earth when He establishes His reign.

Nevertheless, in the meantime, we have been given much of the Kingdom already. This then begs the question, *"What have we done with what we were given?"*

It is high time that we, His Church, grab hold of *the full Gospel* and begin anew to spread it. The Bible says that our God is a consuming fire (Hebrews 12:29), and the Lord said of His ministry:

> *"I have come to bring fire on the earth, and how I wish it were already kindled!"* ~ *Luke 12:49 (NIV)*

This fire was to be kindled in our hearts and through the power and ministry of the Holy Spirit throughout the world. In my secular leadership book, *Lead Like a Superhero*, I ask my readers the rhetorical question: *"What fires have you kindled in the hearts of others because of the inferno in yours?"*

Make no mistake about it; the Spirit of God in you wants to kindle an inferno of God's Holy Fire that will spread to the hearts of multitudes across the globe. The Kingdom is a realm of reproduction and multiplication, and multiply and reproduce we must.

On a personal note, this book is my contribution to share the

Gospel of the Kingdom to the ends of the earth. It is, therefore, my hope that it will honor the King, but most of all, bless His people by re-igniting the fire that Jesus came to set by pointing them once again, perhaps even for the first time, to the Gospel of the Kingdom.

Like you, I am hoping for yet another and mighty great awakening—a great revival. And yet, I am fully aware that it can only come *in Spirit and in Truth*. Both the Spirit of God and the Truth of His Gospel need to be present in order to bring this mighty End-Times revival. This is why I made it my business to try to point you to as much truth as possible through this book.

So, as you read these last few lines, let me ask you once again the same question the King asked me…

Are YOU all in?

I pray you are.

May God richly bless you as you seek first the Kingdom and His righteousness.

Thy Kingdom Come.
Thy will be done on earth as it is in Heaven.
Maranatha! Come, Lord Jesus!

ABOUT SEBASTIEN RICHARD

Sebastien Richard was born in Montreal, Quebec, Canada.

He is a busy author, Bible teacher, and entrepreneur. He is also a certified leadership trainer.

In the course of a tumultuous childhood marked by his parents divorcing and several moves, he had a life-changing encounter with the Lord Jesus Christ at the age of nine.

Despite these various early life trials, the call on his life for the ministry was felt strongly from his late teens well into adulthood.

At age 45, unable to resist God's summon any longer, Sebastien left his full-time government job of 18 years with Canada Post to pursue full-time ministry with his wife, Elisabeth.

Together, they founded *Thriving on Purpose Ministries* (https://www.thrivingonpurpose.com/). From this platform, Sebastien teaches God's people about the Kingdom of God, faith, leadership, personal growth, as he also exposes the many lies that keep believers bound.

A true renaissance man, Sebastien has shared his versatile knowledge by teaching many people in Canada, the U.S., Pakistan, and India. He is a strong researcher, a gifted teacher, and a dynamic speaker who, so far, has authored five books.

When he's not busy with work, or with leading his family to further happiness and bliss, he enjoys masterminding with Elisabeth at breakfast time, family road trips, researching and formulating fringe theories, watching various documentaries, and family movie-night while chowing down pizza.

Sebastien lives in Prince Edward Island, Canada with his wife and three children (Jason, Marissa, and Katelyn).

Check out our Kingdom Apparel, Mugs and Free Resources at Thriving on Purpose Store:

Visit the *Thriving on Purpose* website:
https://www.thrivingonpurpose.com/

Follow *Thriving on Purpose* on Facebook:
https://www.facebook.com/thrivingonpurpose

Subscribe to the *Thriving on Purpose* YouTube channel:
http://bit.ly/TOPTVTUBE

NEW! FROM THRIVING ON PURPOSE:

Record Your Unique Kingdom Journey...

Job lamented that he couldn't record his own words when he said: *"Oh, that my words were written! Oh, that they were inscribed in a book! That they were engraved on a rock with an iron pen and lead, forever! For I know that my Redeemer lives, and He shall stand at last on the earth."* ~ Job 19: 23-25, NKJV

Well, in his defense, Job didn't have access to *My Kingdom Journey Journal Series*; but you DO!

As we advance in our own Kingdom journey, we get inspired, we learn, we sow, we reap, we connect - with God and with people. *But do we record and track all of the God-given insights associated with these experiences?*

It is written in Exodus 17:14, NLT: *"After the victory (against Amalek), the Lord instructed Moses, "Write this down on a scroll as a permanent reminder..."*

And in Psalm 102:19, we read: *"This will be written for the generation to come, that a people yet to be created may praise the Lord."* (NKJV)

Many great men and women of God, explorers, scientists, and inventors of times past recorded their progress in journals. They understood the value associated with journaling for themselves and for future generations. They wrote records, field notes, plans, and tracked their progress to learn from failure, adapt to change, measure their successes, and leave a legacy.

My Kingdom Journey Journals were created with the sole purpose of helping you to do just the same!

As a Kingdom citizen and child of God, your life here matters. Your walk with God is an epic *Kingdom journey* which, if lived in obedience to Him, will leave footprints in the sands of time and impact your life and that of future generations.

When we walk with God and seek first the Kingdom... *Every. Single. Step. Counts.* And now, with *My Kingdom Journey Journals*, you can record...

- Your seed (all of your giving, offerings, tithing, etc.)
- Your field notes (Holy Spirit given ideas, downloads, notes, and inspirations)
- Your decrees (Personalized and inspired prayers, decrees, and declarations over your life)
- Your harvest (all of God's favor, your gratitude, blessings, and answered prayers)

It is a well known fact that *we can only improve what we measure...*

So, measure the progress of your walk with God by recording every single step; for yourself, and for future generations.

The "My Kingdom Journey" Series is comprised of four journals:

- Journal 1: *Seed Journal* (your Kingdom giving and sowing)
- Journal 2: *My Decrees* (your personalized Kingdom decrees and declarations)
- Journal 3: *Field Notes* (your Kingdom Ideas, plans, downloads and inspirations)
- Journal 4: *Harvest Journal* (Your Kingdom blessings, gratitude, and answered prayers)

All four journals can be used independently, but we recommend all four to maximise their impact on your Kingdom Journey.

Available at

https://bit.ly/MyKingdomJourney

Made in the USA
Middletown, DE
30 August 2021